Dale Spender Photo by Jill Posener

Dale Spender is a writer and researcher in the fields of language, education and feminist history. She is an Australian who prefers to live in London, a writer from choice and necessity, a feminist who has set herself the task of drawing attention to the sexist nature of our language, our upbringing and our understanding of our own history.

She taught in Australian secondary schools for nine years and has been involved in teacher training. She has also taught in women's studies courses and is editor of *Women's Studies International Forum*. She is involved in the women's liberation movement and the Fawcett Library.

She is co-editor of *Learning to Lose* (The Women's Press, 1980) and editor of *Men's Studies Modified* (1981) and *Feminist Theorists* (The Women's Press, 1983); she is the author of *Man Made Language* (1980), *Invisible Women* (1982), *Women of Ideas – And What Men Have Done to Them* (1982), *There's Always Been a Women's Movement This Century* (1983) and *Time and Tide Wait for No Man* (1984).

DALE SPENDER

For the Record

The Making and Meaning of Feminist Knowledge

The Women's Press

First published by The Women's Press Limited 1985
A member of the Namara Group
124 Shoreditch High Street, London E1 6JE

British Library Cataloguing in Publication Data

Spender, Dale
    For the record: the making and meaning of feminist knowledge.
    1. Feminism
    I. Title
    305.4′2   HQ1154

    ISBN 0-7043-2862-3
    ISBN 0-7043-3960-9 Pbk

Phototypeset by AKM Associates (UK) Ltd, Southall, Greater London
Printed and bound in Great Britain
by Nene Litho and Woolnough Bookbinding
both of Wellingborough, Northants

For Renate

Theory is not something set apart from our lives. Our assumptions about reality and change influence our actions constantly. The question is not whether we have a theory, but how aware we are of the assumptions behind our actions, and how conscious we are of the choices we make – daily – among different theories.

Charlotte Bunch

There is nothing so emotional as a woman who knows.

with thanks to Phillida Bunkle

The struggle which is not joyous is the wrong struggle.

Germaine Greer

Acknowledgements

Renate Duelli Klein and I were going to write this book together. It was conceived one night when we wondered what we would have when we put 'all' the feminist knowledge of the current movement together: and then we wondered what the feminist knowledge-makers would make of what we had made of them and their work. But for reasons of time – and demands – Renate was not able to work on this project officially: unofficially she has been a source of constant support and feedback, and I must acknowledge a sense of acute discomfort, for I recognise that in other joint projects in which we are involved she has done more than her share (and has frequently done my share) in order that I might be free to write. My dedication of this book to her is but a symbol of my appreciation of her generosity and her strength.

My sister, Lynne Spender, has also been a constant source of support and feedback. As the pages have come hot from that superb typist, Glynis Wood, they have been immediately despatched to my sister in Australia, for her 'stamp of approval', political and personal. Despite the enormous demands of family that are made on her time (for she does my share of caring for our parents), after the required number of days the letter arrives with all its constructive criticisms. Writing would be a much more confusing and isolated task without such a 'sister-reader'.

Likewise it would have been much more difficult without the assistance of Candida Lacey, who has read, checked and edited with the greatest goodwill, attention to detail and valuable recommendations for improvement.

I am also fortunate in the indulgence I receive from my friends. After days of solitude I am inclined to bring up every little detail that has been worrying me, and Anna Coote has listened and advised on many a night that must have left her exhausted; while Margaret Bluman has also been a source of constant replenishment. I value greatly her views on feminist knowledge and what it means. Her smile, her good humour, her insights, have all played a part in the making of this book.

I also have a debt to the women who are represented within these pages and who willingly read what I wrote about their ideas, and quickly responded in helpful and constructive ways.

I am grateful – yes, grateful – to that entity called the women's liberation movement which has made possible not just this book, but the context of sisterhood in which it was written.

Contents

Introduction: All things to all women

This book is really a review of books. When it came to the task of defining the boundaries of feminist knowledge I soon realised that it was not possible to include *all* the feminist ideas to which I have had access in discussions, courses, meetings, and all the many social contexts in which feminist ideas are raised and exchanged. Unless I was going to write volumes (and Ros de Lanerolle of the Women's Press warned against such an eventuality) it was regrettable but clear that I had to limit the scope of my discussion. And so for many reasons I decided to confine my evaluation of feminist ideas to some of the 'classics' of feminism.

One reason for my choice is that I like books. Another is that books have been very influential in my life: over the last decades I have learnt as much – if not more – about feminism from books as from any other source. And I suspect that many of the same books that have influenced me have also made a dramatic difference to other women and to the way they live their lives. So I thought it was reasonable to take books as a guide to feminist ideas; books that have in many respects become standard texts in the women's movement.

In a context as diverse and amorphous as the women's movement it is sometimes difficult to work out the nature of the common ground, and yet groups as far apart as rape crisis centres in Australia, the Manushi editorial collective in India, the panelists at the discussion on racism in the women's movement at the National Women's Studies Conference in New Jersey in the United States, and the executive committee of the Fawcett Society in England, have all had the experience of reading – and of being influenced by – some of the same feminist books. To the extent that these books are available and accessible, women with different priorities on different continents can share the common experience of

1

the exploration and understanding of the whys and wherefores of feminism. And because an analysis of these books can presume a degree of commonality, books seemed to be a good starting point for trying to establish the possibility of a common feminist framework.

But there is yet a further reason why I wanted to review these books – to bring them to attention, again. It is the reason behind the title of this book, *For the Record*. One cannot be a feminist and be unaware of the fate of feminist books. Again and again they have been published over the centuries; and again and again they have been 'lost'. I am not a pessimist, but I can see some of the writing on the wall and I want to take any steps I can to ensure that what happened to feminist writers in the past doesn't happen again. It is no accident that some of the classics of the contemporary movement are periodically out of print . . . and sometimes only reprinted as a result of considerable pressure. Patriarchy will not help keep alive the feminist heritage – *we* have to do it, and we have to do it against the odds. We may have reached the stage where we can produce knowledge, but we are still a long way from influencing the directions that it takes after it is produced. We do not control the many agencies which keep certain ideas at the forefront of social under-standings; we have little access to a fair hearing in the mainstream press; and we are hardly the focus of review periodicals except for the *Women's Review of Books*.[1] From the formulation of the agenda of public knowledge and discussion to the formulation of curricula in educational institutions, women are still denied influence, so that it is not *our* knowledge which informs society. Unless we take preventive measures, feminist ideas which no longer have the appeal of 'novelty' but which are none the less essential to our understandings and a vital part of our traditions, will drift – as they have in the past – to the brink of oblivion. Unless we keep reminding each other of our heritage we endanger it, we risk losing it as we contribute to our own amnesia.

While we are prepared to put much energy into reclaiming women from the distant past, our record is not so good when it comes to preserving our more recent heritage. In fact, we have sometimes been careless about the way we have discarded that very heritage. That nearly all the women whose contributions are evaluated here have given expression to some of the pain they have experienced as a result of the dismissal and denial of their work – sometimes to a debilitating extent – is surely a sign that we should show more care for each other. Care does not exclude constructive criticism.

As it stands, I would not have found it difficult to quote from a multitude of harsh reviews of feminist writing – sometimes by feminists. This is not because there has been an absence of positive comment but because – for reasons that I have no trouble understanding – the 'attacks' gain more visibility and endure longer than the 'supports'.

So this book stands as a testimony. It is a reminder of the radical and riotous ideas women have come up with in the very recent past. It is for now, and for the future, a declaration that women have wonderful ideas.

There are of course numerous limitations in the approach of reviewing these books which have been significant for me. One is that, by definition, the ideas of women who are not in print are not included; their contributions are non-data from the outset. And in this book, where a lot of space is devoted to the way women are defined out of existence and classified as non-data in men's terms, it is as well to have reservations about a feminist framework which defines some women out of existence. Just as men are dominant, and therefore in a position to promote their dominance at the expense of women, so too can the 'dominant' writers within the women's movement have their dominance used to reinforce their position at the expense of those who are subordinate and who continue not to count. I am not unmindful of the pitfalls on the way, but the fact that they are there does not seem sufficient reason for abandoning the journey.

For another strand in this book is the extent to which partial accounts have been accorded the status of complete and unbiased accounts in our patriarchal society. Many of my concerns are not only with what men have left out of their records, but with their assertion that what they have created is a full and accurate account. I do not want to fall into a similar trap. The record that I am presenting is by no means a full and complete account of all the feminist texts – or even of the contents of particular texts; it is a personal and partial account. This is not an apology but a recognition that there is no other way that it could be.

I have read many books which are not included in my discussion, and because I fully accept that no two people are necessarily led to the same view of the world by the same evidence, I presume that much of what I have not covered will have been extremely important to some women who could well be amazed by my omissions. But what I am prepared to assert throughout this book – and what I am prepared to assert here – is that there can be no full and complete account. All knowledge, every record, is by definition partial, and the issue is to acknowledge the partiality, the prejudice – and the politics – to point clearly to the omissions instead of passing them off as the full story. When there can only be incomplete accounts it is not constructive to condemn an account for its incompleteness.

What becomes increasingly clear in this review is that there can be no *one* view, no *one* answer, no *one* record, that can take all the diversity of human experience into account. That under patriarchy men have asserted that there is only one truth – and one 'objective' means of getting to it – tells us more about the power and authority of men in the face of overwhelming contrary evidence than it tells us about what we know and understand of the world. And if we are to have a common feminist framework then it must be all things to all women, it must be able to take account of what all women know and understand of the world even when they know and understand contradictory things. There can be no exclusions within a feminist framework. And the only way to achieve such a framework is to formulate one that is multi-dimensional, which can contain many truths, and which can accommodate many partial accounts.

Again, this is no apology, no qualification of feminist ideas or methodology. A framework that can accommodate diversity and a multiplicity of truths (as a feminist framework can) is a distinct improvement on the patriarchal framework which has room only for the reality and truth of the rulers, and excludes all else as 'meaningless'.

At one level, then, I have acknowledged the unavoidable inadequacy and partiality of my account of the feminist texts, but there is another level where partiality is not at all inevitable and where I can actually do something to ensure that my own prejudices do not go unchecked: this is the area of representation and *mis*representation. I might have been obliged to select out a number of books from my sample and thereby have misrepresented the whole, but I am not obliged to select out a number of issues from those books and to misrepresent the ideas of the writers. It is possible to return to those writers and to ask them if they have been fairly represented; and if they feel they have not, it is possible to offer them the right of reply.

The issue of the misrepresentation of women's ideas in a male-dominated society runs right through this book. I am extremely critical of the way men have used their position as 'gatekeepers' to keep out of the record the ideas of women they find threatening or dangerous, inconvenient or disquieting: and I am extremely critical of the way they

4

have distorted the ideas of women whom they have wanted to discredit. Yet as a writer, representing the ideas of other women writers, I too have a gatekeeping position which I could – even unconsciously and unknowingly – exploit. And as it is my contention that no one is pure, no one free from partiality, prejudice or political bias, so it is my responsiblity to try to ensure that in this area at least I make some provision for checking and validating what I have kept in and what I have kept out.

This is why I have sent a draft of what I have written about each woman to most of those who were willing to respond to my questions about whether or not they have been fairly represented. Initially, it was a theoretical consideration which led me to adopt this method and, in practice, I have learnt that it makes an enormous difference to what one writes. It has astonished me just how much more care I have taken to be accurate, how much more thoughtfully I have perused the texts (and how often I have completely revised my opinion and evaluation) simply because my portrayal of a particular woman's ideas was going to her for comment. I have learnt a great deal from the exercise and I hope that the exchange and comment that this book contains is as useful to the reader as it has been to the writer.

As feminists I think we have a responsibility to encode 'right of reply' in some of our work, so that our omissions do not become exclusions. We need to devise more means of dialogue and validation in a society where these are not readily sought. It would be advantageous to have more departures from the traditional forms and the inclusion of more and varied voices, even when they are critical, for they help to expose the inherent limitations of one's own experience and to point to the *whole* range of meanings which are understandably absent from any single account.

When I began this project I thought it would be a relatively simple task: a review of the texts. I intended to analyse the books and to work out whether there was indeed a feminist framework and, if so, what form it took. But in the very process of putting all these books together, new connections have been made for me. I began to see links that I had not realised existed before. And I came to understand that at the core of feminist ideas is the crucial insight that there is no one truth, no one authority, no one objective method which leads to the production of pure knowledge. This insight is as applicable to feminist knowledge as it is to patriarchal knowledge, but there is a significant difference between the two: feminist knowledge is based on the premise that the experience of all human beings is valid and must not be excluded from our understandings, whereas patriarchal knowledge is based on the premise that the experience of only half of the human population needs to be taken into account and the resulting version can be *imposed* on the other half. This is why patriarchal knowledge and the methods of producing it are a fundamental part of women's oppression, and why patriarchal knowledge must be challenged – and overruled.

1. Who Knows?:
The starting point of Betty Friedan

Betty Friedan helped to start it all when she went and talked to women about their lives. This might not appear to be a dramatic move but it was an unusual departure from the practices of the time. In the late 1950s *men* were the sources of public knowledge about women. It was men who formulated the theories about women, who made the pronouncements and proffered the advice on how women should live their lives. It was mainly men who wrote about women in the academic press and who talked about women in the media. It was men who were primarily in charge of the women's magazines which Betty Friedan believed to be so influential in shaping women's lives.

In this context it was seldom that women were allowed to speak for themselves, and when Betty Friedan forged the opportunity, what they had to say came as something of a shock, for if you were to believe the public image about women you would have expected to find behind every suburban door a housewife devoted to her role as wife, mother, homemaker, a women who was supremely happy and fulfilled, enjoying an unprecedented, perfect life. But if such women indeed existed, they were few and far between: when you actually entered that suburban home and asked the women themselves about their lives as Betty Friedan did, you got a very different story: the housewife was a long way from happiness or fulfilment.

Betty Friedan came to realise that a great gulf separated the well-established public understanding about women from the private and isolated understanding generated by individual women each day, as they lived out their lives: 'There was a strange discrepancy between the reality of our lives as women and the image to which we were trying to conform,' she wrote in *The Feminine Mystique* (1963: 9), and she proceeded to raise some of the issues which were to become a major preoccupation of society in the ensuing years.

It is significant that *The Feminine Mystique* is not presented in the form of a social science treatise deferring to the academic conventions of distance and methodology. Using transcripts from the women themselves, Betty Friedan set a precedent which many feminists were to follow when she used *women's experience* as the starting point for her work, rather than a discrete problem within a particular discipline. (Had she followed the academic model she might not have found what she did.) She wanted to know about women, so she went to women. She did not 'study' the women as a group distinct from herself, but talked *with* women and identified *with* them: she deliberately drew on her own experience as a woman who shared some of the same problems in order to explain what was happening.

Such personal involvement is characteristic of a great deal of feminist research, and is at the centre of any discussion of women's ideas. It is not simply an issue of hard data versus soft data, although that is often how it is presented in academic circles where the *participant–observation* approach of much feminist research is often roundly criticised for its so-called subjectivity. The crucial issue behind this discussion is, *who knows?* Betty Friedan – and many other feminists who followed – was not only putting forward women's versions of experience (her own included), she was indirectly challenging the right of men to encode knowledge about women: when as men they were precluded from being participants in experience specific to women, by what authority did they construct knowledge about women?

'Hard data', as Jessie Bernard (1974 : 13) pointed out, is frequently the knowledge *men* make about women's lives: 'soft data' is frequently the knowledge *women* make (and which helps to explain the inferior status of the method); and any debates on the relative merits of the two can contain a sub-text on whether it is men or women who have the right to encode knowledge on women.

When Betty Friedan let women speak for themselves, and included her own authenticating voice (confirming that she knew what the women were saying), she was in effect revealing just how inadequate and inaccurate was the public and legitimated knowledge of men. Implicitly she asked *who knows* about women, the male experts, or women themselves? (At various times in the pages of *The Feminine Mystique* she returns to the question and criticises the social sciences,

8

the educators, the range of counsellors, the media-makers for their 'mistakes', but she does not embark on any systematic critique.) The question of *who knows* became a fundamental one in feminist analyses of the 1970s.

The model for research – for finding out – that Betty Friedan used may not have upheld the conventions of the academy but it was an effective approach for her purpose: 'My methods were simply those of a reporter on the trail of a good story' (p.9), she wrote. In some ways this method of investigative journalism is particularly appropriate for feminist research and should not be devalued. When there is an official version of knowledge on women (and for this read 'hard data', 'objective', 'public knowledge') which is so much at variance with the reality of women's lives, the notion of a cover-up is not inappropriate, either implicitly or explicitly, and has pointed to the discrepancy between the official version provided by the male authorities, and the 'real story' as told by women themselves.

Betty Friedan did have a good story when she exposed what the official version on women concealed. She encountered housewife after housewife who was perfectly aware of the official version and who knew full well that her life was *supposed* to be the envy of women around the world, who knew that she was meant to be happy, but who actually felt quite lost, incomplete, disappointed, bordering on despair. Informed so frequently and forcefully that women had everything, most women Betty Friedan talked to had difficulty trying to describe or explain what was wrong: 'When a woman tries to put the problem into words, she often merely describes the daily life she leads' (p.27), emphasising that there was no particular label to name this problem in the public knowledge provided by men. With no acknowledgement of the problem, and no credibility given to its existence, it was understandable that the most usual conclusion a woman could draw was that *she* was at fault.

The response to any complaint she may have made helped to reinforce her sense of inadequacy. Betty Friedan describes how dissatisfactions were 'dismissed by telling the housewife she doesn't realize how lucky she is – her own boss, no time-clock, no junior executive gunning for her job. What if she isn't happy – does she think men are happy in this world? Doesn't she know how lucky she is to be a woman? (p.21). Alternatively, they were greeted with shoulder-shrugging and the assertion that 'this is what being a woman means, and what is wrong with American women that they can't accept their role gracefully?' (p.21). Reluctant to be labelled as a failure – or an ingrate – the housewife retreated into silence, diagnosed herself as 'disturbed', and determined not to let anyone else know.

This was the tight-lipped suburban scene that Betty Friedan entered. She listened to women talk around the problem, she listened to the 'surface noise' of difficulties with marriages, children, home-making and chicken soup. And in the process she began to hear what the real problem was:

> on an April morning in 1959, I heard a mother of four, having coffee with four other mothers in a suburban development fifteen miles from New York, say in a tone of quiet desperation , 'the problem'. And the others knew, without words, that she was not talking about a problem with her husband, or her children, or her home. Suddenly they realized they all shared the same problem, the problem that has no name. They began, hesitantly, to talk about it. Later, after they had picked up their children at nursery school and taken them home to nap, two of the women cried, in sheer relief, just to know they were not alone. (p.17)

Betty Friedan described 'the problem without a name', but she displayed little systematic interest in questioning this absence of a name. Unlike Mary Daly (1973) and Sheila Rowbotham (1973), Betty Friedan does not state explicitly that naming – the process of labelling, ordering, making sense of the world – is not only the province of men, but that it is also a fundamental feature of their power.

All human beings have a biased and limited view of the world: biased in that it begins with self, and limited in that it is restrained by experience. This means that theoretically there are many ways of seeing the world: the insistence on *one* view not only leaves out a great deal (and is therefore partial and inaccurate), it assumes considerable privilege for those whose view it happens to be. They are in the privileged position of knowing 'everything': their bias, their limitations, become the yardstick by which all else is measured, and if they have not been exposed to a particular experience – in the way that whites in western society have not been exposed to the receiving end of racist abuse, the employed have not been exposed to redundancy, men have not been exposed to the everyday routine of the housewife – then such experience can be deemed not to exist: it is unreal.

But for Betty Friedan – not a member of the group who knew everything – the problem which was central in women's lives was real enough. Men may have found no need for a name for this pervasive difficulty, but she – and other women – did need a label. She gave the problem a name; she called it 'the feminine mystique'. Later, Daly and Rowbotham among many others named it differently; they called it the oppression of women. And these very different names point to very different definitions of the problem – and call for very different solutions.

Betty Friedan readily acknowledged that the image of woman to which the American housewife was desperately trying to conform was oppressive. But by placing more emphasis on the *image* itself rather than its *origins*, she implied from the outset that a change in the image would mean an end to the oppression. It was 'the feminine mystique' that was at fault, with its insistence on woman's sole function as wife and mother, with its image of woman as 'housewife heroine . . . forever young' whose purpose ended with childbirth and who was therefore denied any life of her own (p.39). In Betty Friedan's frame of reference what was required was a new and more realistic, more fully human, concept of woman, and then the problem would automatically be overcome as more women aspired to the new ideal and were able to lead more fully human lives.

With hindsight it is easy to be critical of Betty Friedan's analysis and solution, but it would be grossly unfair to underestimate the value of her contribution. She *did* open the door on women's experience, she *did* focus on some of the most galling features of some women's lives which had previously gone unnoted. Yet she did *not* push her questions towards the origin of this strange state of affairs where it was acceptable for men to pass as the experts on women. She made few if any connections between power and expertise, between the dominant sex and the dominant explanations. Betty Friedan was not struck by the total absurdity of the situation in which men in their workplaces were declaring that women in their homes were supremely happy. Yet the rest of society was prepared to go along with the idea that, somehow or other, men knew what they were talking about. Nonsensical arrangement that this was, there were not many other challenges to it at the time, and Betty Friedan should not be assessed solely on the absence of questions about the male 'right to know'. But it would be just as culpable not to point out that she made little attempt to investigate the politics of social organisation, to explore the relationship between the dominant sex and their role in providing the dominant meanings for society. Indeed, she passed over this 'arrangement' – and many others – as if somehow it simply arose by accident, and would be ended in much the same way.

Of course, there were images for women *and* men which both sexes strove to live up to, but Betty Friedan barely mentioned that it was *males* who devised the images for *both* sexes and that it was males who derived considerable benefit from this form of organisation: the happy housewife in the home, her husband the centre of her existence, and any dissatisfaction she may have expressed, readily and resoundingly denied. By concerning herself with the image, Betty Friedan overlooked dimensions of male self-interest and power. This is surprising, because Betty Friedan was not unaware that over time the image of woman has changed, while the relationship of women to men has remained much the same. Nor was she unaware that any image – regardless of the form it takes – can become a constraint if it calls for rigid conformity. (She compares the image of white, middle-class American woman in the 1950s with that of the Victorian lady, and notes that, while different, both models are equally restrictive.) She even goes so far as to note that women's achievement of technical sex equality in the 1940s and 1950s coincided with the arrival of an image which effectively prevented them from making use of the new opportunities.

It is more than a strange paradox that as all professions are finally open to women in America, 'career woman' has become a dirty word; that as higher education becomes available to any woman with the capacity for it[1] education for women has become so suspect that more and more drop out of high school and college to marry and have babies; that as so many roles in modern society become theirs for the taking, women so insistently confine themselves to one role. Why, with the removal of all legal, political, economic and educational barriers that once kept woman from being man's equal, a person in her own right, an individual free to develop her own potential, should she accept this new image which insists that she is not a person but a 'woman', by definition barred from the freedom of human existence and a voice in human destiny? (p.60)

Why indeed? What is the origin of this strange paradox which more firmly ties women to the home at the very same time that there is an extension in opportunities for women to enter the workforce and compete with men? If Betty Friedan answers this question at all, it is not in the terms which many feminists were later to employ.

Any blame to be apportioned was laid primarily at the door of Sigmund Freud – and the psychologists, educators and media-makers who put his theory into practice. It was Freud who had insisted that the human virtues were *manly* virtues, and that a woman who wanted to be human was neurotic, moved by a sense of envy in her desire to be a man. Such a woman failed to adjust to her femininity and was to be pitied for her failure. But even here Betty Friedan is concerned that Freud had made a 'mistake': she is much less concerned with *why* he should make this particular – and exceedingly convenient and male-enhancing – mistake.

She does not comment on the cleverness of the image construction – as Phyllis Chesler (1972) and Naomi Weisstein (1970) were to do later – or the convenience of a position where, if a woman does as she is told and conforms to the image of femininity, then she is clearly less-than-a-man, and so, of course, less than fully human; but if a woman defies instruction, refuses to adjust to her femininity, and insists on trying to do some of the things men do then she is still less-than-a-man, and not fully human.

From our standpoint in 1984, when men define humanity and male as one and the same thing, those who are non-male can never qualify as part of humanity. As long as male is 'the norm' then woman must be the 'deviant' whatever she does. But while this definition of the sexes is crucial to any analysis of the relationship between the sexes, it is not an issue that Betty Friedan pursued.

What she did do was make an excellent job of charting the restrictive nature of the feminine mystique for white, middle-class women. Accordingly she noted that one of the fundamental requirements of the image was that women should appear happy and contented; but she does not comment on the usefulness of this arrangement for men. Telling women they are only true women when they are happy and contented is a certain way of suppressing any complaints even before they arise, because any woman brave enough to declare that she doesn't like the life she is required to lead is breaking the rule of happiness and can immediately be branded as *not a true* woman: her opinion, her protest is suspect.

This is precisely the weapon used against Betty Friedan. She was herself condemned as a maladjusted woman: another pathetic woman who couldn't adjust to her femininity and wanted to be a man. With so many penalties for the woman who refused to feign happiness and who dared to complain, it is fair to suggest that it was the very act of protest itself which was one of Betty Friedan's major contributions. When she defied the image of the contented housewife, she found the crack in the mask of uncomplaining, blithely bland womanhood. She paved the way for women to move from silence to expression; by giving voice to women's experience, she indirectly undermined the authority of men to speak for women. She protested, knowing what the penalties for protest were. She knew from her own experience and from the experience of the women she talked with that women were taught that they should want one thing only – to be wives and mothers. She knew that if women showed signs of wanting anything else – and it was perfectly reasonable that they should want something else – they could quickly be branded as human failures. Both at home and at school women

were taught to pity the neurotic, unfeminine, unhappy women who wanted to be poets or physicists or presidents. They learned that truly feminine women do not want careers, higher education, political rights – the independence and opportunities that the old-fashioned feminists fought for. (p.13)

There was no mystery about the sort of response there would be. Women who were silly enough to talk of women's rights left themselves wide open to some of the cruellest and most damaging abuse. 'It has been popular in recent years,' she wrote, 'to laugh at feminism as one of history's dirty jokes; to pity, sniggering, those old-fashioned feminists who fought for women's rights to higher education, careers, the vote. They were neurotic victims of penis envy who wanted to be men' (p.71) To her credit, Betty Friedan went back to those neurotic feminists and reclaimed some of them from the disgraceful category to which they had been consigned, and proudly ranked herself with them.

It is unfortunate that Charlotte Perkins Gilman was not among those whom she helped to reinstate, for had she been familiar with Charlotte Perkins Gilman's work (Women and Economics, 1899; The Home: Its Work and Influence, 1903; The Man-made World or our Androcentric Culture, 1911) it is unlikely that she would have retained her analysis of

14

the problem as that of the 'feminine mystique'. *Women and Economics* is, in some senses, a forerunner of *The Feminine Mystique*, but it is consistently concerned with *why, how* and *by whom* women are confined to their less-than-human existence. Charlotte Perkins Gilman not only mentions money (a glaring omission in *The Feminine Mystique* where all the interviewees are white, middle-class and free from financial want), she refers again and again to the convenience of the arrangement for men, in which women are obliged to perform the unpaid work in the home, while men maintain their monopoly on paid work at the workplace. For Charlotte Perkins Gilman, male power was of paramount importance.

Betty Friedan's wording might have been different from some of the versions of the nineteenth century and earlier, but there can be no mistake about her clear call for rebellion. Her advice to women who were suffering from the problem without a name was simple and straightforward – they 'must unequivocally say "no" to the housewife image' (p.297). If the only sanctioned image for women was that of a housewife, Betty Friedan was inciting insurrection with her call to women to repudiate this role. However, she immediately added the reassuring note that the refusal to be the housewife did not necessarily mean that a woman 'must divorce her husband, abandon her children, give up her home'. Like some of her predecessors who, in their demand for the vote, had tried to mollify men by insisting that women would still want to look after them and their homes and children once they got it, Betty Friedan tried to take the sting out of her demand by declaring that women would *still* want to accept the responsibility of husband and home once they had careers. Without suggesting how the required number of hours were to be found in a day, she stated that a woman

> does not have to choose between marriage and career: that was the mistaken choice of the feminine mystique. In actual fact, it is not as difficult as the feminine mystique implies, to combine marriage and motherhood and even the kind of life-long personal purpose that was once called 'career'. It merely takes a new life plan – in terms of one's whole life as a woman. (p.297)

In the years to come, there were to be two major and contradictory criticisms of this solution. There were those who held her personally responsible for the break-up of the family; and there were those who saw her advocacy of the combination of motherhood *and* career as responsible for the new (and exhaustingly restrictive) image for women – that of 'superwoman'. By not addressing the issue of work in the home, and who should do it, feminists have argued that Betty Friedan was encouraging women to have two jobs, where previously they had had only one. She was proposing, as a solution, that women should enter the paid workforce, but she was not suggesting that men should assume their share of the unpaid work in the home. Nor did she have any advice for the many women who had tried her solution and found it wanting, who were already from necessity doing two jobs, and who could no doubt have told Betty Friedan that it wasn't as easy as she said it would be.

Betty Friedan counselled women to make a 'serious professional commitment' (p.303). It was no good having hobbies and interests, an hour off from home-making: too frequently these were just time-killers and did nothing to promote a woman's sense of worth. '[M]usic or art or politics offered no magic solution for the women who did not, or could not, commit themselves seriously,' for

> 'I have noticed that when women do not take up painting or ceramics seriously enough to become professionals – to be paid for their work, or for teaching it to others, and to be recognized as a peer by other professionals – sooner or later, they cease dabbling; the Sunday painting, the idle ceramics do not bring that needed sense of self when they are of no value to anyone else' (p.303).

Betty Friedan readily acknowledged that 'the jump from amateur to professional . . . is often hardest for a woman on her way out of the trap'(p.301), but it was a jump which had to be taken. For 'even if a woman does not have to work to eat, she can find identity only in work that is of real value to society – work for which, usually, our society pays. Being paid is, of course, more than a reward – it implies a definite commitment'(p.301).

No demand for equal work or equal pay: rather the assumption that women do not directly *need* money in the same way as men do for what it can *buy*, but indirectly, for the legitimacy it lends to their work. She is not challenging the whole value-system which measures personal worth in terms of personal wealth. She simply states that unpaid work is not valued – including housework and her own analysis of it in this category – and that if women want to be valued as human beings, then they must do work for which they *are* paid.

It was quite simple: women should have careers.

She begs the question of who does the dirty work when every woman has a career and, as Sheila Rowbotham (1973) has pointed out, this makes it difficult to take Betty Friedan's solution seriously. Like everyone else, Betty Friedan's view of the world is biased and limited by her own experience. She sees nothing absurd in her unequivocal injunction to *all* women to make a professional commitment. Yet, even in America, a vast number of women are ruled out of her solution from the beginning: 'a job, any job, is not the answer – in fact, it can be part of the trap. . . . If a job is to be the way out of the trap for a woman, it must be a job that she can take seriously as part of a life plan, work in which she can grow as part of society' (p.300). Without any acknowledgement of the inherent absurdity of the advice, she goes on to counsel the career-woman to spend her entire salary if necessary on domestic help and childcare!

The reader might, of course, assume that there is going to be a wholesale reversal of sex roles, that all women will be out at (professional) work, while men become the domestics and child-rearers. Such an assumption would be mistaken, for Betty Friedan envisages few changes for men. What she is advocating (but does not say) is a solution for *some* women.

And the women who cannot take her advice, who from necessity are obliged to settle for 'any job'? The chances are that they will have not one, but two 'hearth and home' jobs – their own, and that of the new career-woman they will be servicing. And if they felt failures when they could not measure up to the old image of the feminine mystique, how are they going to feel about not living up to the requirements of the new image of the career-woman? It may be that the *majority* of women would be – indeed *are* – in this situation. Betty Friedan could well have been opening a way out of the trap for some women; but for others she was constructing a new way in.

In short, Betty Friedan's understanding of the problem she named is biased and limited. But her book is remembered with affection by many for whom it was liberating and exhilarating. Her assertion that being a wife and mother was not a sufficient life-long goal, and that making a serious commitment to work (and financial independence) was not a

17

crime for which you would be ever after punished, was for many women of my generation permission to defy convention and to determine to make use of our education. Her example was also valuable when we were condemned as feminine failures. And her challenge to men's right to know everything, their right to decree women's existence, was one that we heard, took seriously, and developed.

She assumed the validity of the way the world worked – including the premise that the only existence for a woman was with a man – and it is not unjust to state that her aim was for some women to have a bigger and fairer slice of the cake. From her later writing, particularly *The Second Stage*, it becomes clear that she did not appreciate that her protest would inspire not just career-women to organise for reform, but a whole range of women to demand radical changes in society.

I suspect that Betty Friedan was astonished by the many and varied women who took up her call.

2. A Very Good Year:
The women's liberation movement

Many women took over from where Betty Friedan left off. What happened in the years immediately following 1963 is difficult to determine, but seven years after Betty Friedan pushed at the door it had opened to admit a women's movement – with a variety of voices. What must be said of 1970 is that it was a very good year for women.

Kate Millett's *Sexual Politics* preceded Germaine Greer's *The Female Eunuch* by a matter of weeks. 1970 also saw the publication of Shulamith Firestone's *The Dialectic of Sex*, Eva Figes' *Patriarchal Attitudes*, Robin Morgan's anthology, *Sisterhood Is Powerful*, and Alice Rossi's *Essays on Sex Equality by John Stuart Mill and Harriet Taylor Mill*. Between 1963 and 1970 there had been few books which were concerned with an analysis of women's position in society (although this could reveal more about the publishing industry's conservatism than about women's interests and writing), Mary Ellmann's *Thinking About Women* (1968) being a notable exception. Numerous articles were being written during this period – including Juliet Mitchell's powerful and perceptive essay, 'Women: The Longest Revolution' (1966), and Sheila Rowbotham's *Women's Liberation and the New Politics* (1969). But if a conservative publishing industry had been reluctant to risk books by, about and for women – and such angry and unpleasant books at that! – on the grounds that there was no demand for them (Lynne Spender, 1983), prejudice yielded to expediency in the bonanza year of 1970.

It is very seductive to try to plot the course of events after the publication of Betty Friedan's *The Feminine Mystique*, but I suspect that it is impossible at present, even for those who were involved. No doubt when our contrary accounts are resolved by the passage of time, a clear, chronological course will be constructed; but in the interim the most satisfactory explanation I can find for the development from a single voice to a chorus, for the emergence of the contemporary women's liberation movement, is the 'virus theory': women's liberation was in the air and scores of women on different continents caught it. What is possible, though, is to distinguish a number of contributory factors.

One was the publication of *The Feminine Mystique* and the way it brought women's dissatisfaction out into the open, but there were others, too. There was the contraceptive pill as well as the greater participation of professional women in the workforce – although even here I would not be prepared to state which came first. The technology of the pill had been available for some time, and it is just as likely that it now became generally available because women were needed in the workforce as that, once it was prescribed, women were able to enter the workforce. (I am also mindful of the fact that once women were no longer wanted in the workforce, the pill was discredited – which may or may not be a coincidence.)

But Betty Friedan, the pill and paid work do not even begin to add up to the turmoil of the 1960s. There was a great deal of revolutionary fervour at work during that decade: student protests, black protests, anti-war protests, and the flower children leaving home for life on the road or in communes. The absence of women's protest would have been surprising in this context. Indeed, it was the involvement of women in some of the protest movements which led directly to the women's liberation movement, for like the women of the nineteenth century who had fought for the abolition of slavery and who had found that in order to speak for the slaves they had first to defend their right to speak for themselves, many women in the protest movements found that although they were permitted to be workers for the revolution, they were not to partake of its rewards: liberation was for men only. 'Radical politics in the 1960s provided an excellent breeding ground for feminism,' wrote Anna Coote and Bea Campbell in *Sweet Freedom: The Struggle for Women's Liberation* (1982). 'Men led the marches and made the speeches and expected their female comrades to lick envelopes and listen. Women who were participating in the struggles to liberate blacks and Vietnamese began to recognize that they themselves needed liberating – and they needed it now, not "after the revolution" ' (p.13).

The contradiction involved in working for the liberation of others while being treated as a subordinate oneself was not lost on many women who started to ask their own questions and to come up with their own 'disruptive' answers. Attending a women's meeting in 1968 of the Revolutionary Students' Federation in London, Rosalind Delmar recalled that

> A male trade unionist came in and started telling us what to do. We told him to go away, no one was going to listen to him. There had always been a tendency on the student left to defer to industrial workers because they were felt to be more strategically important than anyone else – certainly more than women. I was very impressed with what we had done. (quoted in Coote and Campbell, *op. cit.*: 16)

There was uneasy and unsettled talk among women during the 1960s, not just in overtly political places, but wherever women met: at the school gates, in launderettes, at the supermarket checkout, in play-groups, as well as at the workplace. Reared in some of the richest countries in the world, initiated into society's values of the good life, women in English-speaking countries were becoming disillusioned as they realised that what they had been taught about the good life did not apply to them. They were the poor and the underprivileged, because they were women (see Juliet Mitchell, 1971: 21).

Jan Williams, a young mother in the 1960s, described the experience like this:

> I used to push my kids round and round the duckpond, wishing I could push them in it.... It [a women's club for young mothers run by Peckham Rye council] was really good. We talked about the same things again and again – about children, about sex, about being used. I had started a part-time job and my husband had said he would look after the kids, but he didn't. I began to feel there was something wrong with the unfairness and inequality of it. If you're at home all day and you keep everything together, you feel completely buffeted. Then you're expected to make love and it's just another imposition, another chore. (quoted in Coote and Campbell, 1982: 16)

Women were starting to experience being women in a positive sense when they talked to other women, but there was increasingly the negative experience of trying to inform men about the way they felt. I cannot remember reading a greater indictment of 'progressive' men than that provided by Robin Morgan in *Sisterhood Is Powerful* (1970) when she explained where some of the women had come from to join the women's liberation movement in the United States:

In 1964 Ruby Doris Smith Robinson, a young black woman who was founder of SNCC [then the Student Non-violent Co-ordinating Committee] wrote a paper on the position of women in that organization. It was laughed at and dismissed. In 1965, Casey Hayden and Mary King, two white women who had been active in SNCC and other civil rights organizations for years, wrote an article on women in the Movement for the now defunct journal, *Studies on the Left*. Women began to form caucuses within the Movement organizations where they worked; men's reactions ranged from fury to derision. In 1966, women who demanded that a plank on women's liberation be inserted in the SDS [Students for a Democratic Society] resolution that year were pelted with tomatoes and thrown out of the convention. (p.xxiv).

But such intimidatory tactics didn't work; on the contrary the momentum for an autonomous women's movement began to build up as women confronted more and more explicit evidence of the contempt in which men held them. By the spring of 1972, Joan Cassell (1977) was able to state that 'one informant estimated that every block in Manhattan had at least one consciousness-raising group. Observation tended to confirm this estimate' (p. 34). And while the emergence of consciousness-raising groups in Australia, Britain, Canada, for example, as well as the United States, was a sudden and very dramatic development, it was not without precedent. Similar confrontations had already occurred at Ruskin College, Oxford. Here regular history workshops were organised, and women reacted when once too often they were dominated by men: they decided that the next history workshop would be on women. But that wasn't enough – they would organise a women's conference. In February 1970, the first National Women's Liberation Conference in Britain was held at Ruskin College. It was an enormous success.

This was a visible event which made a reality of the women's liberation movement, but it didn't appear from nowhere. Behind it lay months – years – of increased concern about women, which had found expression in a variety of women's groups and which in itself comprised the formative stages of the women's movement. The geographical, social and political diversity which has characterised the movement was clearly present from the beginning when so many women found, to their astonishment, that hundreds of other women felt the same way. But where did the 600 women who attended this first British conference come from?

There were women from the newly formed women's liberation groups which had sprung up in cities, on campuses, within organisations, and out of existing political groups. There were women trade unionists determined that women should cease to be treated as second-class members of their unions, and who formed the National Joint Action Campaign for Women's Equal Political Rights. There were women from anti-war groups, whose consciousness had not only been raised by their treatment within the group, but by their growing perception of war as an integral part of male values. There were women who had come through the hippie experience and who had rejected an alternative life-style that demanded that women continue to give domestic and sexual services to men: 'Make Love, Not War' might have represented a liberated life-style for the male, but birthing and childcare in primitive conditions hardly qualified as an improvement for women.

There were women who had been motivated by an article or a course – Juliet Mitchell, for example, was a superb catalyst. Her article, 'Women: The Longest Revolution', appeared in New Left Review in 1966, and the following year she ran a course on 'The Role of Women in Society' at the Anti-University. Different groups took it in turns to produce the Shrew, and essays, newsletters and notes, too numerous even to begin to trace, were duplicated. They all had an effect.

Throughout this period, too, were the women of the suffrage movement who must have almost despaired of the present generation challenging male dominance. Their excitement and enthusiasm was rekindled. The Six Point Group (formed in 1920 to achieve six points for women's equality) had survived, and in 1968 its leader, Hazel Hunkins Hallinan, helped edit the group's publication, In Her Own Right. It was a book which again called for the emancipation of women and for the revolution which had begun – but had apparently petered out – to be completed (see Dale Spender, 1982b and 1984a). That women's liberation was once more in the air was their vindication. They also helped to give shape and substance to the issues which once again were finding expression.

In short, to look for a straightforward cause-and-effect model for the re-emergence of feminism in so many different countries is to distort much of the variability of its origins. Particular conditions in one country did not always pertain in another, yet the women's movement materialised at much the same time and with much the same commitment everywhere. For example, my experience as an Australian will not allow me to accept women's experience in the US civil rights movement as a definitive cause of the women's movement, for there was no comparable anti-racist campaign in Australia during the 1960s and yet the (white) women's movement made its appearance. Likewise, the Vietnam war and conscription which was tearing society apart in Australia and the United States was very different from the anti-war movement in Britain and Canada, yet the women's movement appeared virtually simultaneously on all three continents.

What can be said with confidence about this period is that women were dissatisfied, that they were becoming aware of contradictions, that the taboo against their complaining and protesting was breaking down, that they were beginning to give vent to their anger, and that they gained from finding that many other women felt much the same. Central to women's growing consciousness was the recognition that it was men who were presumed to know about women – to act and to speak for women – and with this came the conviction that it was time for women to take charge of their own lives and to claim the authenticity of their own experience. When women on different continents sat down to work out what was wrong – and to speak out – they came to strikingly similar conclusions, which in turn helped to reinforce their stand and encourage them to continue.

There were, of course, great differences in the analyses, just as there were enormous differences among the women writers. Kate Millett and Germaine Greer, for example, focused on literature (as Mary Ellmann had done (1968)), and began to examine the way men portrayed the world in general and women in particular. They drew from their studies the insight that power was a dimension of the relationship between the sexes, that it wasn't the same for women as for men, and that women had a lot less of it than men. This literary and theoretical approach was in direct contrast to Robin Morgan's 'school of hard knocks', where the lessons were based on personal experience and derived directly from the everyday lives of women. Eva Figes put the attitudes and values of a male-dominated society under the microscope, while Alice Rossi undertook an exercise in the history of ideas and looked to the philosophers of the past in order to understand more about the present relationship between the sexes. Shulamith Firestone adapted dialectical materialism on the basis of sex, rather than class, and Juliet Mitchell extended traditional Marxist and psychoanalytic theory to accommodate the oppression of women.

In spite of their different areas of inquiry and sources of evidence, these women had much in common. They were all speaking out, they were all putting forward a view of the world in which women were the starting point, the central reference point, and in which the supremacy of men was presented as a problem. Directly and indirectly they were challenging men's 'right to know everything', they were exposing the partial and self-interested nature of male meanings of the world, they were disputing men's authority and ability to delineate women's reality, and they were establishing women's right to describe and decide for themselves.

This diversity within a common framework now characterises contemporary feminism. But it is not surprising that women should have consciously adopted such an approach because it is closely related to their experience as women. Aware that one of the most fundamental problems they faced was that women's views of the world had for so long been suppressed, the last thing responsible women wanted was another, *single* view which would suppress the experience of those women who did not share it. Nothing would be gained by continuing in the male tradition of *one* explanation and *one* truth, in which difference was thereby denied. So often at odds with the dominant view, so sensitive to the bias and limitations of any one view no matter how 'official', so concerned with the issue of *who knows?*, and *by what authority?*, it would be little short of a double-standard for any one feminist or group to declare themselves in possession of the only 'truth'. Feminists, therefore, have had to break with the conventions in which they were reared, and come to terms with the possibility that *there is more than one truth*. This is not always an easy lesson to learn, and perhaps is easier learnt by some than others, but it is one of the reasons why there are not – and cannot be – any 'official' explanations in feminism. (The official verdict is that there will be no official verdicts!) Instead, there is a multiplicity of interpretations, and far from being accompanied by a flurried search to find them right or wrong, there is an acceptance – in varying degrees – of the coexistence of diverse and even contradictory explanations. A feminist framework which took women's experience of the world as central could hardly go any other way.

To come from a context in which one of the greatest indignities was that women's experience did not count, it would not have been sensible to set up a system for ordering the world – in which the experience of some women did not signify. Of course, the principles haven't always worked perfectly, and no doubt the multiplicity of truths can be confusing, but the intention behind the principle is a worthwhile and necessary one.

The notion that there are many truths is no more difficult to sustain (and probably less so) than the notion that there is only *one* truth, with its powerful demand for the denial of contradictions. And with women having been so systematically *left out* of the descriptions of humanity, what is *left out* of any explanation – including those of women – has become for feminists as crucial, and on occasion more crucial, than what is *left in*. It is the *absence* of the acknowledgement of the full humanity of others that is the source of so much bias and prejudice, be it based on dimensions of race, class, sex, age or sexuality.

It is not a question, then, of right or wrong, of true or false. The removal of this judgement leaves the way open for an examination of what is left out, what is unaccounted for: it allows for the exploration of everyone's biases, limitations, value-judgements. For while no *one* view may be the truth this does not mean that all views are equally valuable. Some are more helpful, more illuminating, and even more just than others; but this is a very different matter from true or false.

Yet all this discussion is more a comment on the developments of the bonanza year of 1970 and afterwards, and is therefore somewhat premature. Before the publication of all those books in 1970 there was only an embryonic network, and the probability of Kate Millett, Germaine Greer, Shulamith Firestone, Eva Figes and Robin Morgan each knowing what the other was doing or thinking was remote indeed. In 1984 we can examine the multiplicity of feminist explanations and derive benefit from their rich diversity; but in the late 1960s the women who were developing these explanations were, in one sense, very much on their own.

3. On Changing Thinking: Ask a feminist

Betty Friedan had helped to describe the realities of women's lives: the next step was for women to explain them. By 1970 this analysis was well under way and a variety of explanations for women's position were being advanced. But there was one respect in which all these women writers were in agreement: women's position was untenable. Whether the reference was to Kate Millett's analysis of the power-base of the sexes, to Germaine Greer's inventory of misogynistic assertions, to Eva Figes' exposure of entrenched patriarchal beliefs, to Robin Morgan's documentation of personal tactics for supremacy, or to Shulamith Firestone's views on the uses and abuses of reproduction, the picture of women's existence which emerged was stark and insupportable. The plight of women could be held up as an indictment of the whole of society and one response was predictable. If the situation was as awful as these feminists were claiming, why weren't more women aware, incensed, and making every effort to protest and to free themselves? Why was it such a pressing and painful issue now, if only last week it hadn't been noticed?

It may be helpful at this point to consider the role of social theory in general. All human beings are influenced by the particular belief-system in which their culture has initiated them, and this system helps to circumscribe their view of the world. Members of one culture, for example, will see as a delectable food what members of another culture find repellant; similarly, members of one society may see as erotic what members of another society find distasteful. Even the colours of the spectrum are experienced differently according to the linguistic and cultural concepts of the observer.

Thus, human beings tend to project onto the objects and events of the world the value-system they have learned, selecting evidence from the world which fits into, and reinforces, the belief-system of their culture. Depending on the society in which we live, we are 'programmed' for a particular and limited set of meanings, and we then proceed to respond only to that which is meaningful to us. Contradictions tend to be censored, and we continue to see only that which is consistent with our established world-view. This theory helps to explain why it is that human beings from different societies – or from different groups within the same society – are not always led to the same world-view by the same empirical evidence.

If this were *all* we could do, then the prospects for change would be bleak indeed, but fortunately we are not confined by our original value-system. It is not an entirely closed system; there is some room for conflicting evidence – the contradictions – to creep in. Sometimes we come to see as meaningful and significant something which previously went unnoted.

The development of feminist theory has been specifically concerned with understanding the way we think, and how we can think differently. The very existence of feminist theory is evidence that human reasoning is not a completely closed system, because if we could not see beyond our accepted societal values, if we were totally locked into a patriarchal value-system, we would not have been able to conceptualise a feminist alternative. But there is considerable debate about just how *far* we can break free from our conditioning, and many feminists, including Mary Daly (1978) and Margrit Eichler (1980), argue that we don't get very far at all, that we are constantly hampered by our patriarchal assumptions even while we formulate our feminist theory. A slow process it may be to 'decode' our minds, but the crucial issue is that we can begin.

Feminist theory is essentially concerned with consciousness and conditioning, because these are the very realms in which women have been expressly disadvantaged. Men have developed the mode of thinking in our society[1] on the basis of their experience, so it is precisely the experience of women – *if it stands in contradiction to the male view of the world* – which is omitted or ignored. If we want to have women's experience incorporated then we have to change the way society thinks. This means that feminists have a vested interest in understanding the processes of thinking and reasoning, and, in order to develop a feminist theory, have to begin by exploring and explaining human consciousness and the reasons why the vast, varied and valid realms of human experience that pertain to women have been left out.

It is no coincidence that the contemporary women's movement was ushered in on a wave of *consciousness-raising*, which specifically challenged our socialisation and ways of thinking. Such consciousness-raising activities can help to reveal the extent to which our minds can be 'colonised'; but they can also demonstrate the rapidity with which 're-programming' can take place. The feminist literature on consciousness-raising is full of accounts of the sudden and spectacular way the perception of the world can change shape when the 'mind-set' of conditioning is broken: Jessie Bernard (1972) calls this the 'click phenomenon', when, in an instant, a woman sees the world differently.

This *switch* from one world-view to another raises a number of important questions. Within a framework where only one truth is recognised and where the world is divided into right and wrong, the exposure of patriarchy as a false world-view can – with limited and circular reasoning – lead to the conclusion that feminism is the *true* world-view. Is this conclusion justified?

In my terms, a feminist framework need be no more 'true' than a patriarchal one, but this does not mean that it isn't a good deal better!

The patriarchal world-view begins – and ends – with male experience of the world, and takes little or no account of women's experience where it differs from men's. The feminist world-view, however, begins with women's experience of the world *which includes the experience of patriarchy and the limitations of male reasoning*. It therefore offers a broader and more encompassing world-view than patriarchy.

While it is understandable that men who are given no reason to believe that there is anything valid outside their known male experience and have no 'programme' to make sense of women's experience should be puzzled by women, there is little likelihood that men's views and values will remain a mystery to women, for women have to live in and operate in a patriarchal reality defined by men, and are therefore familiar with its meanings.

But this is not the only ground for claiming that the feminist framework is better: it is also better because it is more just, because it offers half of humanity a means of explaining their oppression in terms other than that it is their own fault. It is a framework which offers the potential of change and is a better view of the world in that it seeks a better world.

The assumption of society that feminism has focused on is that of male supremacy. Prior to the efforts of comtemporary feminists, this belief virtually went unquestioned. Members of society assumed that it was *natural* for men to enjoy the privileges that they did, and *natural* for women to be dependent on the greater male resources. Being part of the *natural* world there was nothing that could be done about this. For men to be seen as superior was just as normal as the once-held belief that the world was flat, or that it had been made in six days. To think of changing the nature of man was as inconceivable as it had once been to think in terms of a world with a different shape or an alternative account of creation. These were the givens and it was madness to propose alternatives. As Shulamith Firestone states in the opening paragraph of *The Dialectic of Sex* (1970), *'That*? Why, you can't change *that*! You must be out of your mind!'

'Out of your mind' is not such a bad representation of feminists, for in a sense we do have to get 'out of our minds', out of the mind-set we have been socialised into. It is a mark of feminist achievement that male supremacy (patriarchy, male dominance) can now be recognised as a part of social reality in English-speaking societies as a round world and the theory of evolution are. And because feminism has necessarily been concerned with the way we think and how we change our patterns of thinking it has made a contribution to our social understandings of the nature of consciousness and knowledge.

4. Men as the Enemy: Kate Millett's politics

In 1970, Kate Millett may not have been aware of all the variations on the feminist theme which were even then in the process of construction, but she wasn't completely without guidance when she wrote *Sexual Politics*. There were the lessons of an earlier women's movement to be studied (and her discussion of this historical background comprises the longest section of her book), and there were also the more recent scholars, among them Simone de Beauvoir, Viola Klein,[1] Betty Friedan and Mary Ellmann.

But if Betty Friedan had exposed the discrepancy between the official version of women's lives and women's own version, Kate Millett went one step further: she systematically stripped men of their authority to speak for women and declared that it was nothing other than male self-interest which was at the root of so many 'official' pronouncements on what women should be. Part of her considerable achievement lies in the fact that she made her case in the academic mode in which she had been educated – that of 'objectivity' and 'proof'. Using these to discredit the 'knowledge' that men had created she proposed the reasonable hypothesis that there is a power dimension in the relationship between the sexes. Her move was both brave and brilliant – brave because it exposed her to all manner of censure; brilliant because it helped to indicate just how partial and prejudiced was previous scholarship. In *Sexual Politics* Kate Millett made it very clear that what the knowledge-makers left out not only revealed their limitations, but pointed to the self-interested nature of their knowledge-making – the very discipline which they held to be value-free and objective.

Her first task was to present a convincing case for the existence of this power dimension. She thus begins with 'Instances of Sexual

31

Politics', in which she turns to literature and the worlds created by three men – Henry Miller, Norman Mailer and Jean Genet. She lets them speak for themselves, with the result that her book opens with three stark examples of male exploitation of women. She provides a new angle for the examination of their writing, but lets these male writers establish her case for the existence of power relations between the sexes. Once the existence of power as a dynamic of the relationship between the sexes has been documented by the men, she then accounts for the origin and particular manifestations of this power.

Things have changed since Kate Millett brought the consideration of power into the discussion of what she termed 'sexual politics'. It was an idea that was unthought of by Betty Friedan, for example; and at that time most people did not understand what the term signified. Today there may be those who disagree with the concept of sexual politics, but there aren't very many who don't know what it means. Much of the credit for this must go to Kate Millett, who defined this dimension of male power so clearly, concisely and convincingly.

It is not easy to step into the unknown, to introduce a new vocabulary to define something which has not been formulated before, but this was what Kate Millett did, and many women have benefited from her pioneering work. Giving shape to women's view of the world, changing old habits of thinking, and finding the words to bring a new world-view into existence was, and still is, a primary feminist task. Virtually every feminist is aware of the significance of 'naming' and some have made it the central concern of their work, including Mary Daly (1973, 1978), Elizabeth Janeway (1980), Cheris Kramarae (1981), Adrienne Rich (1980), Sheila Rowbotham (1973) and Dale Spender (1980).

For women who are continually trying to put back what men have left out there is not just the problem of the absence of a vocabulary to define what we mean, there is also the difficulty that existing words carry the meanings of the dominant group and are therefore precisely what we do *not* mean. Yet if we are to communicate we must make use of the words that are available, even when they are resistant to our purposes. As Sheila Rowbotham (1973) has said, 'As soon as we learn words we find ourselves outside them' (p.32). Because we have no alternative but to use them, our meanings are restricted and our dependence on the language of the dominant group is reaffirmed.

To express our submerged alternative meaning is a daunting task, but it is one which Kate Millett undertook, and with few known precedents to guide her, her achievement is impressive. With her descriptive outline and her reference points, she provided the foundation stones of a feminist theory, and the women who came after her were able to build on and expand the concept of sexual politics: in all the concepts and explanations that have since become part of feminist theory, there are few which cannot be found in Kate Millett's framework. This is one of the reasons why her description and explanation warrant such close attention.

The rule of our society, stated Kate Millett, is that of *patriarchy*: it is the rule of men over women, and it is a blatant political system which provides one sex with power and resources, while it denies them to the other, and thereby ensures that those who have power keep it. Patriarchy is no different from any other political system in which those who rule enjoy power and privileges which are unavailable to those who are ruled. Because the rulers wish to continue to rule, they have different priorities from those who are ruled. As in other political systems, then, there are not only two groups with unequal resources and different priorities; there are two groups with a *conflict of interest*.

This conflict, however, can be submerged or denied because those who rule have the ruling ideas, one of which is that they have a right to rule and that it is for the good of the whole society that they should do so. Their rule is not recognised as a problem for the simple reason that it poses no problem for them, and they have the power to identify what the 'problems' of society are. Thus men, as rulers, can dispute the very existence of sexual politics, and do so because it is in the interest of maintaining their power. If they are to maintain the *status quo* which provides them with benefits and presents them with no problems, then it is not in their own interests to undermine their own authority by trying to establish that there is a conflict of interest between the sexes. Besides, argues Kate Millett, it's not just a matter of self-interest, it's also a matter of capability. So great is the difference between the rulers and the ruled that women and men inhabit completely different cultures (which she likens to apartheid), with the result that those who occupy the institutions of power – 'the military, industry, technology, universities, science, political office and finance – in short every avenue of power within society including the coercive force of the police is entirely in male hands' (p.25) – are not capable of comprehending the realities of the world of those who are ruled, and who must daily contend with that power. This exercise of male power is not a superficial or partial system; partriarchy is the basic means of rule: 'However muted its present appearance may be,' she writes, 'sexual dominion obtains nevertheless as perhaps the most pervasive ideology of our culture and provides its most fundamental concept of power' (p.25).

In a society where the relationship between the sexes was posited on the highest values of civilisation – mutual respect, cooperation, even love – this analysis of an undisguised power-play met with resentment, anger, outrage and a great deal of denial. Secure in the idea that the overriding rationale was *love*, many were affronted with the idea that power and not love was the guiding principle of public and *private* alliances. Such a reality, so far removed from what they had been 'programmed' to accept, was too harsh a change to be welcomed or adopted by many women and men. With the simple premise that men were the rulers and women were the ruled, and that this was the basis of all relationships between the two, Kate Millett's description gave rise to distressing implications for women, and threatening implications for men.

In effect what Kate Millett was doing in outlining the conflict of interest between the rulers and the ruled was drawing up sides. Unlike Betty Friedan who had stopped short with a restrictive image of women, Kate Millett went on to look at who was responsible for this image and who it was who required their conformity. She identified men as the power-group which established different rules for themselves and for women, and who did so on the basis of promoting and perpetuating their own advantage. In short, there was a conflict of interest.

Since the publication of *Sexual Politics* the notion of 'men as the enemy' has been widely discussed and has roused considerable controversy, partly because of the implications it has for personal relationships between the sexes. To some who have analysed the construction of women's dependence in sexual and economic terms, it is perfectly clear that women and men have opposing political interests and that, therefore, for women this view of men is appropriate and acceptable (see discussion on Adrienne Rich, pp.184-200). But to others, such a crude representation of half of humanity, in which no reference is made to individual characteristics, is nothing less than offensive; and because it can raise the level of hostility and exacerbate the tensions between the sexes, the designation of men as the enemy can, in this view, be counter-productive.

The same evidence – that men have power and use it to deny power to women – can lead to very different conclusions among feminists themselves. Some assert that the way forward is to challenge men for their power, while others are equally insistent that women should cooperate with men, so that men will see the benefits of power-sharing. This difference in approach is not new, of course: a similar controversy arose in the nineteenth-century women's movement in both Britain and the United States when one group became militant and engaged in a battle between the sexes while the other persisted with their efforts of peaceful persuasion.

But apart from the interesting illustration this historical background provides, there is another matter which calls for attention: why is it so difficult to represent the opposing interests between the sexes in our society? Why is it seen as anything from unpatriotic to unreasonable for women to express their grievances against men and to portray men as being on the other side? The same objections do not seem to have been raised in other contexts where the ruled have protested against their rulers and taken measures to put an end to an unjust regime. Women who protest about *male* rule are rarely praised for their sense of justice and their intentions.

Sheila Rowbotham (1973) suggests that the source lies in the fact that 'the relationship of man [sic] to women is like no other relationship of oppressor to oppressed' for 'after all, the two often love one another' and this is 'very different from the relationship between worker and capitalist' (pp.34–5). Granted, the worker and the capitalist are not required to live together, love one another, or link their genes, but is this the best explanation we can find? 'Love' of the oppressor and hetero sexuality no doubt complicate the 'politics' of the relations between the sexes, but surely the idea that power can be exercised at these intimate levels of existence reveals a great deal about the nature of our society and its value-system, and is not just an obstacle to coherent and fruitful debate. In Kate Millett's terms, this relationship between the sexes is the crucial model of power relations for society, and I do not think it mere coincidence that it is made difficult for women to identify, comment upon, and object to this form of rule.

Still, recognising why women can have trouble naming men as the enemy does little to help solve the problem. There are women for whom it is valid for men to be represented as the enemy, and women for whom neither men as a class nor men as individuals are the enemy, and there is little point in trying to decide which is the true representation, for any one view would leave out the contradictions and be only a partial description. What is required is a representation which validates both views. The only way this can be achieved is by acknowledging the multiplicity of interpretations.

This is not all that difficult. In my own case, I have little trouble with the idea that some men are my enemy and some are not, that I am against men as a social category but not against their humanity, that I object to the institutionalisation of male power but not *a priori* to all men. When it is a matter of politics it is clear to me that I am on a different side from men who, no matter what their individual characteristics or their propensity for utilising their power, derive benefit from patriarchy: but then, politics is not the sole dimension of existence and it would be restrictive and distortive to reduce human affairs to a simple politicism.

If one believes that male power is not sustained by deliberate intent but is more a matter of ignorance which can be overcome by education, then the categorisation of men as the enemy is neither sensible nor serviceable. But if one sees the problem in terms of power and politics (as Kate Millett did) and recognises that no ruling group has ever readily surrendered its power (as Kate Millett did) then categorising men as the enemy is plausible and practical.

This was not all that Kate Millett did, of course. In her construction of a feminist theory she provided illuminating insights into thinking, and her observations on patriarchy at work are noteworthy. She focuses on the belief in male supremacy throughout society and then documents the way in which this supremacy is constructed as individuals select the evidence and forge the meanings so that male supremacy 'comes true'. Patriarchy doesn't *depend* on men being superior, she argues, because once the concept of male supremacy is built into the social code, men are automatically accorded supremacy since any contradictory evidence is left out. She implies that male dominance will not end until the concept of 'male-as-superior' is eliminated from the belief-system that is used to find meaning in the world. Given the problems of changing the patterns of thinking, this frame of reference is pessimistic. But Kate Millett acknowledges and finds remarkable that men have for so long been able to maintain their primacy without reference to their performance: there is 'cause to admire the strength of a "socialization" which can continue a universal condition "on faith alone" ' (p.31).

To Kate Millett there was little that was random about patriarchy: it

36

is a complete system of interlocking parts, which perpetuates itself by socialising its members in terms of temperament, role and status (p.26) – girls being prescribed a very different temperament, role and status from boys.

The concept of socialisation became popular after the publication of *Sexual Politics*. One school of thought held that the initiation into appropriate sex roles was equally restrictive for both sexes because each was confined to only half of human qualities. This reasoning, which takes the politics out of socialisation, has little to link it with Kate Millett's analysis for she never lost sight of the issue that, while both sexes are socialised, one is socialised to assume and exercise power and the other is not. She would have no part in a framework which left out power and suggested a spurious sex parity. Even sex roles could not become apolitical entities in Kate Millett's hands: she defined them as a code of conduct for each sex which assigned 'domestic service and attendance upon infants to the female, the rest of human achievement, interest and ambition to the male'. And added, 'The limited role allotted to the female tends to arrest her at the level of biological experience' (p.26).

Once more Kate Millett challenges cherished assumptions about women's disposition for the care of hearth and home, and men's endowment which supposedly destines them for achievement. Men see domesticity as low-status work, whereas achievement offers them rewards. In this analysis there is nothing 'normal' or 'beautiful' about sex roles, they simply reflect men's self-interest. That women are seen as 'close to nature' while men are granted the role of 'creators of culture' (an issue which recurs in feminist debates) is another axiom which gets short shrift in Kate Millett's book: if women are disproportionately associated with the biological world, she states, it is because men have permitted them no other realm.

Her criticisms of the asymmetry – and its origins – in the formation of sex-appropriate personalities or temperaments are equally caustic. The division into masculine and feminine is 'based on the needs and values of the dominant group and dictated by what its members cherish in themselves and find convenient in subordinates: aggression, intelligence, force and efficacy in the male; passivity, ignorance, docility, "virtue" and ineffectuality in the female' (p.26).

This is the touchstone of Kate Millett's thesis: that men have the power and use it to take what they value and need for themselves, and allocate what they don't want to women (see also Jean Baker Miller, 1978). Feminists who subscribe to the theory of sexual politics recognise that while existing social arrangements are limiting to both sexes, these are limitations which men desire and which they are in a position to modify: women are not.

But for Kate Millett, sex role and temperament are not the full story: there is also the matter of status. An underlying principle of her thesis is not only to expose the discrepancy between the official explanations of the social order and the workings of power that such an ideology helps to mask, but also her revelations on male status. She scoffs at the notion of a predestined order in which men 'unfold' as superior creatures: on the contrary, they take so much more than their share of resources that it would be surprising if they had not emerged as superior. Their status has little to do with individual or collective merit. After exposing the shortcomings of the 'official' explanations, Kate Millett outlines one of the most convenient 'conclusions' of the circular arguments of the dominant group. The final indignity that women must suffer is that it is not enough that men should take all the high-status opportunities for themselves: they then go on to *blame* women for possessing only those things which men do not want.

Holding women responsible for events over which they have no control (rape being a primary example) may not be sound logic, but it makes sense in a patriarchal society, for it allows men to retain their high status no matter what they do. This practice has been referred to as a *scapegoat* mechanism and is a common topic in feminist analysis: many feminists, including Mary Daly (1973), have pointed to the contribution made by Judeo-Christian religion which established Eve as the first scapegoat. Making women scapegoats allows men to continue to enjoy their high status no matter what they do, and women to continue to be confined to their low status – no matter what they do. Feminists have labelled this reality of women the *double-bind*.

From linguistics (Robin Lakoff, 1975) to mental health (Phyllis Chesler, 1972) the double-bind which women daily confront has been clearly outlined. In *Sexual Politics* the double-bind is not an accident, but an integral part of male rule: women are damned if they do not become 'feminine' but they are no less damned if they follow the precepts of femininity, for this disqualifies them from participation in high-status, male activities.

The force of Kate Millett's analysis lies not just in what she says, but in how she says it. This is no 'feminine' expression seeking approval from those in power, nor is it a sanctioned view of the social order. On the contrary, it is an act of insurrection against male rule. Kate Millett wilfully breaks the code. To her, patriarchy had not developed haphazardly; it was a purposeful system which men had evolved, from which they profited, which they preferred, and wished to preserve. Patriarchy would not be easily dislodged, she claimed, because of the hold it has over our minds as well as the methods it has established for the unequal distribution of resources.

One of the most significant contributions Kate Millett made was to begin to break the hold that patriarchy has over our minds.

Where the 'official' ideology is one premised on the autonomy and uniqueness of the individual and free will, as in most western societies, then any alternative ideological interpretation which stresses the mechanistic and political nature of socialisation and programming appears inconsistent, if not alien. Kate Millett's view of society makes a mockery of some of our most cherished beliefs: it exposes the sheer absurdity of the idea that women choose to be deprived of their share of resources and are content to be dependent on men; it derides the idea that women willingly enter domestic service and freely take up responsibility for the young, that they want to stay out of high-status occupations and gladly forfeit the financial rewards, that they are deservedly responsible for the behaviour of men over whom they have no control, that their status is of their own making.

With its almost acultural description of power, its ruthless elimination of the gloss of sentiment and its indictment of our gullibility, it is no wonder that many find Kate Millett's ideology difficult to understand and difficult to accept. It demands a change in thinking, it demands that we inhabit a very different and much harsher world. It is not a peaceful and harmonious world-view, but one where power and conflict predominate.

While Kate Millett has presented a convincing case for the reality of sexual politics, there is one aspect of her analysis which calls for clarification. In her version men are heading in one direction while women are sent in another, with the inference that men reap the riches and the rewards while women are enjoined to settle for anything the men don't want. This implies that what men appropriate is valuable in itself and that conversely, what women are left with is of little or no value. However, this dichotomy reveals more about the value society places on the status of the sexes than the inherent value of their activities. In present society warfare may be glorious, and childcare a chore, but in a different society, war could be regarded as worthless and childcare worthwhile – particularly if women were sent to fight and men put their energies into rearing the next generation. Allowance needs to be made for men bestowing 'supremacy' on anything they undertake.

The understanding that status can reside in the sex and not the activity is not new: Margaret Mead (1938/1977) and other anthropologists have shown through cross-cultural studies that men undertake a variety of activities from cooking and weaving, to making magic and experiencing labour pains, and that wherever men perform such activities they are accorded high status; wherever women perform the *same* activities they are not of high status. So it's not simply a case of men taking the absolute 'best' in society for themselves: some of the things they do are only ranked 'best' because men do them.

It is not a feminist principle that women should have half of what men have because it's not a feminist belief that men are the yardstick, or even that what they do is desirable. The issue is to construct a new frame of reference and a new society, and this is why it is difficult to propose straightforward strategies for change. There are no simple measures that can be taken today – from the removal of sexist images in educational literature to the passing of the Equal Rights Amendment in the USA – which will eradicate patriarchy. It is more a matter of transformation in our *thinking*, a change in the way we organise the world. The sort of society this would create is unknown, and the business of explaining how it is to be achieved is further complicated by the fact that we can only refer to the unknown in terms of the known. But Kate Millett made an excellent beginning.

If Betty Friedan looked at the lives of individual women and encountered 'the problem without a name', then Kate Millett looked at the collective lives of women, at the position of women under a system of male rule, and named the problem 'sexual politics' – a structural position of women, which surveys the many facets of existence where male power impinges on women's lives.

Always Kate Millett's analysis works on two levels: the material and the psychological – although perhaps the terms 'ideological' or 'consciousness' would be more appropriate. On the material level she vividly describes the reality of sexual politics, the unequal distribution of resources; the asymmetrical division of human characteristics (whereby women are denied the possibility of action in the world, for example); and the physical oppression that women are subject to (whereby women are treated as sex objects or are the recipients of male violence). But with this discussion of the material world there is always an analysis of why this should be so, of how such ruthless politics could be made palatable for women, so that we are beguiled into believing that male rule is just.

Kate Millett holds up the conventional rationales for the existing order and repudiates them. That men should claim a greater share of right on the grounds that they are bigger or stronger is just so much nonsense:

> Male supremacy, like other political creeds, does not reside in physical strength but in the acceptance of a value system which is not biological. Superior physical strength is not a factor in political relations – *vide* those of race and class. Civilization has always been able to substitute other methods (technic, weaponry, knowledge) for those of physical strength, and contemporary civilization has no further need of it. At present, as in the past, physical exertion is generally a class factor, those at the bottom performing the most strenuous tasks, whether they be strong or not. (p.27)

Women do most of the world's dirty work.

One of the characteristics of our western pattern of thinking is that we continually seek to know *the cause* (or, more precisely, continually construct causes). It is not surprising then that this pattern should produce the question, 'How did it all start?' Considerable space has been devoted to this issue, inside and outside feminist circles, and it is fascinating to attempt to find the *first cause* of anything. It is perfectly possible that patriarchy didn't always exist, that it started at some particular point in time and for some particular reason; it is even quite plausible to put forward the proposition that before patriarchy, there was matriarchy. Kate Millett is prepared to entertain this possibility and to speculate on the social arrangements which prevailed before men were able to establish paternity: not familiar with the role men played in reproduction 'humanity would perhaps find the most impressive evidence of creative force in the visible birth of children, something of a miraculous event and linked analogically with the growth of the earth's vegetation' (p.26).[2]

Yet we do not need definitive evidence of the first cause to know that men have power, that they have had it for a very long time, that they seem to have it in every known human society, and that they now use it to keep their power. The *status quo* argument holds that because men have power now, this is the way it should be. This is probably the weakest argument of all to justify patriarchy, but, as Kate Millett points out, it is probably the most difficult to overcome. 'Perhaps patriarchy's greatest psychological weapon,' she suggests, 'is simply its universality and longevity. A referent scarcely exists with which it might be contrasted or by which it might be confuted' (p.58).

But what Kate Millett does not need to speculate upon is the manner in which male dominion is exercised in the present. She identifies *the family* as the basic unit of male rule and a primary source of women's oppression. It is in the family that women are subsumed (under the head of the house), where they are exploited by working for no pay, and where they are prevented from organising by their physical isolation and the extent of their workload.

If women are oppressed by the structure of the family, then one solution is for the family to go, and there have certainly been moves in this direction over the last decade: 'Only 5 per cent of households [in Britain] are made up of working husband, economically inactive wife and two dependent children' (Equal Opportunities Commission, *The Fact About Women Is*, 1983 edition). But where are women to go? To even more isolated conditions, and with dependent children? As many feminists have recently suggested – Judith Stacey (1983) among them – if the traditional family is to go, it is necessary to find some other form of organisation to put in its place. Our failure to provide an alternative means that now 'we are paying quite a costly political and personal price' (Stacey, 1983: 576). She sees much of the contemporary backlash against feminism as a response to this failure to provide an alternative so that while the family has its faults, many women will settle for it 'as the last bastion of intimacy in an alienating world' (p.563).

Not that the blame for this can be laid at Kate Millett's door: she was presenting an analysis of patriarchy, not a blueprint for an alternative society. In fact, she constantly points out just how difficult it is to conceptualise and bring into existence alternative social arrangements. But Judith Stacey's assessment helps to show how feminist theories do not automatically lead to the provision of a viable alternative.

No comparable criticisms of the gap between feminist theory and practice have arisen, however, in the wake of Kate Millett's analysis of women's access to education and paid work in a technological world. She gives a derisory account of economics as a discipline with its inherent bias which allows men to be paid for the work they do but not women, and she covers all the features of what was to become the domestic labour debate of the early 1970s: 'In terms of industry and production, the situation of women is in many ways comparable both to colonial and pre-industrial peoples,' she writes,

> for women do not participate directly in technology or production. What they customarily produce (domestic and personal service) has no market value and is, as it were, pre-capital. Nor where they do participate in production of commodities through employment, do they own or control or even comprehend the process in which they participate. (p.41)

When *Sexual Politics* was written, a third of women were already in the workforce, and their average wage was half that of men (p.40). Since that time there has been a marked increase in women's participation in paid employment, but no commensurate increase in their overall financial position. Indeed, there is mounting evidence that women's poverty is increasing (see Hilda Scott, 1984). Currently, it would be extremely difficult to substantiate the belief that 'women have never had it so good' and easy to demonstrate the veracity of the claim made by the nineteenth-century feminist, Matilda Joslyn Gage, that the harder women work, the poorer they get.[3] The issue is not just one of paid work for women, but *which work*, and *what pay*.

Kate Millett certainly foresaw the present deteriorating state of affairs. Women are intentionally excluded from knowledge of the technical processes of society, she claimed in 1970, to the extent that 'in the absence of males, women's distance from technology today is so great it is doubtful whether they could replace or repair [any] machines (including domestic ones) on any significant scale' (p.41). It is interesting to note that Betty Friedan did not recommend her new career-women to take up engineering. Her examples were predominantly associated with the arts. Yet to Kate Millett, Betty Friedan's was no solution; on the contrary, it was part of the problem: 'In keeping with the inferior sphere of culture to which women in patriarchy have always been restricted, the present encouragement of their "artistic" interests through study of the humanities is hardly more than an extension of "accomplishments" they once cultivated in preparation for the marriage market' (p.43).

Kate Millett also sets out the parameters for the ensuing debate on whether women are excluded from technology, or whether they choose to boycott it on the grounds of its inhumanity. She pre-empts the possibility that all will be well once women have a more technical education and get involved in technology: there can be no easy solutions for the transformation of patriarchal society.

Systematically, she dismantles the ideology of male rule. She dismisses the rationale that women reap their rewards through true love (admittedly not a taxing intellectual task), and advances instead the assertion that women are offered romantic love as 'a sporting kind of reparation to allow the subordinate female certain means of saving face' (p.37), adding that the belief in romantic love also serves to overcome the sexual prohibitions that are placed upon females. She undermines the notion that it is through motherhood that women achieve a sense of significance, by revealing just how little control women have over their own bodies. When it comes to reproduction and sexuality women are without autonomy, the female is 'more often a sexual object than a person' and she is still denied sexual freedom and the biological control over her body through the cult of virginity, the double-standard, the proscription of abortion, and in many places because 'contraception is physically or psychically unavailable to her' (p.54). In short, women are permitted to be mothers only on men's terms.

For women to accept patriarchy it has been necessary to convince them that they do have a 'valued' place within the political system. In *Sexual Politics*, Kate Millett takes as one of her primary tasks that of exposing the debased nature of this 'value'. She reveals the absurdity of the idea that women can be valued and achieve high status via personal beauty (p.55). Through her analysis of the images of women (and who is behind them), and of the representation of women in the media, she shows the extent to which women are seen – and treated – as objects in a male-dominated society which accords value and normalcy to maleness, and defines all that is not male as available for male use.

The 'divide and rule' technique which the dominant group employs by requiring women to compete for men is also denounced. Men have set up 'a lively antagonism between whore and matron . . . between career woman and housewife' (p.38). She does not flinch from facing the fact that many women feel they have a vested interest in the existing political arrangements, because so many can 'identify their own survival with the prosperity of those who feed them' (p.38). Her treatise also helps to raise the issue (more fully elaborated by Adrienne Rich, 1981) that if women do find men necessary to their existence, why is it that the social organisation must be geared to ensure that women align themselves with men? One does not have to investigate very fully to realise that women are denied so many opportunities (including that of equal work and equal pay) that they are frequently channelled into dependency upon men. This naturally results in making men very important in women's lives; it can facilitate directing their energies towards a concern with helping their 'provider' succeed in the world, rather than towards changing that world. But it still leaves unanswered the question of why it is that the rulers have found it necessary to construct their centrality in women's lives. Could it be that they are frightened of being superfluous if women are autonomous? This is an explanation that was later advanced by Adrienne Rich (1981), but it is one which was foreshadowed by Kate Millett. (It could also be a possibility anticipated by men, for many in the male medical establishment are currently engaged in a frenetic race to *produce* children; see Arditti *et al.*, 1984.)

Kate Millett's exposé of (male) myth and religion, and the weight they have predictably lent to the justification for male rule, undermines some of the most sanctioned beliefs (p.53). Her critique of the social sciences in general, and of Sigmund Freud in particular (all products of the patriarchal mind-set, and instrumental in the devaluation of women), is acerbic. And while she makes her way through the maze of 'proofs' and 'justifications' men have given for their right to rule, she also keeps to the forefront of her account the understanding that, although it may be desirable for us voluntarily to accept patriarchy and its ideology, our willing agreement is by no means essential; we can always be induced to conform by force.

So perfect is patriarchy's 'system of socialization, so complete the general assent to its values, so long and so universally has it prevailed in human society that it scarcely seems to require violent implementation' (p.43). But if we think that patriarchy does not rely on force, then we reveal yet another instance of the way we are programmed to see and make sense of a limited range of events. For it is indisputable that we are surrounded by violation – from images of women in misogynist literature, to force and violence in the form of rape and women-battering. Yet we have been socialised to explain or even excuse such actions 'as the product of individual deviance, confined to pathological or exceptional behaviour, and without general import' (p.43). It takes but a slight shift in focus, however, to see the *numerous* cases of violence against women not as pathological and idiosyncratic events, but as the *normal pattern* in a patriarchal society.

It isn't necessary that *all* women be victims of force for force to be effective. The fact that *some* women experience physical violence can be sufficient to intimidate *many*. We are deceived if we believe that patriarchy operates solely on the basis of consensus. If the system could not resort to force or make use of the threat of force, it, like any other political system, would be inoperable.

This is Kate Millett's encompassing theory of sexual politics, designed to describe and explain the system of rule of men over women, and to account for its origins and its operations in all its myriad forms. It not only casts new light on the reality of women's lives but illuminates some of the actions of men that have previously gone unexamined and even unobserved. By taking example after example of women's conditions from this altered perspective, Kate Millett is able to propose and document a political theory as the meaningful rationale which shapes social arrangements. She proposes a framework consistent with the academic conventions in which she is working, and locates within it the actions of men as a group and women as a group, and the connections between the two – that many of the cultural understandings about power and rule have been forged by men, and are based on structures and relationships among men – but these can be used by women and applied to the structures and relationships between men and women.

The notion of a power relationship between the sexes has gained credence since the advent of Kate Millett's thesis, but it would be wrong to claim too much for it. Her interpretation has not been widely or unquestioningly accepted *in full* – that the issue of 'men as the enemy' can still be divisive reveals some of the reservations that some women (and men) have about categorising patriarchy in purely political terms. I suspect that much of *Sexual Politics* is as shocking today as it was fifteen years ago. I also suspect that many feminists today have not read *Sexual Politics*, and that if they did, they would be more than surprised by its contents. Kate Millett might be a symbol of contemporary feminism but this has not prevented much of her analysis from being overlooked.

It is contradictory for society both to accommodate her thesis and to maintain the *status quo*, so that any who have a vested interest in the *status quo* are likely to resist her analysis. Not only is it difficult for many men to accept her representation of them, it is also difficult for many women to accept her delineation of men, and of women. Some women do not want to see the world in Kate Millett's hostile terms. They prefer, and seek, a more harmonious interpretation based on cooperation rather than conflict. Some women cannot afford to see the world she describes because they do not have the free choice to dissociate themselves from those who control the resources and who are necessary for their survival. Some women simply do not want to entertain the possibility of a world-view in which the position of women is so appalling and the prospects for change so remote.

For Kate Millett's ideas to have been taken up in full would have meant the emergence of a new society. Had there been widespread recognition within society that one group had power which they were prepared to use in their own interest, the other group would have been unlikely willingly to align themselves with the powerful and invite exploitation. Instead, they would have sought to redistribute resources among themselves, allowing a greater chance of reciprocity. Given such a development, the relationship between women and men would have been transformed.

Because Kate Millett's theory cannot be incorporated in full without resulting in radical social repercussions, only part of it has found accommodation in the social fabric. It is clear that her thesis has had some impact: sexual politics is an issue and can be debated, and there are now understandings in some circles about power and the sexes; perhaps more understandings will come. One consequence of her efforts has also been that there is now (in some circles) greater understanding about consciousness: how it works and how it changes. Perhaps the way is being prepared for yet further accommodations. Only time will tell if the inroads have been made.

5. Facts are Irrelevant: Germaine Greer's power

One of my research methods when I was re-reading these early texts of the contemporary women's movement was to make a card-index of quotable quotes: when I had finished by far the biggest pile belonged to Germaine Greer. She has a superb command of language and, in her short, pithy statements, excels in turning the world upside down. I should like to have some of her aphorisms printed in appropriately bold letters and placed above my desk, partly because they would serve as such useful reminders in the daily task of sustaining a feminist reality in a patriarchal world, but partly too because they are such shrewd examples of women's wit and so well illustrate her own point that if the struggle is not joyous it is the wrong struggle. However, in lieu of the printed signs I shall give some indication of Germaine Greer's style of feminism by quoting some of her illuminating maxims:

> The fact that there are no such storehouses of jokes against fathers is not because women have no sense of humour. (p.271)

> Romance has been the one adventure open to her and now it is over. Marriage is the end of the story. (p.186)

> Women...must refuse to marry. No worker is required to sign on for life: if he did, his employer could disregard all his attempts to gain better pay and conditions. (p.319)

> As it stands, divorce works in the male interest, not only because it was designed and instituted by men, but because divorce still depends on money and independent income. Married women seldom have either. (p.320)

Frigidity for women is regarded as a common condition, resulting from bad luck and bad management: in men impotence is treated with the utmost seriousness. (p.47)

Women have very little idea how much men hate them. (p.219)

The cornerstone of the Freudian theory of womanhood is the masculine conviction that a woman is a castrated man. (p.91)

Most educated women have simply been admitted to the masculine academic culture. (p.107)

If women understand by emancipation the adoption of the masculine role then we are lost indeed. If women can supply no counter-balance to the blindness of male drive, the aggressive society will soon run to its lunatic extremes at ever escalating speed. (p.114)

These shafts of wit cover a wide expanse and are characteristically bold and barbed: but there can be no hiding their serious purpose and no denying that they do not hit their mark. *The Female Eunuch* is replete with such aphorisms, and my difficulty is to desist. (I cannot refrain from including one more: 'The notion of a curve is so closely connected with sexual semantics that some people cannot help sniggering at road signs' (p.33).) It is demonstrably clear that Germaine Greer can encapsulate the essence of women's grievances simply, strikingly and stingingly.

It was a strange sensation for me, rereading *The Female Eunuch*, because it was such a significant book in my life. Going through it again now has taken me back to a person who was dissatisfied, at loggerheads with the world, and who was utterly convinced that it was all her own fault. It was also the book that marked a change in my relationship with my mother for if it supported my sense of injustice, it also challenged the reality of her conventional 'contentment'. I deliberately chose to challenge her (she has long since understood) rather than to exclude her from this 'new knowledge'. We talked for hours about *that book*, which changed the lives of everyone in my family (my father included), and came to the realisation that before *The Female Eunuch* we had each made the best decisions that we could in the framework of what was known to us. From *The Female Eunuch* we knew different things, and different decisions were demanded of us. So *The Female Eunuch* is very much part of my family history, to the extent that we used a particular term to signify the changes that took place within our value-system: 'BG' – 'Before Germs'.

Alongside the knowledge that *The Female Eunuch* dramatically altered what I believed and the way I led my life, however, rests a more recently acquired understanding: on re-reading the book both my mother and I decided that much of it now sounded so sensible that it was difficult to remember what the fuss was about at the time it was published. It follows, then, that some of Germaine Greer's ideas may have been incorporated into cultural reality.

I must also admit that I now think I have been more influenced by *The Female Eunuch* than I have ever fully acknowledged. I have always been ready to declare that it changed my life, and I have always recognised that its style struck sympathetic chords within me, even if I did take issue with some of its stands. But I had not been aware of how closely some of my values and views resembled those of Germaine Greer, particularly not when it came to my own research. I would have been prepared to swear that no one pointed me in the direction of men being the talkative sex and women being the listeners, and yet there it stands in 1970: 'Communication is not advanced by the *he-talk, me-listen* formula' (p.42). Likewise, I would have stated that I had, after long and arduous research, come to the realisation that women's 'gossip' was not the despicable activity that it was deemed to be, but often genuine *political* talk. And yet I find in *The Female Eunuch*: 'The sight of women talking together has always made men uneasy: nowadays it means rank subversion. "Right on" ' (p.13). There is much that I have given myself credit for which should rightly belong to Germaine Greer.

I have placed *Sexual Politics* before *The Female Eunuch* in this book because that was the order in which they were published. It was not the order in which I read them. I came to *Sexual Politics* having been enlightened by *The Female Eunuch* and as a result I was well prepared for Kate Millett's analysis of patriarchal ideology and the hold it has over consciousness, for of central concern to Germaine Greer was the extent to which women have been duped by the male belief in males themselves. In her view, women are *conditioned* into checking their own action, into holding back and abstaining from exercising any influence in the world. She not only insists that it is imperative that women break free from this belief-system which inactivates them, she also indicates how this can be done.

'The key to the strategy of liberation lies in exposing the situation, and the simplest way to do it is to outrage the pundits and the experts by sheer impudence of speech and gesture, the exploitation of cliché "feminine logic" to expose masculine pomposity, absurdity and injustice. Women's weapons are traditionally their tongues, and the principal revolutionary tactic has always been the spread of information' (p.328).

Germaine Greer lives up to her own exhortations: *The Female Eunuch* is intentionally shocking and misses no opportunity to puncture masculine pomposity.

In a form that has come to be characteristic of feminism, Germaine Greer sets out to challenge male authority, to challenge men, their judgements and their right to make such judgements. There are no holds barred in *The Female Eunuch*: from Sigmund Freud to Norman Mailer she sets up male authorities and knocks them down; she strips them of their trappings and reveals the shallow, self-interested and women-hating nature of much of their value-system.

And male dominance is a *value*-system for Germaine Greer, a belief-system which isn't based on 'facts' and won't be altered by 'facts' (an assertion which has far-reaching implications for feminist research and education). This gives rise to the question that if a value-system cannot be discredited or overturned by the facts, how can it be changed? The answer is, through different values, by means of a different belief-system. If it is obvious that religion declines once people cease to believe in God, it follows that male dominance will decline when people cease to believe in male supremacy and authority. One of the quickest ways of ending the belief in male supremacy is to demonstrate just how silly and sorry are many of the activities of the 'superior' sex.

The conditioning to which women have been subjected is expressly directed towards discouraging women from taking this simple stand. Germaine Greer outlined the tactics that are used against the woman who dares to protest and comments on 'the refusal to consider the content of her grievance' and the counter-measure of charging her with 'penis envy or frustration or perversion' (p.293), which can readily be employed to keep woman in her passive place. In giving voice to her own protest, in defying the male prescriptions of what a 'proper' woman should be (and what she should think and say), Germaine Greer risked and received (as did Betty Friedan and Kate Millett) the full force of censure. Yet ironically, because she was protesting, she was breaking with that conditioning which pre-empts protest, and so by her very act

51

of defiance she established her freedom to act.

It is this audacious, 'unfeminine' action which Germaine Greer advocates as one of the first steps towards ending the restrictive confines of femininity. She dissociates herself from some of the earlier feminists who, in her view, mollified, rather than menaced, when they denied that when women had equality, society itself would change: 'In the good old days, ladies were anxious to point out that they did not seek to disrupt society or to unseat God' (a reference to the 'constitutional suffragists' in Britain). 'Marriage, the family, private property and the state were threatened by their actions but they were anxious to allay the fears of the conservatives, and in doing so the suffragettes [sic][1] betrayed their own cause and prepared the way for the failure of emancipation' (p.12).

'Votes for Women – and Chastity for Men' was Christabel Pankhurst's rallying call as she foreshadowed what would follow women's political autonomy: she left no room for misinterpretation but in Edwardian England went round warning that men's demands on women would no longer be legitimate, once women had the power to resist them. And for her rebellion she received much the same reward as Germaine Greer.

This strategy of abandoning meek and mild femininity for mischief, mockery and mayhem, for outrageous acts of impudency, on the grounds that such defiant action in itself constitutes freedom from some of the restraints of patriarchy, is not a new one but can be found in women like Aphra Behn (1640–89) and 'Sophia' (who wrote *Woman Not Inferior to Man* in 1739)[2] and includes among its many proponents Christabel Pankhurst and Rebecca West.[3] It is a strategy which has its origins in women's view of the world which takes account of the implications of imposed inactivity and deference: it is based on the understanding that liberation can begin with *action* when it is accompanied by the deliberate intention of defying the decrees of the dominant group. Had such a strategy been devised by men, no doubt it would now be elevated to the status of legitimate theory. But this tradition among women – typically – isn't even dignified by a name, despite its current adoption by two such prominent women as Germaine Greer and Gloria Steinem (see *Outrageous Acts and Everyday Rebellions*, 1984).

The concept of power is certainly there in Germaine Greer's understandings about the relationships between the sexes but she concentrates on the suppressed power of women, and not the power of men. This is not the same concept of power that Kate Millett posits, but whereas *Sexual Politics* is the itemisation of the political nature of the system of rule of men over women, *The Female Eunuch* is an elaboration of a much more intimate nexus whereby potentially powerful women are coerced into surrendering their power to men, primarily through marriage and heterosexual commitments. The process of *convincing* women that it is desirable and necessary for them to give up their power in order to please men, and to become dependent on men, Germaine Greer calls conditioning; but she has great faith in the ability of the individual woman to discard her conditioning and begin anew: 'Women are contoured by their conditioning to abandon autonomy and to seek guidance' (p.20), but it is within the scope of every woman to bring about change 'by reassessing herself' (p.14). When sufficient women step out of their conditioning and change themselves then the world will necessarily change and will abound with strong, independent women, instead of dependent women who have sacrificed themselves for men.

This is an attractive prospect and a plausible approach – an aspect of the premise that the personal is political – and completely consistent with the feminist principles which insist on a *private* as well as a *public* dimension in revolution, and would have one taking place in every home. This strategy for change accredits women with the ability to act and to be influential, and assumes a positive outcome. This makes it a much more inviting rationale than those which emphasise the enormous obstacles which lie in the way of change.

Germaine Greer does not brush aside the issue of conditioning, nor does she underestimate how deeply it goes; but she does have great faith in every woman's ability to break free from its pernicious influence. In her view, each woman has a duty *to herself* to refuse to perpetuate the pattern of women's passivity. Her description of the way women are entwined with men is interesting. She begins with women's conditioning which teaches a woman to abandon her will and resources in order to please a man. But when a woman gives up so much of herself and has so little left that she can call her own, she becomes obliged to live vicariously through a man; she needs a man to make her 'complete'. And if she is to get and keep a man, she must 'labour at making [herself] indispensable' to him so that he doesn't leave her. And how is she to become indispensable? By abandoning her own will: women 'are self-sacrificing in direct proportion to their incapacity to offer anything but this sacrifice' (p.151).

53

Yet it doesn't have to be this way. Such conditioning, and the cycle it sets up, cannot work if women won't conform to it. If women 'withdraw their labour' the present unfair, complex arrangement between the sexes will come to an end. Germaine Greer is adamant that it lies within the power of every woman to end her own subordination and bring about the individual changes which in total will add up to social change.

But there are some women, ensnared in a web of economic dependence, who dare not 'withdraw their labour'. In whom a pattern of reinforced failure is imposed when, for *reasons beyond their control*, they are unable to exercise their strength and independence, by breaking away from their conditioning and their conditions. This is not to detract from the *logic* of Germaine Greer's stand, only to suggest that it isn't appropriate for all women. The impression should not be given that Germaine Greer is prescribing *the* way to liberation. She is meticulous when it comes to making it clear that she is proposing *one possible* way out: 'It is not a question of telling women what to do next, or even what to want next. The hope in which this book was written is that women will discover they have a will: once that happens they will be able to tell us how and what they want' (p.21).

What Germaine Greer brings to the forefront of the discussion is the recognition that even when women are in a position to walk away from self-sacrifice, many of them don't, and they don't because they are so locked in to the patterns of femininity. Because women's *will* has systematically been undermined by their socialisation, they are not always aware that it is possible to recover their own resources and use them for their own ends. *The Female Eunuch* is a forceful reminder that women are quite capable of taking back what has been taken away.

Nothing could be more obvious than the way women's will is taken away throughout their education, asserts Germaine Greer. A female who shows seriousness of purpose, who wants to commit herself to hard work, to develop her creative or intellectual potential soon finds that society does not approve her aspirations. Instead, numerous obstacles are placed in her path to deflect her from making use of opportunities that are technically available and to confine her to superficialities:

The constant recriminations, the lamentations that she is missing out on what makes being a girl such fun, on dating and pretty clothes, that she will waste her training by getting married and so forth, the whole tiresome rigmarole, wears down her resistance from day to day.

The pressure of home duties which are spared a boy in her situation is not relieved, unless she goes away to study . . . an expedient which may meet with parental disapproval. (p.133)

With such an explanation for the absence of great women philosophers or artists (or engineers, artisans or merchant bankers) it is not surprising that Germaine Greer should have entitled her later book on women painters *The Obstacle Race* (1979). In *The Female Eunuch* she itemises the obstacles that are placed in the path of women's achievement: 'insofar as she escapes or rejects her conditioning, the little girl may excel in those kinds of intellectual activity that are called creative, but eventually she either capitulates to her conditioning or the conflicts become so pressing that her efficiency is hampered' (p.102).

This is an excellent description of the process of undermining women's will but it is not a full explanation for the absence of women among the 'great'. There is the additional issue that men have historically reserved for themselves the arena of the greats and by a variety of means have kept women out. In the organised professions and trades this has been relatively easy – women have been barred from entry – and this accounts for their 'failure' to be among the prominent architects or engineers, doctors or lawyers, for example. In the areas less amenable to organisation and imposed entry qualifications (art, music, literature, for example) men have achieved much the same ends by setting themselves up as the experts, and are therefore in a position to judge greatness where they find it. It is thus no coincidence that men comprise the 'great' artists, musicians, men of letters, and in their opinion it is predominantly other men who qualify as 'great'.

That women are excluded from the male realms of achievement, action and influence does not dispute the claim that they are also discouraged from putting themselves forward in the first place. But when they find their participation both criticised *and* blocked, what other aspirations are available to them? Once more, alleges Germaine Greer, we are back in the vicious circle: deprived of other uses for their energy, women are encouraged to set their sights upon a man. They are induced to make their goal the attraction of a man. Furthermore, men have decided ideas about what they find attractive, what they want in a woman. The result is that no matter how distasteful or disfiguring women may find men's desired image to be, to achieve this image becomes for many women an overriding necessity:

Demands are made on them to contour their bodies in order to please the eyes of others. Women are so insecure that they constantly take measures to capitulate to this demand whether it be rational or not.... In each case the woman is tailoring herself to appeal to a buyer's market; her most exigent buyer may be her husband who goes on exacting her approximation to the accepted image as a condition of his continuing desire and pride in her. (p.35)

A woman, then, becomes a sexual object because she is taught that it is only through her sexual attraction that she is permitted any influence. But because being a sexual object becomes her primary focus (at the expense of other forms of self-development), she is seen by others, and comes to see herself, as nothing other than a sexual object.

Thus woman is a sexual *object*, not a sexual *subject*. The question is not whether a man (or a woman) attracts her, but whether she is attractive; it is not whether she likes, but whether she is liked. This is the difference between subject and object, between active and passive; woman's force, energy, will are denied; she is placed in the position of *receiver*. Even her physical sexual characteristics assume this mantle of receptivity in a society which sees women's role as waiting passively for men:

What happens is that the female is considered as a sexual object for use and appreciation by other sexual beings, men. Her sexuality is both denied and misrepresented by being identified as passivity. The vagina is obliterated from the image of femininity in the same way that the signs of independence and vigour in the rest of the body are suppressed. (p.15)

Women are therefore given a most difficult feat to perform: on the one hand they are enjoined to get a man, but on the other hand they are forbidden to do anything active about getting him. They must, like the spider, weave their web – and wait. And society will accord them status on the basis of the importance and value of their 'catch'. Of course it is perfectly possible that, on closer inspection, she might not like what she has caught.

For a woman who finds herself in this predicament, Germaine Greer has unequivocal advice: 'Marriage cannot be a job as it has become. Status ought not to be measured for women in terms of attracting and snaring a man, for it is not necessarily the man who gets "caught", and "the woman who realizes that she is bound by a million Lilliputian threads in an attitude of impotence and hatred masquerading as tranquility and love, has no option but to run away' (p.19). More importantly, she should not feel that she is running *from*, but running *to* – running to her own life and the opportunity to take her own actions in the world. Running away is the beginning of such action: it is not irresponsible, but responsible to leave an arid, stultifying and even brutalising confinement: it should not be accompanied by feelings of guilt.

Germaine Greer is not so simplistic as to suggest that this is a mere matter of making a decision that defies the established orthodoxy and of then proceeding to carry it through without qualms. She does not gloss over the hold that social beliefs have over us all, so that even when we can intellectually repudiate the validity or usefulness of a custom, we can still find ourselves tied to it. She gives the example that although we may recognise the absurdity of the notion that the right man will solve all our problems, we may still continue to look for him. That we may be aware of the silliness of the expectation that a man should be taller, stronger, older (convenient inputs for the structuring of male supremacy), doesn't necessarily stop us from seeking a taller, stronger, older man: 'The strength of the belief that a man should be stronger and older than his woman can hardly be exaggerated,' she acknowledges. 'I cannot claim to be fully emancipated from the dream that some enormous man, say six feet six inches, heavily shouldered and so forth to match, will crush me to his tweeds, look down into my eyes and leave the taste of heaven or the scorch of passion on my waiting lips' (p.180).

Germaine Greer elaborates on the hold that romance has on women's minds, partly by reference to romantic fiction – that 'drug' that can lure women into the realm of fantasy: 'If women's liberation movements are to mean anything at all,' she warns, 'they will have to cope with phenomena like the million-dollar Cartland industry' (p.178). *Romance* is the sugar coating on the marriage pill: without it, women wouldn't swallow marriage. And as far as Germaine Greer is concerned, marriage is one of the primary means by which women are oppressed, which is why women's liberation movements must deal with all the devices designed to deceive women about its debilitating nature.

If they knew what they were in for, no rational human beings would willingly take on such hard and unrewarding work, putting all their energy into making the spouse's lot an easier one, into looking after a (misnamed) partner, into building up the confidence of someone else. Yet a woman is required – and is trained – to serve a man 'faithfully for a menial's wage or no wage at all so she can increase his earning power and cloak his mistakes' (p.125).

Whether she is describing women at home or in the workplace, Germaine Greer's emphasis is always on the *individual* dimension. In this respect she is markedly different from Kate Millett, who focuses more on the *collective* experience of women as a class. So at the workplace, for example, Kate Millett is more concerned with theoretical explanations of the structures which operate against women, whereas Germaine Greer is more concerned with the personal dimensions of what each woman gives up. Again, Kate Millett starts from the premise that men have collective power and use it, while Germaine Greer begins with the premise that women have personal power – and don't use it.

In the workplace, women can surrender their resources to men in much the same way that they do in marriage, claims Germaine Greer. There are few women who do not know the demands that are made over and above the job description and which induce women to provide emotional support for the men they work with – not to mention the additional services which may range from tea-making and minute-taking to sexual favours – all of which have since been termed *sexual harassment* (see Lin Farley, 1978; Catherine MacKinnon, 1979; Liz Stanley and Sue Wise, forthcoming). Germaine Greer witnesses this behaviour but describes and explains it as women yet again channelling their resources into men. This is one of the reasons why 'The pattern that emerges is that of an inert, unvalued female work force which is considered as temporary labour, docile but unreliable' (p.116).

Another reason why women in the workforce can be regarded as 'inert' and 'docile' is that they may be simply exhausted. Germaine Greer does not set up an image of superwoman, who is obliged effortlessly to meet the demands of home and paid work. There are many women in the workforce doing *two* jobs, she states, and often the paid one is the easier of the two: 'For many women, sitting down to a machine, be it a type-writer or a power sewing machine, is a rest after the unremitting employ-ment of all their physical strength and energy in the service of a young family. The lunch hour of a secretary who has to do the shopping and the bill paying for her family is the most strenuous part of the day' (p.122).

When women are exploited both at home *and* at the workplace –

and where a substantial dimension of women's exploitation is the requirement that they undertake two jobs instead of one – the first and most obvious solution is to eliminate one set of demands. In an economistic society such as ours, Germaine Greer sees the demands made by the home as the ones that can be dispensed with. Women must refuse to marry, she declares.[4] If women are to free themselves from one set of tyrannical demands, then marriage must go or, more precisely, regular heterosexual relationships must go. Only by not engaging in heterosexual relationships in which they are required to sacrifice themselves for men, will women be in a position to cultivate their own development.

If the only source of women's oppression were the home, if women enjoyed the same status and opportunity in the workplace as men, then it would seem feasible to suggest that women's position would be greatly improved once they rejected the demands made by personal heterosexual relationships. But of course home is *not* the only place where women are exploited (and not all women have heterosexual relationships): women are also discriminated against at work and in pay, and a predictable outcome of women refusing to link their lives with men could well be the situation where there were a lot more poor women. The increase in the number of single-parent families headed by women – and the fact that in Britain and the United States they are the biggest group among the poor (Hilda Scott, 1984) – reveals that the problem is already with us. Not that all the women in this category have *chosen* their single circumstances: many have found that, despite their self-sacrifice, they are deserted or divorced.

Yet another fallacy, however, in this entanglement of economics is the notion that women who do live with men do so for financial support. This belief is persistently challenged by feminists who assert that with or without men, women are the world's poor (see Hilda Scott, 1984), and that this aspect of women's oppression demands immediate attention.

Although Germaine Greer called on women to refuse to marry, she saw this only as a first step, not as the complete solution. Sweeping changes in the economic system – even in the way we think about economics – were needed for women to be both psychologically and financially independent. She went so far as to warn against trying to get a better deal for women within the existing framework, and pointed out that many reforms, no matter how well intentioned, could be used against women if the value-system itself was not changed: 'equal pay', she wrote, 'might mean that where women did not have the advantage of being cheaper, they might not be employed at all, and women's work might become more and more segregated in the semi-skilled and unskilled categories' (p.117).

Germaine Greer thus foresaw the development of the present economic crisis for women, and her opinion was then – as is Hilda Scott's now – that 'Unless the concepts of work and pay and reward for work change absolutely, women must continue to provide cheap labour', and, rejecting the conventional distinctions between public and private, and preserving the concept of the totality of women's work, women will continue to provide 'free labour, exacted of right by an employer possessed of a contract for life, made out in his favour' (p.22). In relationships with men at home and at work, in the way we think about home and work, about paid work and 'labours of love', Germaine Greer wanted a revolution.

There are certain areas, however, where many women would suggest that Germaine Greer's revolution does not go far enough. While she deplores the way women are exploited by 'heterosexual love', her strategies are directed towards improving this relationship, rather than towards challenging it. She counsels women to refuse to marry, to refuse the demands of heterosexuality, but this is for the purpose of strengthening their bargaining position within the heterosexual framework: she does not propose a viable alternative.

'Men,' she asserts, 'have commandeered all the energy and streamlined it into an aggressive, conquestatorial power, reducing all heterosexual contact to a sado-masochistic pattern' (p.16). If this is what it is like when women 'love' men, then clearly women are better-off without such love: but this does not pre-empt women from loving women. Yet in *The Female Eunuch* this possibility is conspicuous by its absence. This is surprising, for given Germaine Greer's philosophy that women accord men too much significance and centrality, there is the expectation that she should pursue this line of reasoning to its *sexual* conclusion. Lesbianism, however, is not proffered as a practical solution or even as a chosen way of life, although it is acknowledged as a form of protest and can 'be understood as a revolt against the female role of passivity, hypocrisy and indirect action, as well as the rejection of the brutality and mechanicalness of male sexual passion' (p.293).

Germaine Greer has very little to say that is positive about sex as it applies to heterosexuality. Sex is harnessed as a force of counterrevolution, she argues (and she develops this case more fully in her later book, *Sex and Destiny*, 1984), so that members of our society are led to the conviction that a full life means a full *sex*-life, and in the interest of pursuing the ever-elusive sexual satisfaction, they are diverted from serious political consideration and activity.

Her questioning of sex and the role it plays in the social order is perceptive and far-reaching, and it represents a challenge to the assumption that more freedom means more sex. But her assumption is that no matter how bad heterosexuality is, it's all we have. This assumption, too, is open to challenge.

Many questions are raised in *The Female Eunuch*, and some have since been translated into household words – literally – with one of the biggest debates in its wake being that of the injustice of women's workload in the home. The insistence it contains, that women themselves could enforce change by the withdrawal of their labour, was well founded[5] and to Germaine Greer must go some of the credit for awakening women to the possibilities of their own power and to being able to use it to assert their own demands for a more equitable division of labour in the home.

Women's work, however, was not the only issue that Germaine Greer raised and although some of the dimensions that she outlined have since been incorporated into cultural understandings, some of the other issues to which she gave equal attention have not been taken up, and seem just as alien and shocking now as when she first put them forward. It is significant that her chapter 'Loathing and Disgust' has been overlooked: and when I re-read this section I still found it chilling.

'Women have no idea how much men hate them' (p.219), Germaine Greer wrote, and in retrospect it seems that there is still resistance in women to the idea. This is understandable. Male dominance rests to some extent on women wanting to make much of men, and if it were to be widely recognised that men hated them, women might decide that 'getting a man' was neither a sound nor a safe option – the point Germaine Greer repeatedly makes. Her discussion of the relationship between male loathing and disgust of women, depicted in pornography, violence and rape, makes gruesome reading and is tantamount to Kate Millett's assertion that men are the enemy. Both descriptions are equally unacceptable to a society that relies on women seeking to link their lives with men and explains why the full force of these meanings cannot be accommodated within the existing cultural understandings.

It is worth noting the distance that Kate Millett and Germaine Greer had travelled from Betty Friedan. Neither Kate Millett nor Germaine Greer flinched from describing the brutality and exploitation they witnessed, despite the fact that society would prefer to ignore these. Partly for this reason, feminists since that time have been assisted in bringing these issues to the forefront. There is a direct link between Germaine Greer's chapter on 'Loathing and Disgust' and Andrea Dworkin's work (*Woman Hating*, 1974; *Pornography: Men Possessing Women*, 1981; *Our Blood*, 1982) as well as with Susan Brownmiller's analysis of rape in *Against Our Will* (1976).

When *The Female Eunuch* was written, few of the prevailing explanations for rape had been challenged. When its reality wasn't denied ('there's no such thing as rape'), the generally accepted rationale was that 'women asked for it', that in the face of powerful temptation, some men just couldn't control themselves. Germaine Greer would not let this pass. 'It is a vain delusion,' she wrote,

that rape is the expression of uncontrollable desire or some kind of compulsive response to overwhelming attraction. Any girl who has been bashed and raped can tell how ludicrous it is when she pleads for a reason and her assailant replies 'Because I love you' or 'Because you're so beautiful' or some such rubbish. The act is one of murderous aggression, spawned in self-loathing upon the hated other. Men do not know themselves the depth of their hatred. (p.251)

That rape can be the product of 'love', Germaine Greer challenges when she includes the perspective of women for whom such an argument is 'ludicrous'. However, she does not hold men wholly responsible for their actions. They too are the victims of a value-system, and have been initiated into a code of hatred for women so that they 'do not know themselves the depth of their hatred'; they too are influenced by personal despair, and can, from 'self-loathing', force their actions on women and the world. (An alternative view would be to ask where this value-system comes from and who wants to sustain it. The answer is unlikely to be women.)

Another area in which Germaine Greer exposes the dimensions of hatred and contempt towards women is that of language (and again I must acknowledge a debt). Without entering the debate over whether words give rise to meanings or meanings give rise to words, Germaine

Greer identifies some of the many terms of abuse for women in the English language for which there are no male equivalents. Her list helps to reveal the loathing for women that is embodied in our language. If these words only described women who had offended men it would be bad enough, she argues, 'but the terms of endearment addressed to women are equally soulless and degrading' (p.265): whether women please or displease, the vocabulary is equally vicious.

Women's humanity is taken out of language – even the vocabulary of heterosexual relations is offensive, with its insistence on labelling men as active sexual beings who exercise themselves on dehumanised, inanimate women: 'All the vulgar linguistic emphasis is placed on the *poking* element: *fucking, screwing, rooting, shagging* are all acts performed on the passive female,' states Germaine Greer. She also shows the extent to which heterosexuality is described in male terms, 'the names for the penis are all *tool* names' (p.41). Words are revealed as being used against women; even in intimacy there is no acknowledgement of women's experience and emotion.

Germaine Greer helped to open women's eyes to their *absence* in the vocabulary and meanings of society; later feminist analyses developed this understanding, providing example upon example to demonstrate that language is oriented to express what is *done to* women rather than to signify what women *do*. Such linguistic restraint helps to pre-empt and undermine women's self-concept as positive and active, and this can be illustrated with reference to heterosexuality. As Susan Brownmiller (1976) emphasised, prominence is given to the male view of the world even in activities where both sexes are participants. And she asks why sexual intercourse is named as *penetration*: if women were in charge of sex and the language, she argues, it would be more accurate to speak of *enclosure* (p.334).

This brings us back to where Betty Friedan began, to the relationship between knowledge and power, a crucial feminist issue. We can see that because women are without power they are not represented in the language and meanings of society. We can also see that because women are not represented in the language and meanings of society they are deprived of power. Both these aspects of the relationship between knowledge and power need to be kept in mind if we are to retain a comprehensive view of women's absence from these areas.

But no *one* feminist explanation can account for all we can know: all contributions to our understandings have to be held in mind, and it is a culturally limited and unproductive question to ask whether the source of women's oppression lies in either men's hands or women's heads. Up to a point both views can be substantiated; to insist therefore on *either* one or the other is to move into the realm of dogma. What we do know is that men's meanings predominate and that this is part of women's oppression; that men are their own reference point, and assume their own supremacy; that they then proceed to encode the meanings of society and to enforce their meanings on those who don't share them, so that their supremacy is realised at the expense of women. This process – the double-standard – ensures that no matter what they do, men are perceived as better than women.

For a feminist framework to be useful it must consistently take into account that the two sexes are not the same: they are ascribed different values and are subject to different rules. The same event can assume entirely different meanings according to the sex associated with it. Menstruation serves as a particularly good example. We are aware of the meanings that society has constructed for menstruation: it is dirty, shameful, and should be concealed. Germaine Greer says of it:

> we still have a marked revulsion for menstruation, principally evinced by our efforts to keep it secret. The success of the tampon is partly due to the fact that it is hidden. The arrival of the menarche is more significant than any birthday, but in the Anglo-Saxon households it is ignored and carefully concealed from general awareness. (p.50)

To treat this natural process as unclean – with, as Kate Millett has pointed out, all the negative consequences this has for the female psyche – is unreasonable, unfair and unhealthy, and many women want to decode the meaning of menstruation. But in order to change a meaning it can be helpful to know the source of its associations. Is the negative meaning of menstruation associated with the event itself, or with the sex that menstruates?

In an extremely witty article, 'If Only Men Could Menstruate', Gloria Steinem (1984) helps to answer this question. If men could menstruate, she writes, 'Clearly menstruation would become an enviable, boast-worthy, masculine event'. She then lists all the changes which would take place when '*men*-struation' became associated with the superior sex. 'Men would boast about how long and how much' and, far from being ignored, the onset of menstruation would be celebrated with gifts, religious ceremonies and male-only parties. Scientists would prove that men performed better – at everything – during their periods; generals would insist that only men could serve their country '("You have to give blood to take blood")'; religious leaders would insist that only men could be priests, ministers, God himself, or rabbis: '("Without a monthly purge of impurities, women are unclean")'. Men would be adamant that sex was better at 'that time of the month' and lesbians would be declared to be afraid of blood and therefore of life itself.

> Of course, intellectuals would offer the most moral and logical arguments. Without that biological gift for measuring the cycles of the moon and planets, how could a woman master any discipline that demanded a sense of time, space, mathematics – or the ability to measure anything at all? In philosophy and religion, how could women compensate for being disconnected from the rhythm of the universe? Or for their lack of symbolic death and resurrection every month? (Gloria Steinem, 1984: 338–9)

Same events, but different sex – and very different meanings! This is how reality is constructed and there can be no denying how powerful such constructions can be, and how necessary it is for women to bring about change: if women could be represented as positive and powerful in the social reality women could become positive and powerful.

Both Kate Millett and Germaine Greer are convinced of the need for a women's view of the world, which assumes women's centrality and significance, to become (at least) an equal part of social reality. However, they differ in their views on how this can be done. While I do not want to imply that Kate Millett does not acknowledge the complexities, it is fair to say that she places emphasis on *male* power, and she urges women to take some of this power for themselves so that they can be in a position to insist on their own positive meanings. Germaine Greer, however, while not ignoring some of the ramifications of male power, advocates *female* power; she is adamant that women already have power and will realise it once they cease subscribing to male meanings.

These are, of course, two views of the same problem. Kate Millett sees women as a class who must seize the power that men have usurped, while Germaine Greer sees each individual woman as capable of taking back the power she has been conditioned individually to surrender to a man. Both explanations add to our understandings. There is much sense in Kate Millett's demand for women to confront the institutionalised power of men and to fight for their freedom, but there is certainly substance in Germaine Greer's claim that, for a woman, the strategy in a personal relationship with a man lies 'not so much [in] assailing him as by freeing herself from the desire to fulfil his expectations' (p.18).

For Germaine Greer, it was fundamental that a women should start with herself; that she should cultivate self-respect, self-esteem, and self-love. From this base of psychic autonomy, free from the bondage of the need for male approval, much more would flow, although it would not be easy: 'In the struggle to remain a complete person and to love from her fullness instead of her inadequacy, a woman may appear hard,' she warns, and 'She may feel her early conditioning tugging her in the direction of surrender' (p.224). But despite the difficulties she appeals to women to cease sacrificing themselves for men, and instead take responsibility for and control of their own destiny. She counsels women to be the strong, independent and happy human beings that it is within their power to be, and in the process they will be doing their community a service.

Placing the power for women's liberation in women's own hands is both a strength and a weakness of Germaine Greer's argument. One of its strengths is that it accords women power in a male-dominated society bent on denying that power, and as such it represents a challenge to male dominance not just because of the greater status it gives women, but because it takes away and minimises some of the supposed power of men. But the problem with this approach is that it raises the question of how far women's oppression resides in women's minds, and can be changed – when women change their minds.

Rather like Rebecca West a generation earlier, who also said that women take men too seriously, Germaine Greer surmised that male power is exaggerated and that it is better for women to scorn it than succumb to it. She has repeatedly suggested that men would not act as if they had power if women treated them as if they didn't. When women adopt this policy, this in itself could produce startling changes in behaviour and the relationship of the sexes. In an interview with Frances Cairncross (the *Guardian*) Germaine Greer illustrated her argument with reference to rape. Having made the distinction between the physical and psychic dimensions of rape, she claimed that changes in the psychic dimension would not only change people's minds, but

66

their behaviour as well. Rape is an area where women accord men power, she stated, and while a woman continues to believe that a man has the power to do her *psychic* harm by raping her, this expectation will be fulfilled – men will continue to exploit this power-base and to do women physical harm as well. But if a woman rejects the idea that rape is psychically harmful, if she starts to see rape not as powerful but as pathetic, and refuses to be psychically violated because some contemptible man manages to 'put his dick in her', then a whole bastion of male power is swept away. Rape would no longer be a way for males to exercise their power and might be committed less frequently. This view, while an extension of her premises, is none the less consistent with them.

The spectacle of women behaving as if men did not have power has its appeal (in some ways it is another version of Adrienne Rich's strategy of playing on the fear of male irrelevance). But there are flaws in this approach: men *do* have material power and there are millions of women who are not free to develop their own power and to repudiate that of men; and, for the very same reason that men's confidence and ability to act would be undermined if they were treated as though they had no power, so too are women *now* in the position of having had their confidence and ability to act undermined, after centuries of being treated as if they didn't have power.

These reservations do not invalidate Germaine Greer's thesis but simply point to some of its limitations. But I have yet another reservation. I endorse the concept that women can reclaim their own power and can use it, but I would like this understanding to be set in a context of qualifications, otherwise the woman who tries to assert her own strength and independence, who tries to change the behaviour of a particular man (or men in general) might find that she is unable to achieve her aim, and could well feel that she had *failed*. Women actually have no control over men's behaviour and it is an example of the 'blame-the-victim' syndrome if women are held responsible for what men do. Admittedly, the price of action is the risk that it will not work, and the price of the removal of risk is to remain inactive. But women can be encouraged to see the directions that can be taken – and also can be warned of the dangers on the way.

'The way is unknown,' writes Germaine Greer, 'and so no ultimate strategy can be designed. To be free to start out and to find companions for the journey is as far as we need to see from where we stand. The first exercise of the free woman is to devise her own mode of revolt which will reflect her own independence and originality' (p.20).

Germaine Greer's concept of human beings is one of the powerful, creative, conscious individual: it is this energy which she sees suppressed in half the population and which she wants released. In 1970, it was her view that it was possible for women to begin to unchain themselves and to start their own revolution, wherever they may be. This is in marked contrast to established notions of revolution.

Has her analysis stood the test of time? Predictably, the answer is not all that simple. In 1985, when it can be substantiated that there are many women throughout the world engaged in their own personal revolution, when there are thousands of women's groups in which women are realising their own power and are bringing about changes in their own communities, then it is clear that Germaine Greer's understandings and predictions were soundly based. The part that is left out, however, is the equally well-substantiated evidence (provided in part by the United Nations) that conditions are getting worse for women, that on every index from poverty to illiteracy, from mobility to workload, the position of women is deteriorating. There is more than one truth.

No matter what combination of truth we accept there is a long way to go. Germaine Greer has advised:

> The end cannot justify the means: if she finds that her revolutionary way leads only to further discipline and continuing incomprehension, with their corollaries of bitterness and diminution, no matter how glittering the object that would justify it, she must understand that it is a wrong way and an illusory end. The struggle which is not joyous is the wrong struggle. The struggle is not hedonism and hilarity but the sense of purpose, achievement and dignity which is the reflowering of etiolated energy. (p.20)

6. The Living Evidence: Robin Morgan's personal/political

The *personal* revolution which a woman could achieve was Germaine Greer's starting point, while for Kate Millett the *political* end of the spectrum was the focus for her analysis of women's oppression. With Robin Morgan there comes an end to the polarity between these two positions: for Robin Morgan, the *personal is political.* I do not know whether her inclusion in this book at this point is in strict chronological order, but, with her synthesis of the personal and the political, she provides, conceptually, the next step in the development of feminist theory.

> Women's liberation is the first radical movement to base its politics – in fact, create its politics – out of concrete personal experiences. We've learned that those experiences are NOT our private hang-ups. They are shared by every woman and are therefore political. (p.xx)

This description of the women's liberation movement reveals that more than the personal and the political have been fused to provide the framework: gone too is the distinction between theory and practice as women in consciousness-raising groups – everywhere – *do* liberation. Gone too is the distinction between women as individuals and women as a class as each woman finds her own meanings with the help of other women. Rather like Betty Friedan, Robin Morgan states that 'The Women's Liberation Movement exists where three or four friends or neighbors decide to meet regularly over coffee and talk about their personal lives.' Such meetings become a source of knowledge and a political act as they reveal the distance between the dominant explanations and the experiences of the women. Wherever women are they can use the personal to be political, states Robin Morgan, and she lists all the possible places from the bed to the streetcorner, from the supermarket to the convent, from the maternity ward to the workplace. The women's liberation movement 'exists in your mind', she says, it exists 'in the political and personal insights you can contribute to change and shape and help its growth' (p.vxli), making it clear that it is possible for every woman to participate in this collective movement.

Because Robin Morgan emphasises the *collective* nature of women's personal/political experience, to single out her contribution from *Sisterhood Is Powerful* is to misrepresent her. But by providing a unifying context for the enormous range of articles that followed, her introduction embodies many of the understandings that have become characteristic of feminist thought and action. So although convenience influences my decision to treat her work in semi-isolation, accuracy demands that I acknowledge that this could well distort the meaning of much of what she has to say.

And what she did say in 1970 was electrifying. Robin Morgan overturns the whole patriarchal frame of reference with her refusal to abide by its rules. First, she breaks the cardinal rule about the presentation of knowledge which requires an 'authority' to remain outside a process and to comment on it from a distance. Robin Morgan reports on what it is like in the most personal and political terms from *inside* women's liberation, and it is this which gives the sense of immediacy, community and authority to her account of *doing* women's liberation. If Kate Millett and Germaine Greer conceptualised the significance of consciousness and outlined the potential of women to reclaim their own minds, then Robin Morgan is the concrete evidence of their abstraction. And not only does she set out a rationale of what consciousness-raising is, and how it can work in practice, she then proceeds to do it in her own writing. 'This book is an action' (p.xv), she claims; there could be no disagreement.

This is her second sin against patriarchy which would not only force a distinction between theory and practice, but which would elevate theory above practice (and, of course, imply that it was the province of men). Robin Morgan, however, blends theory and practice into a multifaceted process which leaves theory without action or practice without theory looking limited, absurd even. A theoretical activist, she defies the rules by making women's actions the substance of theory.

To think of theory as a prescribed set of meanings imposed from

70

'above', as a 'line' which must be adhered to even when it denies the knowledge of life (as does every lecture I have ever heard on child development) is to be constrained by the meanings of our patriarchal society which are based on legitimating *one* view and disallowing the contradictions. Outside such a patriarchal framework there is no reason why theory cannot be formulated communally, the product of every woman having her say, and of having that say incorporated, so that theory is developmental, an explanation that expands to accommodate all the diverse accounts and contradictions fed into it. Theory can grow from the sources of personal knowledge, which are in turn validated by becoming part of the theory.

This process of explaining the world in all its diversity, inter-connectedness and multiplicity of constructed meanings is not a *substitute* for theory but another form of theory markedly different from conventional theory. It contains and accommodates the views of many, rather than one; it also takes account of its own existence as distinct from the accepted belief that it fell from heaven ready made.

For Robin Morgan there was no static and prescriptive theory; from her vantage point inside the women's movement she could see that there was no one feminism, no single movement that women could join, and no simple, pat solution that would end women's oppression. Her personal documentation was a political challenge to patriarchy and the dominant explanations for making sense of the world: the point of the challenge was the challenge itself. This is why she made it – this was *doing* women's liberation.

One of her most useful contributions is her account of what women were doing at the time, for it helps to show the diversity and the vitality of women's action to reclaim their power and to use it against patriarchy:

It is now the spring of 1970. During the past few months, wildcat strikes by women at General Electric, Bendix, and the New York Bell Telephone Company surprised both management and labor: the women felt they had been sold out by the union, which was more concerned about its male members . . . . Housewives in Stockton, California, went on strike for wages and a clear definition of their 'job' – in writing. Women's caucuses have been formed or are forming in the American Political Science Association, the Anthropological Association, the Modern Language Association, the History Association and the American Association for the Advancement of Science

71

.... Welfare mothers have been disrupting welfare centers all over the country.... Roman Catholic women are in revolt over the Pill, and Catholic nuns demand greater autonomy from the male clerical hierarchy .... Miss USA exposes the commercial way she has been used, and denounces her exploiters. Women are marching, picketing, and mounting a variety of actions against abortion laws in every state. Boycotts have been started ... and all the major magazines have had stories on the Women's Liberation Movement .... Women's Liberation Centers are being set up by local groups all around the country.... And in the first 'occupation and barricade' action done by women ... women ... were demanding that the millions of dollars earned from pornographic books that degrade women go to set up childcare centers for community and working mothers, a bail fund to free prostitutes, and training programs to prepare women for decent and well-paying jobs. (pp.xxxii–xxxiv)

In years to come, if the present women's movement is masked by the same misapprehensions as previous women's movements and is passed off as a 'reform' movement interested only in a single issue (such as the passing of the Equal Rights Amendment in the United States), it will be important to have this documentation of Robin Morgan's *for the record*.

In outlining the scope and the pace of change, however, Robin Morgan doesn't confine herself to what other women are doing. Speaking unashamedly from her own experience, she says that during the year it took to put the book together, 'I twice survived the almost-dissolution of my marriage, was fired from my job ... gave birth to a child, worked on a women's newspaper, marched and picketed, breastfed the baby, was arrested on a militant women's liberation action, spent some time in jail, stopped wearing makeup and shaving my legs, started learning karate, and changed my politics completely' (p.xvi). Most of the other women who collaborated on the book experienced just as much change, and there is even a warning about taking as given the information the book contains: 'By the time you read this, some groups referred to in articles might have changed form or name, and judging from the astonishing rate at which new groups are proliferating around the country – indeed the world – our list can hardly be considered exhaustive or definitive' (pp.xix–xx).

At the same time that Germaine Greer was suggesting that women could exert their power and become a force to be reckoned with, Robin

Morgan was showing women doing just this. And like Germaine Greer, it was clear to Robin Morgan that women couldn't both be positive and powerful, *and* surrender their resources to men. Women were positive and powerful only when they withdrew their labour from men and used it to support each other. Placing more emphasis on the collective process of support than on the individual demands of heterosexuality (although these were not overlooked), Robin Morgan's counsel was not for women just to refuse the demands of a male-dominated *relatio₁ship*, it was for women to refuse the demands of male domination and, where possible, to work with women only. This included the work for women's liberation.

What Robin Morgan was urging was an autonomous women's movement where women could be free from the definitions and demands of men, where women could decide for themselves on the basis of their experience (which men were so quick to discount) what they wanted and how they would achieve it. It was her own experience of working with men for a new society which helped her to reach this conclusion.

Describing her own involvement in the men's movement, she writes that, 'Thinking we were involved in the struggle to build a new society, it was a slowly dawning and depressing realization that we were doing the same work and playing the same roles IN the Movement as out of it; typing the speeches that men delivered, making coffee but not policy, being accessories to the men whose politics would supposedly replace the Old Order. But whose New Order? Not ours, certainly' (p.xxiii). Align yourself with the oppressor, in other words, and you shouldn't be surprised that you are oppressed.

This was a personal/political stand which had many consequences. First, it represented women as positive and able to exert influence, a repudiation of the prevailing opinion that a woman was not complete without a man and that the only serious actions (and, indeed, the only significant conversations) occurred in the company of men. Secondly, the claim for an autonomous women's movement was the beginning of the celebration of an independent women's culture: it ushered in the growing realisation that women could produce their own meanings, their own cultural forms, and use them for the further replenishment and inspiration of women. This recognition of women's culture, from books to art, from courses to centres, from plants to politics, is one of the most significant and least publicly acknowledged gains of the women's

73

movement, and Robin Morgan helped to prepare the way for its development with her insistence that women did not have to meet the requirements of men but were in a position to define for themselves what their representations – and standards – would be.

But thirdly, and predictably, because Robin Morgan advocated that women work in their own interests, she and other radical feminists whom she was seen to represent were branded with a new pejorative term – that of *separatists*. This is another variation on the 'men as the enemy' theme, another attempt to discredit a view which does not assume the centrality and necessity of the male. While it is obvious that if women are to break with the dominant meanings which distort them they must form their meanings outside the influence of the dominant, the concept of women doing without men remains a threat. The resistance to women-only groups (and the use of sex-discrimination legislation against them) reveals how entrenched is the concept that women should remain in the company of men. *Separatism* in the way the term was used against Robin Morgan is an infringement of patriarchal order. Like other names that are used to force women to conform (from bra-burner to man-hater, to bitch), this too could be seen for what it was – and defied.

Aware that there was little future for women's liberation while women were dominated by men, Robin Morgan was also aware of the contradictions of her position and was not averse from making her doubts and ambivalence explicit: 'I haven't the faintest notion what possible revolutionary role white heterosexual men could fulfill,' she declared, 'since they are the very embodiment of reactionary-vested-interest-power. But then I have great difficulty examining what men in general could possibly do about all this. In addition to doing the shitwork that women have been doing for generations, possibly not exist? No, I really don't mean that. Yes I do. Never mind, that's another whole book' (p.xl).

From her personal experience Robin Morgan forged her own political conclusions that women paid a high price for heeding the meanings of men. Even working on the book (which was an all-woman project) it was the women who worked within the publishing industry who had the least influence: they were 80 per cent of the workforce and all at the bottom of the ladder (p.xix), Robin Morgan stated. If it was possible to choose, she decided, then she was going to choose to work outside male influence, she was going to choose her independence in conjunction with other women who had made the same decision.

In the presence of men, she argued, male meanings and male priorities predominate and women become appendages, encouraged to put aside women's concerns until the men have sorted out the latest 'skirmish' among themselves (for their revolution, 'were it to occur tomorrow, would be no revolution, but only another *coup d'état* among men' (pp.xxxv–xxxvi)): women's concerns are a luxury – and can wait. The fact that men define their own actions as *revolutionary* and women's demands as *reforms*, reveals more about the status of the sexes than the nature of their political activities.

But refusing to work with men or to accept men's meanings and priorities does not end the story, for women are not left to develop their own strengths. Tactics aimed at discrediting such women are soon brought into play, and it is interesting to see the list of charges Robin Morgan draws up that were made against the women's liberation movement, for they haven't changed much since 1970.

One of the most common accusations levelled at women in the liberation movement then was that they were being misled, for the women's movement was *over*. She also draws up a long list of labels that are used against women: 'bra-burners', 'lesbians', 'neurotics', 'destroyers of home and family', 'runaway wives', and one, designed to play on guilt and which is rarely used by men about their own 'progressive' groups, that the women's liberation movement is 'white, middle-class and young'.

Robin Morgan does not ignore the issue of colour: she notes the parallels between racism and sexism and there is nothing in her framework which confines feminism to white women. But then, as now, this is probably one area of the women's movement where there *is* a discrepancy between theory and practice and this should be contended with, not omitted. One solution is not to give up, but to change.

The charge of middle-class she finds easier to deflect. When all women are required to marry 'up', she states – echoing the sentiments of Susan B. Anthony – we may appear deceptively middle-class.

One reason for the previous image was that working-class women are of course compelled to strain after middle-class values (what mothers call 'marrying well' and sociologists call 'upward mobility') and to *act* middle-class. We all began to discover that a large percentage of the movement comes from working-class backgrounds. (p.xxx)

This defence aside, I have always been intrigued when confronted with the assertion that the women's movement is middle-class – how does the critic know? With the women's liberation movement taking so many different forms in so many different places, *no one* knows its class composition. This is not to deny the class differences among women, but they are very different from the class categories formulated by men and for men. The differences among women in terms of finance, education, articulacy and security, for example, are of paramount importance: we need to understand them. But in 1970 – and now in 1984 – these differences remain speculative: a devastating indictment of social science.

What Robin Morgan did know in 1970 was what the women's movement could be with its commitment to the common experience of women:

> It is ... the first movement that has the potential of cutting across all class, race, economic and geographical barriers – since women in every group must play essentially the same role, albeit with different sets and costumes; the multiple role of wife, mother, sexual object, baby-producer, 'supplementary income statistic', helpmate, nurturer, hostess, etc. (p.xx)

And the 1970 charge that the women's movement was 'wrong' because it was young? Fifteen years later, with a lot of us still around and not, therefore, quite so young, this charge has given way to the new accusation that the women's movement is middle-aged!

Robin Morgan not only deflected the accusations of the present, she also looked to the past for guidance. Concerned to learn from history, she had much against the development of the women's liberation movement into a middle-class movement, more interested in bourgeois reform than in creating a new society:

> I fear for the women's movement falling into precisely the same trap as did our foremothers, the suffragists: creating a bourgeois feminist movement that never quite dared enough, never really reached out beyond its own class and race. For example, with a few courageous exceptions, most of the suffragists refused to examine the family as a structure oppressive to women. Because of this type of failure, they wound up having to settle for the vote. (p.xxvi)

76

This fear was also expressed by Germaine Greer, as we have seen, but is one which, with the benefit of fifteen years' research and the restoration of women's traditions, we can see as a version of women's history within the framework of *men's* history. In the light of our present understandings it would be grossly inaccurate to suggest that the women of earlier movements were concerned with reform, not revolution. *Women's* demands in the past – irrespective of how radical they were – have ultimately been judged as reforms within the male framework.

When in the 1850s Barbara Bodichon in England claimed the right of married women to own property and Elizabeth Cady Stanton in the United States claimed the right to vote, these were *radical* demands which men believed would revolutionise society: the measure of the threat of these demands lies in the nature of their response. They declared that if married women owned property, voted or decided when and how many children they would have, society would collapse. These radical demands were finally achieved after many years, and, as we know, there was no great alteration in the relationship between the sexes. But so too were some of the radical demands of Karl Marx, such as a reduction in the working week and the introduction of workers' compensation, without there being any great alteration in the relationship between the classes. Rarely, however, is Karl Marx branded pejoratively as a reformer: he remains a revolutionary; but the revolutionary women have become 'unattractive reformers', an example of failure, and a model that present generations of women should seek to avoid.

This is how women are turned away from our own history. It is not a criticism of Robin Morgan that she should have accepted in 1970 what women had been taught of women's past. It is a criticism of male dominance which is strengthened when women of each generation have to start again without the advantage of learning from the positive women who went before. We cannot afford to continue to subscribe to this myth that our foremothers failed – but that we have it 'right' and are going further than they dared.

Fifteen years after Robin Morgan expressed her fears that the women's movement might fall into the trap of not questioning the source of women's oppression in the family, we have considerable evidence that, historically, this has been one of the most frequently challenged forms of oppression. As early as 1696 Mary Astell, in England, was cautioning women against marriage in terms that would still shock today. Throughout the nineteenth century it was marriage that figured at the top of the scale of women's oppression; even John Stuart Mill (1869) gave it considerable attention. And when women started demanding the vote, this was no disqualification from working for radical changes in the family structure as well. Elizabeth Cady Stanton and Matilda Joslyn Gage, both editors of *History of Woman Suffrage*, didn't leave the family out of their analysis and Matilda Joslyn Gage's theory has not been surpassed today; Charlotte Perkins Gilman's *Women and Economics* (1899)[1] remains a classic text on the exploitation of women in the family. In England, Josephine Butler wanted the vote and education for women, but was more concerned with women's sexual oppression; in 1909 Cicely Hamilton wrote her scathing critique, *Marriage as a Trade*, in which she claimed that women were deprived of every other possibility in order that they could be coerced into marriage and obliged to trade themselves in exchange for board and lodging. If required, hundreds of women who have challenged marriage, the home and the family – in much the same way as we do today – could be quoted. And these would be only from the *written* record.

Robin Morgan epitomises the plight of all of us when she presumes that women are confronting some of these issues for the first time, for we have all been systematically denied the historical insights which would help to illuminate our present predicament. None the less, Robin Morgan does an excellent job of outlining the predicament women find themselves in. She knows that women work harder for less financial rewards. 'In essence, women are still back in feudal times. We work outside capitalism as unpaid labour – and it is the structure of the family that makes this possible, since the employer pays only the husband and, in fact, gets the rest of the family's services for free' (p.xxxvii).

In 1970 when women were looking to existing analyses to try to add to their understandings about the exploitation of women's labour, it was clear that, in the accepted theories of the time, the position of women had largely been ignored. There were, of course, theories about the exploitation of labour and the means by which it could be overcome, and there were some who believed (and still do) that while these theories did not originate with women and paid scant or no attention to women, they could still be extended to encompass an understanding of women's position. Robin Morgan was not convinced by this argument. She objected to the idea of trying to fit women into a framework designed for men, and looked instead for more appropriate explanations for women's exploitation for, in practice, she concluded, these theories did not work for women: 'We know that two evils clearly pre-date corporate capitalism, and have post-dated socialist revolutions: sexism and racism' (pp.xxxv–xxxvi). It would therefore be misguided for women to place their faith in socialism or a socialist revolution. This rejection of the accumulated wisdom of men on the grounds that it was only useful for men, and the commitment to creating theories – and wisdom – for the good of women, was a characteristic which was later used to designate a 'radical feminist' or a 'separatist': it was also a major impetus for the growth of women's studies courses.

From the tone of Robin Morgan's writing, I suspect that she encountered (as I did) some of those critics who, confronted with the assertion that men hadn't begun to conceptualise the dimensions of women's position – let alone the possibility of a solution – would respond heatedly with the counter-argument that if women did not like a male frame of reference, what would they put in its place? Such a question reveals a basic lack of comprehension. It would be futile to explain that we didn't know – but were thinking about it. As Robin Morgan states, it's as if they 'expected us, like tidy housekeepers, to come up in five short years with the magic remedy cleaner that will wipe clean the mess men have created from their position of power during the past 5,000 years' (p.xxxv).

Even where some men did acknowledge the existence of the issue their ideas for 'improvement' were on their own terms, did little to undermine their own privileged position, and were generally hopelessly inappropriate. Holding up sexual freedom as the way for liberation was part of this particular pattern and Robin Morgan was not taken in: '[the] so-called sexual revolution was only another new form of oppression for women. The intervention of the Pill made millions for the drug companies, made guinea-pigs of us, and made us all the more "available" as sexual objects; if a woman didn't want to go to bed with a man *now*, she must be hung up. It was inconceivable, naturally, that she might not like the man, or the Pill, or for that matter sex' (p.xxxv). Despite our years of research, in some respects our understandings have not progressed greatly since Robin Morgan set them out in 1970. She even refers to the harassment of women by men (p.xxxv), a topic taken up and developed more fully later (see particularly Catherine MacKinnon, 1979).

Her description of sexism, its all-pervasive nature, and the way it erodes women, was brilliantly perceptive and it is the personal/political dimension that gives her account much of its reality and force. It is

Everything from the verbal assault on the street, to a 'well meant' sexist joke your husband tells, to the lower pay you get at work (for doing the same job a man would be paid more for), to television commercials, to rock song lyrics, to the pink or blue blanket they put on your infant in the hospital nursery, to speeches by male 'revolutionaries' that reek of male supremacy – everything seems to barrage your aching brain which has fewer and fewer defenses to screen such things out. (p.xviii)

Knowing all this, 'I couldn't believe,' she states, 'still can't – how angry I could become, from deep down and way back, something like a five-thousand-year buried anger' (p.xvii).

Not surprisingly *Sisterhood Is Powerful* soon became many women's bible – 'Genesis' was about the psychologists' creation of the female (' "Kinder, Küche, Kirche" as Scientific Law: Psychology constructs the Female', Naomi Weisstein, pp.228–44); the 'Book of Revelations' included 'The Politics of Orgasm' (Susan Lydon, pp.219–27); and chapter and verse explained what was going on with housework, and why ('The Politics of Housework', Pat Mainardi, pp.501–26). Her view from inside the women's movement was one of the most valuable additions that could have been made, and although her later contributions – *Going Too Far: The Personal Chronicle of a Feminist* (1978) and *The Anatomy of Freedom* (1982:1983) – develop some of her earlier ideas, it is fair to say that she hasn't been given due credit for her multidimensional understandings which are the substance of *Sisterhood Is Powerful* and which, with their blend of the personal and political, have become the touchstone of feminist understandings and visions. One of the temptations that feminists have to resist is the patriarchal predilection for finding the 'correct' political line and the single, simple solution. In 1970 Robin Morgan openly acknowledged that the contributions in *Sisterhood Is Powerful* were 'uneven and contradictory (p.xx) and, what's more, that that was the way it was going to be. Her unapologetic defiance of conventional wisdom was both a means and a source of the liberation she envisaged for each individual woman who could experience the collective power of sisterhood.

7. Women and Children: Shulamith Firestone's solution

It may have been a coincidence but with the publications of Kate Millett, Germaine Greer and Robin Morgan, the scope of feminism had been plotted and future explanations were – and in the main still are – within this territory. Shulamith Firestone's book, *The Dialectic of Sex: The Case for Feminist Revolution*, is an elaboration of some of the concepts already set out, and although it includes many original insights, her thesis is primarily located within the boundaries that the other women had charted.[1] Like Kate Millett, she sees men as having power – although she does not think it is a fixed power; like Germaine Greer, she sees women as having their resources drained by men, and is convinced that women themselves can reclaim their power; and like Robin Morgan, she blends the personal and the political, and writes from within the context of doing liberation and can therefore comment authoritatively on consciousness-raising.

Again like Kate Millett and Robin Morgan, she places sexual oppression at the centre of her analysis of oppression. *Sexual* oppression is the most fundamental form of oppression, and from this other forms of oppression flow. Having learnt the model of sexual oppression from birth, she reasoned, further forms of oppression will seem reasonable and normal. Because, from infancy, the individual is taught the justice and necessity for some human beings to have power over others, because the lesson is the legitimacy of male power over women and children, then it does not come as a shock but more as the 'unfolding of the natural order' to find this principle extended to race and to class. Making the oppression of women (and children) the prototype for all other forms of oppression was the hallmark of the radical feminist, a label that Shulamith Firestone unapologetically claimed.

Her stand allowed feminists to deal with the allegation that the *real* issue was class, and that they were therefore not only splitting the genuine movement (read *men's* movement) by failing to support as supreme the class issue, but they were on the wrong track, and couldn't possibly get to the roots of oppression if they persisted in thinking only in terms of women. Shulamith Firestone countered this particular argument by asserting that only by beginning with women could the origins and complexity of oppression be understood. Revolutionaries who confined themselves to the overthrow of class on the grounds that other forms of oppression would then presumably wither away not only failed to deal with racism and sexism, they failed to come to terms with the nature of power itself, and were therefore engaged in nothing other than a redistribution of power among the rulers rather than a revolution which would transform power – and relationships.

With this line of reasoning, it is apparent that Shulamith Firestone had much in common with the feminists whose frameworks have already been outlined. Where she differed was in her understanding of history or, more precisely, her understanding of women's history. It is this difference which influences many of her conceptualisations of power, how it works, and how women can contend with it. First, she is aware that there have always been women rebels who have protested against male domination (p.23), but without great success, so if the aim is to end male domination then it isn't enough just to have women rebels. Secondly, she sees through the received wisdom of a male-dominated society that dismissed earlier women's movements as bourgeois and reformist: according to Shulamith Firestone, the nineteenth-century women's movement in the USA was a radical and grassroots movement (p.24), which had made revolutionary demands and, over time, some of them had been achieved: but there had been no revolution – males still dominated.

Shulamith Firestone was concerned to make sense of women's past. That radical women came to be so misrepresented was not at all difficult to explain: men were in charge of history and could decide what it would and would not include, so that the portrayal of women in unflattering and non-threatening terms – as far as men were concerned – was not at all surprising. More perplexing, however, was why such radical demands as equal education and political recognition for women had not led to the transformation of society when they were achieved as many women had intended they should.

It could be that the women had got it 'wrong' – a not uncommon explanation in a male-dominated society; it could be that when they focused on education and the vote, for example, they did in fact make a mistake. Yet it was not only women who had concluded that education and the vote were power sources: men too had feared that if women were educated on equal terms with men and allowed the same political rights they would soon lose the status of being the superior sex. This is why women put so much energy into obtaining education and the vote. But men without doubt remained the superior sex. So what other possible explanation could there be?

It could be that power is not a constant; that is to say, it is not fixed in specific skills or structures. This would help explain how women could get the vote, for instance, and still not achieve a real shift in power. But such a concept requires illustration, and the example which follows is my own, not Shulamith Firestone's.

Let me take war as an example. In our male-dominated society, men go to war and, ideologically, war is presented as a glorious activity. But because war is the province of men, men present a myriad of reasons for preventing women from being warriors. Given the association between dominant males and warfare, it might be surmised that being a warrior is a source of power, and that women will only be full members of society when they are full members of the armed forces (some contemporary arguments are based on this premise). Women therefore make the radical demand of full admission to the armed forces, and men protest vehemently on the grounds that if the armed forces are full of women,[2] not only will it mean a loss of efficiency, it will be the end of society as it is known – the end of male supremacy. So they resist.

But imagine that women put real energy into their campaign and, after (many) years, are given equal representation in the armed forces. Will the last bastion of male power crumble? Will women be on equal terms with men?

I foresee a very different outcome, based on lessons learnt from the past campaigns for education and the vote. If these are any guide, then women would not occupy the top jobs in the armed forces; women would be the troops. Would it feel like equality and power, I wonder, if, in the event of threat, the (male) officers sent the (female) troops into the areas of greatest danger? I hardly think our grand-daughters would be grateful for the rights we had won for them.

Because of the lessons she had learnt from women's history,

Shulamith Firestone was aware of the limitations of the line of reasoning that fastened on any *one* attribute of male power, and then attempted to attain it for women. Such a strategy did not allow for the shifting focus of power, she argued. For example, once women were admitted to education in general, then the power shifted to a *particular form* of education; although it was acknowledged that women could be educated, technological education was erected as the stumbling-block which separated (and justified) power and powerlessness.

Berit Ås, a contemporary Norwegian feminist philosopher with an illuminating turn of phrase, has summed up this problem another way. Men are the officials who run all the events in our society, and every time women look like qualifying, *men change the rules*. There's no point in women trying to enter on the grounds that men prescribe, she insists, because as soon as women look like fulfilling the requirements, men present a whole new set of rules – and there's no referee to appeal to. Women have to start again to meet the new criteria.

Looking at what's happened in education, I think she's probably right. Women are no closer now to being full members of that educational élite which helps to set the social agenda and determine priorities, than they were 150 years ago, when in England Greek and Latin were the 'entry tickets' to positions of influence – and it was a well-established 'fact' then that women couldn't *do* Greek and Latin.

But back to Shulamith Firestone and her lessons of history. Not only did she want to find a way of conceptualising power with all its shifts, she also wanted to account for the fact that 50 years after the demands for revolution, women didn't even know that their fiery, feminist fore-mothers had existed, and, what's more, they had swallowed the myth that equality had been achieved when the vote was won. There was a great deal of explaining to be done.

Shulamith Firestone was among the first to begin to ask awkward questions about the 'disappearance' of feminist theorists. Looking back we can see clearly that some very impressive feminist ideas were being formulated during the 1940s and 1950s, but with little effect. There can have been little that was more startling than Simone de Beauvoir's *The Second Sex* (published in English in 1949) or Margaret Mead's *Sex and Temperament in Three Primitive Societies* (1935) and *Male and Female* (1950). Yet what happened to these challenging ideas? Publication alone isn't enough – such books have to be made visible, they have to be reviewed, quoted from, referenced if they are to be available to women. As it is they are so infrequently taken into the mainstream, they are so unlikely to become part of public knowledge, that in effect they cease to exist for women's purposes.

With such precedents we should be able to appreciate the absolute necessity of keeping to the forefront of our understandings the contributions made by feminist theorists fifteen years ago. If we do not, they too will disappear (or be *made* to disappear) and future generations will be puzzled by our failure to quote and make use of the remarkable ideas of our own generation, just as we can puzzle over the 'failure' of women of the 1950s to make use of Simone de Beauvoir, Margaret Mead, Viola Klein, Mary Ritter Beard and many more.[3]

For Shulamith Firestone, the 1950s were the worst decade of all in the twentieth century, for women: 'All authentic knowledge of the old feminist movement by this time had been buried' (p.34). Over a 50-year period the 'Myth of Emancipation' had anaesthetised women's political consciousness so that women coming to maturity in the 1950s were lost indeed, with little positive legacy to bequeath to their daughters:

> By 1970 the rebellious daughters of this wasted generation no longer, for all practical purposes, knew there had been a feminist movement. There remained only the unpleasant residue of the aborted revolution, an amazing set of contradictions in their roles: on the one hand they had most of the legal freedoms, the literal assurance that they were considered full political citizens of society – and yet they had no power. They had educational opportunities – and yet were unable and not expected to employ them. They had freedoms of clothing and sex mores that they had demanded – and yet they were still sexually exploited. (pp.36-7)

In short, just about every revolutionary demand that had been made had been achieved, but there had been no revolution.

In seeking to explain what had gone wrong, there was one thing that Shulamith Firestone was definitely not going to do: she wasn't going to blame the victim. She wasn't going to hold women responsible for the failure to transform society. Instead she sought an analytic method which would encompass contradictions, be dynamic, and which could help to account for the ever-moving shifts in power. She therefore turned to the methodology of Karl Marx and Friedrich Engels, to the methodology of dialectical materialism.

Shulamith Firestone was perfectly aware that their analysis had applied to class oppression only, but she was confident that she could use their methodology fruitfully for an analysis of *women's* oppression. It was the claims that were made for this methodology that were the attraction: the possibility of conceptualising human affairs not in linear, monodimensional terms, but in their multiplicity of interconnections and simultaneously opposing occurrences, and all in the context of their material origins. Shulamith Firestone wanted to represent and analyse the complexity of interrelationships and contradictions which are the fabric of women's position: an aspiration shared by virtually every feminist theorist who has taken the view that there is more than a simple cause-and-effect explanation.

Shulamith Firestone likened her approach to dialectical materialism; Robin Morgan, in *The Anatomy of Freedom* (1982), likened her method to the viewing of a holograph.[4] It is important to note the 'set of rules' that Shulamith Firestone adopted for interpreting women's position, because they played an influential role in the formulation of her solutions which were very different from those recommended by most other feminists at that time, although she started with the evidence common to the feminist frameworks that have been discussed so far – that of the reality of male power and its relationship to the meanings and knowledge of society. And, as with her rebellious sisters, there was no hint of a quest for male approval in her approach. While acknowledging her debt to Marx and Engels, Shulamith Firestone was not at all reluctant to point accusingly at what they had left out. On the contrary, she asserts that Marx had left out a great deal more than Engels, who had at least recognised

> that the original division of labour was between man and woman for the purpose of child breeding; that within the family the husband was the owner, the wife the means of production, the children the labour; and that reproduction of the human species was an important economic system distinct from the means of production. (p.14)

But while the 'class analysis is a beautiful piece of work', there 'is a whole sexual substratum of the historical dialectic that Engels at times dimly perceives, but because he can see sexuality only through an economic filter, reducing everything to that, he is unable to evaluate it in its own right' (p.14). What's more, she insists, 'Engels has been given too much credit for these scattered recognitions of women as a class' (p.15). He could be credited with noting the phenomenon, but it would be inappropriate for women to accept his pronouncements because his intention had been to explain the system of production, not of reproduction; he 'acknowledged the sexual class system only where it overlapped and illuminated his economic construct' (p.15).

Such words were hardly deferential; such priorities – women and children *first* – were hardly acceptable, inside or outside the doctrine of historical materialism. And even the habit of taking from a particular doctrine the bits you liked and thought you could use while leaving the bits you considered were unsatisfactory – was deemed by many to be breaking the rules of the game. (I can remember when the charge of 'eclectic' was a most intimidating one: there was a lot of pressure against the feminist practice of taking from established theories only those parts that were considered useful.) But Shulamith Firestone was undaunted – she took from Engels what she found helpful, and without qualms left the rest.

One of her principles was 'know the enemy', with the result that she devotes considerable space to an analysis of men, to their patterns of thinking and to their material circumstances, which she sees as giving rise to a 'psychology of power'. While later feminist researchers might have favoured the premise that feminist research consisted primarily of research about women, Shulamith Firestone was not of this school, partly because she was convinced that it was a distortion to view women in isolation when every aspect of their existence was governed by the power of men (see also Liz Stanley and Sue Wise, 1983). Rather, she tried to preserve the pattern of interconnection between the sexes, which meant that men – and their power – had constantly to be kept in mind, even at the risk of perpetuating the patriarchal pattern of placing men at the centre and women at the periphery. According men such significance did not, however, preclude her from advocating an autonomous women's movement: on the contrary, it was *because* she recognised the extent to which male power impinged on women that she believed it was crucial for women to be able to avoid the clutches of men, and to set up their own space and develop their own independent cultural forms.

Shulamith Firestone firmly believed that our society has a fundamental assumption, that the world is 'split in two', and that this dichotomy, which is the basis for making sense of the world, is predicated on and justified by sexual division. By distinguishing themselves from women, and by appropriating power for their own kind, men had set up a framework in which there was a right and a wrong. In this she was greatly influenced by Simone de Beauvoir's assertion in *The Second Sex* (1949) that men were the reference point for humanity, which made women 'other' and 'in the wrong'. This concept of male-as-norm, by definition, casts women in the role of deviant and deficient, so that our way of seeing the world is, from the outset, through the lens of 'man as right' and 'woman as wrong'. This 'Representation of the world, like the world itself,' Shulamith Firestone writes, 'is the work of men: they describe it from their own point of view, which they confuse with absolute truth' (p.148). The authority they claim, this capacity to be the knowers in possession of the true view of the world, does much to enhance and reinforce their privileged position. What they know, what forms they create from their knowledge, they would have us accept is *all* that there is to know or be, states Shulamith Firestone, yet 'this culture is not universal but rather sectarian, presenting only half the spectrum of experience' (p.122).

Being in a position to know everything might be reassuring and validating for men, but can be disastrous for women, declares Shulamith Firestone. When women try to interpret their own existence and the only code for interpretation is that provided by men, then

> women have no means of coming to an understanding of what their own experience is, or even that it is different from male experience. The tool for representing, for objectifying one's experience in order to deal with it, culture, is so saturated with male bias that women almost never have a chance to see themselves culturally through their own eyes. (p.149)

If all else were equal, so oriented is our existing culture towards the greater significance of men in its language, meaning and knowledge, that it would be impossible to sustain even the concept of equality, because men would be seen as authoritative and women's experience would slide into the realm of non-data. In our culture, the world of men counts, that of women doesn't: and this basic inequality, argues Shulamith Firestone, spirals, justifies, and comes to be realised in everyday reality. It is at the heart of our cultural knowledge about the world, including all the true and objective knowledge which is produced in academic institutions (p.175).[5]

The division of academic endeavour into arts and sciences is, to Shulamith Firestone, further evidence of the manifestation of sexual dichotomy (and inequality) with both branches of learning deprived and distorted by these restrictions (p.179). The arts and the humanities are diminished, and 'The catalogue of scientific vices is familiar: it duplicates, exaggerates the catalogue of "male" vices in general. This is to be expected; if the technological male develops from the male principle then it follows that its practitioners would develop the warpings of the male personality in the extreme' (p.173). This understanding (later illuminatingly elaborated by Carolyn Merchant, 1982) has become well established in feminist knowledge. Like Kate Millett, Shulamith Firestone states that women's exclusion from the process of formulating the values, agenda, direction and methods of scientific enterprise has been so complete that 'We can hardly find a relationship of women to science, worthy of discussion' (p.161).

Shulamith Firestone is devastatingly critical of male control of science, and the one-sided and linear pattern of thinking that typifies its processes. She denounces the absurdity of empiricism which leads logically to the 'process' of nuclear bombs: 'Why are there disciplines or branches of inquiry that demand only a "male" mind?' she asks, and turns the question round so that it suggests that only a man could be sufficiently limited to develop such destructive, anti-human products – and then to hold them up as achievements! 'Why should a woman, to qualify, have to develop an alien psychology?' she demands. 'How and why has science come to be defined as restricted to the "objective"?' (p.162).

Her greatest anger, however, is reserved for schooling, which she sees as the major tool of indoctrination in the inferiority of women. Her assertion is that schooling is inextricably linked with the oppression of women and children, and that it retards the development of human beings in order to make them more 'manageable' (p.84). The apparently absurd practices of schooling (the segregation of human beings according to age, provided with a curriculum as a substitute for experience of life, and kept under control) only make sense when seen in the light of being a production process designed to turn out people who can fit into the dichotomised and unequal positions which society depends on for its maintenance.

There was a time, she states, when young members of society were simply smaller members of society, and education was not necessary as a means of social control. But with the introduction of 'childhood' – a relatively recent invention – which separated them from adults and the real world, education became essential:

> The school was the institution that structured childhood by effectively segregating children from the rest of society, thus retarding their growth into adulthood and their development of specialized skills for which the society had use. As a result they remained economically dependent for longer and longer periods of time. (p.86)

It is the relationship between childhood and womanhood that prompts Shulamith Firestone to declare that women cannot be liberated unless this is accompanied by the liberation of children. She insists that it is by the oppression of children – only made possible since the establishment of childhood – that inequality is internalised. But whereas boys are permitted to *grow up*, there is nothing for girls to grow up *to*; this state of affairs has been reflected historically in the use of costume (p.81): 'Here is an astonishing fact,' she states, looking at patterns of the past, and making use of the research of Philippe Ariès:

> *Childhood did not apply to women.* The female child went from swaddling clothes right into adult female dress. She did not go to school.... At the age of nine or ten she acted literally like a 'little lady'; her activity did not differ much from that of adult women. As soon as she reached puberty, as early as ten or twelve, she was married off to a much older male. (p.181)

The model was that of the oppression of children, but for women this became their permanent state, and it was because Shulamith Firestone was concerned to make oppression a *meaningless category* that she was determined to have all its forms removed. It was no good advocating the liberation of women while any prototypic model of oppression remained, she argued, because in the end it would be used against women. And she was convinced that the oppression of children constituted a fundamental model.

Like women, children were supposed to be innocent and pure, and for this they warranted 'respect' and required protection from the harsh realities of the 'adult' (that is, male) world. Both children and women were placed in a position of economic dependency, were contained, obliged to be servile and to find pleasing the touching and fondling of those who had power over them: 'The special tie women have with children is recognised by everyone. I submit however that this bond is no more than shared oppression' (p.77); 'I say this knowing full well that many women are sick and tired of being lumped together with children', she adds, and 'that they are no more our charge and responsibility than anyone else's, will be an assumption crucial to our revolutionary demands' (p.102).

Shulamith Firestone concludes that there are certain 'categories' which are used as foundation stones on which layers of meaning are erected. So with the construction of the distinctive category of childhood, for example, comes the construction of all the meanings which make the oppressive treatment of children seem reasonable and unexceptionable, as part of 'the way the world works', with the result that we find it difficult – if not impossible – to imagine a world without these categories and meanings. Yet it hasn't always been this way, she argues, for there was a time when the category of childhood did not exist and – in her frame of reference – this meant that the specific oppression of children did not exist either.

How does this understanding relate to the oppression of women? Is it possible for the category 'woman' not to exist? If the distinctions between childhood and adulthood, which serve as a rationale for oppression, can be removed, is it possible to eliminate the distinctions between 'woman' and 'man', which also serve as the rationale for the oppression of women? If there is no way of distinguishing 'woman', there is no basis for the construction of the *oppression* of women.

The major stumbling-block, of course, was that *only* women reproduce. It was this clearly perceptible, unmistakeable and necessary quality which was the fundamental distinction between 'woman' and 'man', and which, in Shulamith Firestone's terms, was at the root of women's oppression. But she also suggested that this was not an immutable distinction. If women ceased to be the human beings who gave birth – by no means an impossibility given the increasingly sophisticated methods of reproductive technology – there would be no way of constructing the social meanings of 'woman' and of creating and justifying women's oppression. No difference between women and men means no difference, and therefore no basis for oppression. The use of reproductive technology – *under the control of women* – was therefore the answer: 'To free women thus from their biology would be to threaten the *social* unit that is organised around their biological reproduction and the subjection of women to their biological destiny' (p.193); even the family, that major instrument of women's oppression, would be destroyed (p.195).

This was the explanation that could take account of shifts in power: this was how it was possible to make sense of women's achievements of revolutionary demands – without the occurrence of a revolution. If demands such as equal education, political rights, justice, representation in the armed services or political office were achieved, only for women to find that, before they arrived, the power had been 'relocated', then the fundamental issue was to remove the origin of power itself. It was to end sex distinctions, and with their abolition would come the end of duality and the end of structured inequality. There would be no basis then for 'male-as-norm' and 'woman-as-deviant', because any differences that there were between women and men would be insignificant once women ceased to be mothers.

This 'objective' solution met with a somewhat 'subjective' response – which Shulamith Firestone anticipated. She recognised that motherhood was accorded a reverence in a patriarchal society: it was even seen to be the sole source of women's power by some. There was also the ideology of motherhood which caught women in its web of meanings with its rationale that all 'true' women wanted children.[6] Given the range of pressures on women to have children, it was extremely difficult for a woman to voice a negative opinion, but it should at least be possible to have 'an honest re-examination of the ancient value of motherhood' (p.189), where women could begin to assess the pros and cons of their distinctive capacity:

At the present time for a woman to come out openly against motherhood on principle is physically dangerous. She can get away with it only if she adds that she is neurotic, abnormal, childhating and therefore 'unfit' . . . . This is hardly a free atmosphere of inquiry. At least until the taboo is lifted, until the decision not to have children or to have them by artificial means is as legitimate as traditional childbearing, women are as good as forced into their female roles. (pp.189–90)

However, Shulamith Firestone left out of her analysis the possibility that when women were no longer necessary for reproduction, women themselves might no longer be necessary! This is a possibility which is beginning to haunt many women today for, far from *removing* the distinctions between woman and man, artificial reproduction *under the control of men* is getting closer to being a distinctive capacity of the male: future generations could be *produced* by *men*, not *reproduced* by *women*.

Shulamith Firestone is sometimes portrayed today as 'that feminist who wanted test-tube babies'; indeed she is even unjustifiably held responsible, on occasion, for the frightening developments within reproductive technology. But central to her recommendation was the insistence that *women* should control the technology, that *women* should *seize the means of reproduction and use it to liberate themselves* from the oppression which had been constructed on the basis of their biology. There was no ethical argument about this being unnatural, she claimed, for the history of society was one of the development of technology to 'improve on nature'. Where there was an ethical argument, was in relation to who *controlled* the technology, and here she was clear that if it were in the hands of women it could be a means of their liberation: in the hands of men it could become yet another instrument for the oppression of women. But the possibilities of this new technology are so frightening, she acknowledges, 'that they are seldom discussed seriously. We have seen that the fear is to some extent justified: in the hands of our current society and under the direction of current scientists (few of whom are female or even feminist) any attempted use of technology to "free" anybody is suspect' (p.193).

Yet if women did seize the means of reproductive technology, they could use it to end their oppression and to transform society, she argued. It would mean the end of romance, love, the family: there would be no further need for 'romance' – which is nothing other than the tool of male power that keeps women from understanding their oppression (p.139). And there would be no further requirement for 'love', the pivot of women's oppression. Love, as the term is currently used in relation to heterosexuality, is the means by which women give up their resources for men, it is the raw fuel of the male cultural machine (p.148): 'male culture is parasitical, feeding on the emotional strength of women without reciprocity' (p.122), but with no 'male', there will be no '*male* culture', and no demand for women to service the culture-makers, for they will themselves as human beings be participants in the production of culture.

Gone too will be the need for a woman to find herself in a man, to be capable only of loving herself after a man finds her worthy of love (p.126). There will be no reason for a woman to seek to align herself with a member of the ruling class in the belief that some of his privilege will rub off on her (p.132). How far removed is this from the present, she notes by way of contrast, where women are beguiled: 'To participate in one's subjection by choosing one's master often gives the illusion of free choice: but in reality a woman is never free to choose love without ulterior motives. For her, at the present time, the two things, love and status, must remain inextricably intertwined' (p.132).

Sex stereotyping, which coerces women into looking alike so that they can readily be identified as a class and differentiated from men, would serve no useful purpose when there were no sex distinctions, Shulamith Firestone states. It would be the end of the process whereby women 'look alike, they think alike, and even worse, they are so stupid they believe they are not alike' (p.144). And no more would 'Women everywhere rush to squeeze into the glass slipper, forcing and mutilating their bodies with diets and beauty programmes, clothes and makeup, anything to become the punk prince's dream girl' (p.144), because the enormous penalties for failure to conform which are exacted from women now would not apply when human beings were simply human beings, all members of the same species.

One of the most destructive aspects of women's present oppression which she notes is the obligation women are under to reassure their masters that they really *like* being oppressed. Betty Friedan had observed a similar 'problem' which prevented women from protesting, and which she diagnosed as an unfortunate part of the image of 'the feminine mystique', but Shulamith Firestone sees this as a vicious practice which damages women for the definite purpose of preserving the peace of mind of men. Because it makes men 'uncomfortable to know that the woman or the child or the black or the workman is grumbling, the oppressed group must also appear to *like* their oppression – smiling and simpering though they may feel like hell inside' (p.89), she writes, opening up an area of future meanings which have since been commented upon but not systematically pursued.[7]

Shulamith Firestone used her personal experience to suggest the potential meanings for women of this line of inquiry:

In my own case I had to train myself out of that phony smile which is like a nervous tic on every teenage girl. And this meant that I smiled rarely, for in truth, when it came down to real smiling, I had less to smile about. My 'dream' action for the Women's Liberation Movement: a *smile boycott*, at which declaration women would instantly abandon their pleasing smiles, henceforth smiling only when something pleased *them*. (p.89)

The picture that Shulamith Firestone paints of the present society is bleak. Her description is fuelled by a deep anger, and the only real prospect for change that she offers is the obliteration of primary sex differences, and a feminism that is 'a revolutionary ecological movement' with the aim of 'control of the new technology for humane purposes' (p.184).

Meanwhile, the hatred of women by men will continue; a hatred that expresses itself in everything from Norman Mailer's vituperative prose to the sexist assaults of the media; a hatred that women find so difficult to deal with: 'To overhear a bull session is traumatic to a woman; so all this time she has been considered only as "ass", "meat", "twat" or "stuff" to be gotten a "piece of", "that bitch" or "this broad" to be tricked out of money, sex or love. To understand finally that she is no better than other women comes not just as a blow but as total annihilation' (p.143).

Of all the books published in 1970, *The Dialectic of Sex* is the only one which leaves me with the feeling of despair, because I believe her 'solution' will not work. For while I do not 'know' the dividing-line between the 'real' world and the one we construct, what I do 'know' is that it is perfectly possible that *physical* distinctions that do not exist in other cultures could well be created in our own[8] if desired: I also 'know' that where physical distinctions do exist, they can be used either positively or negatively according to the belief-system which ordains and interprets the shape of our world. Look what would happen if men could menstruate: think what would happen if women were no longer *re*producers!

But this leads me back to the premise that once values are encoded in the belief-system they work to create the world we inhabit: in order to become human we must learn the language and take on that belief-system, so we are trapped into continuing to construct the world in accordance with those values. We take on the progamme that has male supremacy built into it, and while we use that programme we help perpetuate male supremacy. And I share with Shulamith Firestone the belief that there is no simple cause and effect, no single or logical solution. I can offer no better rationale than that of Shulamith Firestone, and I have no explanation for why I should feel more optimistic than she does in *The Dialectic of Sex: The Case for Feminist Revolution*. What does distress me, however, is that Shulamith Firestone today no longer participates in the debate, and we do not have the opportunity to benefit from her farsighted analysis. The difficulties which she encountered after the publication of her book took their toll: as Phyllis Chesler has said, 'We commit sororicide daily – sometimes in the name of "feminism" ' (see p.210).

8. Suspect Woman: Eva Figes' attitude

'It was intended that this should be a book about women,' states Eva Figes in the opening paragraph of *Patriarchal Attitudes*, another publication of 1970. But 'It has turned out to be a book largely about men' (p.7), she adds. Setting out to understand more about women and ending up finding out more about men was not, then, an experience confined to North America. Eva Figes – the first British contributor to be introduced in this context – had much in common with her sisters in the United States, particularly with Shulamith Firestone, but she had her significant points of departure as well. What is interesting, however, is that her contribution generally corresponds with the framework that has already been outlined.

Eva Figes starts with woman and, of course, immediately confronts the problem that woman is man-made (p.12). Her description is based on the understanding that men are in possession of power and are therefore in a position to decree what woman shall be; and women, who do not enjoy such power, are in no position to do anything but oblige (p.15). There is no shortage of evidence when it comes to men's instructions on how women can 'measure up' to meet the requirements of the ideal, she writes, but there is a noticeable absence of evidence of any reciprocity. Few indeed are the public injunctions of women which set out the steps for men to attain approval: in fact, she claims, one of the indices of patriarchy is that such counsel coming from women would be ludicrous – akin to children laying down the law to their parents. In a patriarchal society it is men who are the authorities, and who know: 'Thousands of books have been written about women, many studies have been made of them, many poems written, dozens of philosophical and psychological essays written. And in almost all cases the author has been a man,' writes Eva Figes, echoing the feelings of Virginia Woolf who wrote about

97

her experience of examining the books on the shelves of an Oxbridge library.[1] And, 'So consistently has the author been male, that the point has been totally overlooked, taken for granted. Certainly the idea of bias is never entertained. But the moment a woman sets pen to paper it is another matter. I was accused of bias even before I had written a word of this book, simply on the grounds that I was a woman' (p.16). Here we have one of the fundamental issues in a nutshell: in our society the assumption is that a man is authoritative, a woman is suspect.

Eva Figes launches straight into the web of meanings where so many other women have tried to find their way. From the outset she identifies the principle of 'male-as-norm' in our culture, the principle that defines woman as deviant. Men are the ones who know, who start with themselves in the right; any differences which women display can therefore conveniently be used as evidence of their deficiency. This allows for the wholesale dismissal of women's unique experience as meaningless, abnormal or unreal: 'Thinking man orders his universe, builds a pyramid with himself placed automatically at the tip. All other living creatures are placed in a descending downward slope beneath him' (p.120).

This male value of male value permeates our way of knowing and understanding our world, according to Eva Figes, without our being conscious of the extent to which our judgement is being swayed. We do not allow for the fact that our language system – like mathematical and musical systems – has been constructed by human beings (p.18), and so we often fail to take into account the fact that the human beings who have been in the position to construct language have primarily been males. Because both sexes use the same language we can lose sight of the origins and interests of our system of representation: we assume the neutrality of a language and culture which is geared towards enhancing the value of men. While we continue to be 'brainwashed', there is little escape from this system of male dominance, she asserts: 'We are born into a world where the great discoverers, philosophers and scientists have almost all been male. Male law-makers, male conquerors, even the God perpetuated in tradition, who still somehow haunts the early days of childhood, is male. Our whole code of morality was formulated by men' (p.17). There is little provision for the existence of half of humanity in this arrangement.

One obvious question which arises from this description of the bias and limitations of male patterns of thinking and forms of representation is why men themselves are not aware of the constraints under which they operate. How can they continue to insist on their right to be right, on their authority and all-knowingness, when they have access to only half of the experience of humanity, when they can see only one side of the story?

Women, of course, are often in the position to see both sides; they are *taught* the official version of experience, the world of men, and they *live* the unofficial version, the world of women. Because they have realms of experience which are not male, it is possible for women to get outside the male frame of reference, to be 'anthropological observers' of members of a culture whose values they know but do not share. From this vantage-point women are able to assess the limitations of the male frame of reference which does not take them into account. But how can men get outside their value-system?

If a condition of their frame of reference is that it is the *only* frame of reference and the repository of truth, then in male terms it is an absurdity even to suggest that it might be profitable for them to do so. Indeed, if women suggest that men are missing something, they are more likely to be considered 'crazy' than to be given credit for having valid criticisms of the male mind: the more evidence feminists can produce on the partiality of male 'truth', the more evidence we provide of our failure to know and understand in men's terms. We are thus left being in the wrong. Besides, claims Eva Figes, it's not just that it's difficult, or a contradiction in terms, to urge men to get outside their own value-system and its limitations, it's not desirable either – as far as men are concerned:

the male population has little enough motivation to stand aside and analyse the accepted body of opinion at any one time. By questioning it he has nothing to gain and everything to lose; he would lose not only social and economic advantages, but something far more precious, a sense of his own superiority which bolsters his ego both in his public and his private life. (pp.19–20)

So the male is *committed* to his particular value-system, for the reason that it makes him feel good: but in a system where it is the male prerogative to make up the rules and apportion the values, this passes under the name of objectivity.[2]

To Eva Figes it was abundantly clear that men left a lot out of their

99

reasoning and hence ended up with circular arguments.[3] She turns to historical evidence to illustrate that while women have made many demands for their rights, the male defence against granting them has consistently taken the form of a circular argument – more often than not accompanied by peevishness: 'One is struck, regardless of the intervening centuries, by the similarity of the arguments which, in spite of great developments in logic and the sciences, remain illogical and circular, and by the similarities of tone which is usually aggrieved. Such words as "annoying" and "insufferable" occurred frequently in the writings of people opposed to an extension of women's rights in the nineteenth century' (p.24). When it comes to registering their resistance to women's demands, men, it seems, have not progressed much over the centuries.[4]

Throughout her book, Eva Figes documents and analyses male reasoning which insists on the logic of one rule for men and another for women. She quotes Margaret Mead's[5] assumption-shattering insight: that the world over, no matter what men do, it is perceived as important and when women perform the same activities they are not regarded as important (p.55) – indeed, they can be a positive source of shame when women undertake them, as Ann Oakley (1972) later demonstrated. The exploration of the *double-standard* is a unifying theme throughout *Patriarchal Attitudes* for, after all, the double-standard *is the manifestation* of the fundamental patriarchal attitude, which proclaims the superiority of men under all circumstances.

Eva Figes sets herself the task of examining and exposing the unfounded nature of the many patriarchal attitudes which persist, not by virtue of their logic, but because of their desirability if the pre-eminence of the male is to be preserved. Her method is to take some of the many 'facts' that abound about women and to reveal their underlying fallacies. One example which appeals to me – partly because of its current usefulness – is that of the much reiterated precept that women's purpose in life is to reproduce and that women, therefore, should confine themselves to this activity. With impressive effect, Eva Figes turns this argument around:

> one could just as well argue that men merely exist for the impregnation of women, after which they can be gobbled up like male spiders. The idea that bearing children is the primary reason for a woman's existence has always been very widespread and is still with

us. One could almost say that it is a fundamental tenet of the male mind. (p.82)

One could almost say that it is the most convenient rationale for keeping woman in her place, that it establishes her fitness for one purpose only, which can then be used as evidence of her *un*fitness for any other. But in the absence of a double-standard this rationale has little to do with logic.

One of the best illustrations that Eva Figes provides of male logic at work in the interest of male supremacy is that of 'The Great Brain Debate'. The issue of brain-size was virtually an obsession among nineteenth-century scientists who first insisted that men's brains were bigger and better. There was a flurry of embarrassment, however, when Havelock Ellis pointed out 'that brain size has to be assessed in relation to body size, in which case woman actually wins the day' (p.126). The next step the scientists took was to suggest that it wasn't the overall size, but the size of a specific area that determined intelligence. But at a time when it was also believed that the frontal region of the brain was the seat of abstract reasoning, it would have been extremely awkward to have found that the frontal region was, in women, relatively greater. Fortunately, however, a new discovery was made – in apes, the frontal region was relatively greater than it was in man, so suddenly it was *smallness* that mattered. After this discovery the way was open to allow the relatively greater size of the frontal region of the brain in women. I have no way of knowing the outcome of the current research on sex differences in the brain; what I can state with confidence, though, is that it is the rule of patriarchal society to find in favour of males, and that its findings, which are the products of patriarchal attitudes and values which construct a male supremacist society, are therefore qualitatively no less partial or subjective – or male supremacist – than most other knowledge constructed in academic institutions.

While Eva Figes does not present a systematic critique of the construction of knowledge, nor an evaluation of the bias that cuts across academic disciplines, she does, by her reference to the various 'mistakes' that have occurred, put her finger on the relationship between patriarchal attitudes and the knowledge we generate in our society. She concentrates on individual philosophers, pointing to the initial prejudice with which they began, which then becomes part of their reasoning, and is built into the fabric of their work. By identifying the flaw which runs through what we know, she calls into question everything we do know.

Charles Darwin, for example, whose ideas have been extremely influential in shaping our current view of the world, did little for women. His theory of the survival of the fittest was hardly a suitable platform for the construction of an egalitarian society or a source of inspiration for women seeking equal rights (p.120). A product of the capitalist system, his theory fed back into and validated the belief that it was perfectly proper for 'he who has, to get more', a 'truth' consistently used against women. Not only did he help to legitimate the inequality of the sexes, as Eva Figes indicates, but, as Ruth Hubbard (1981) was to establish later, at the heart of his explanation was the assumption that *only men evolved.*[6] We were 'lucky' *as women* to get a fresh supply of man's evolved and superior genes, for without their contribution to each generation we would fail in the evolutionary race.

As with the other feminists whose work has been discussed, Sigmund Freud was also a prime target for criticism. At his feet could be laid much of the responsibility for the new form of women's oppression for, according to Eva Figes, 'Of all the factors that have served to perpetrate [sic] a male-orientated society, that have hindered the development of women as free human beings in the Western world today, the emergence of Freudian psychoanalysis has been the most serious' (p.159). Like Shulamith Firestone, she sees Freud's ideas emerging at just the right time for patriarchal society. Some of the old values that had protected male supremacy were beginning to break down – women were entering education and the professions, and were setting their sights on some of the same privileges enjoyed by men; they were demanding sexual freedoms and even the right to be free of men. Freud would acknowledge that all these 'achievements' *were* technically possible for a woman, but any woman who opted for them would not be a *true* woman: she would be maladjusted, suffering from penis envy, and an object of pity, if she were to pursue such a life (p.145).

But the barriers erected by Freud's philosophy were by no means explicit: it was each individual woman who was now required to erect her own barriers to participation, who was enjoined to restrict her horizons and abilities in order to qualify as a 'real' woman worthy of social approval. This was the new form that the oppression of women took: it was internalised, and it placed on woman the onus of renouncing her full humanity instead of having it denied her. This constitutes but another example of men changing the rules, and, in practice, has shown itself to be much more insidious and much more difficult to combat, as it is based on an illusion of freedom in which a woman is *free* to do anything, but, because of her nature, *chooses* to stay in a woman's place and insists that she is content to do so. With this particular ideology at work, comments Eva Figes, it is easy to see how the myth of women's emancipation could be constructed (p.182): emancipation implied a technical equality; the myth, that as true women they didn't want to make use of it.

While not denouncing education as Shulamith Firestone does, Eva Figes is none the less critical of the institution of education and especially of one of its founding fathers, Jean-Jacques Rousseau. Eva Figes sums up his guiding principle as 'man is born free but woman should definitely be kept in chains' (p.107). It was Rousseau's belief that women were not capable of abstract thinking, and he developed his educational philosophy in accordance with this conviction: men should be educated for the world – and women for men. Females 'must be trained to bear the yoke from the first, so that they may not feel it, to master their own caprices and to submit themselves to the will of others' (p.106).

In Eva Figes' view, this principle has become enshrined in educational philosophy, and she analyses some of the many pronouncements that prominent educationalists have made – and continue to make. When educationalists assume that women and men are destined for very different roles in this world (and, after all, they can be expected to hold this assumption, for it is one on which their society is predicated), then they can be expected to devise the best system for helping male supremacy to come true. It is also the way education helps racism to come true (p.115).

Eva Figes also comments on the extent to which the idea of male supremacy takes hold in our minds, influences our judgement, and helps to construct our reality, but she rarely refers to 'consciousness'; nor does she write from her own experience of participation in the collective process of consciousness-raising. Her evidence takes the form of a reflection upon the male bias in knowledge and in life, which she attributes to the residual nature of patriarchal attitudes which persist long after the rationale for their existence has passed, or has been repudiated: 'The further we move into the realm of modern ideas, the more we discover that patriarchal attitudes can survive intellectual change: the attitudes are transmuted, adapted but remain fundamentally what they had been for generations' (p.118).

Her explanation for the occurrence of male supremacist values is couched in more passive terms than those of Robin Morgan or Shulamith Firestone, who see consciousness as a dynamic process and who, from their own experience of consciousness-raising, can testify to how quickly and dramatically some of the initial patriarchal assumptions can be changed and can lead to a very different world-view. In contrast, in Eva Figes' conceptualisation of 'attitudes' we encounter something more fixed, more obdurate, a framework which is 'there', which constrains what we think today, has constrained what has been thought in the past, and may constrain what we think in the future. This is a long way from Germaine Greer's plea to women to reclaim their consciousness, but it is still very much part of the pattern of 1970 when women began to recognise that male supremacist values reigned – at women's expense.

The most significant attribute that males claimed under the male supremacist values was that of intellectual superiority, in Eva Figes' terms. Of course, she was by no means the first woman to make the link between supremacy in general and the ostensibly greater intellectual competence of men. In 1792, Mary Wollstonecraft had made a similar deduction.[7] But by 1970, when Eva Figes was writing, Mary Wollstonecraft's particular dream of equality had been realised, and *still* males were considered intellectually superior. So how could this idea of their greater intelligence persist? Eva Figes stated that this was a male claim – without a lot of substance:

One of the most enduring ideas men have passed down through the centuries in order to bolster their own feeling of superiority is the notion that women are intellectually inferior. It is an assumption that many intellectual thinkers have made quite baldly, without any inkling that there might be some need to prove such an assertion. One might almost say that the men who have set the greatest store by their own intellect have tended to be misogynists in the same degree, as though they could only raise themselves up by pushing someone else down. (p.22)

This is *why*, but there is also the issue of *how*, because it is no mean feat for men to sustain the image of their intellectual supremacy. One way it is sustained is through the operation of the double-standard, whereby, as several recent pieces of research have shown, what men do is presumed to be of greater intellectual stature.[8] But is it 'faith' alone which is responsible for ascribing greater intelligence to men? Is there no way to break down this belief in greater male intelligence which undoubtedly serves to justify as well as to maintain male supremacy? I think there is. The crucial issue is not, in my opinion, male intelligence: it is male authority. While the assumption that male-is-the-norm and knows everything holds, then he will continue to be seen as more intelligent and more important, more authoritative. But, as Germaine Greer emphasised, male power is not all there is: there is also the potential of women to reclaim their resources. *Patriarchal Attitudes* is part of this rebellion.

When it comes to male power and women's oppression, Eva Figes' view is that it does not take the same form from one era to the next, as she demonstrates with the post-Freudian era. Since the introduction of capitalism, she argues, women's position has deteriorated; and she substantiates her argument with a somewhat rosy picture of marriage in feudal society as a 'working partnership'. Then capitalism divided the world into public and private, and placed men in the public realm (with its financial rewards) and women in the private realm (with the responsibility for unpaid labour). Needless to add that this view of marriage was not one which was always shared by the women who experienced it, as the many publications of the seventeenth, eighteenth and nineteenth centuries testify to. Unlike the other feminist writers referred to so far, Eva Figes suggests that 'The rise of capitalism is the root cause of the modern social and economic discrimination against women which came to a peak in the last century' (p.70), and she implies that the end of capitalism will be the end of the discrimination against women.

In the last 100 years or more an open battle of the sexes has been waged, states Eva Figes; women have known it, and men have known it too, and have reacted accordingly: 'Man has always known, if only subconsciously, that there was a fight going on, and he blames women for it on the grounds that there would be no war if only she would give in. And because man has refused to abandon an inch of ground more than necessary, having so much to lose, he has been afraid of the dormant power he has subdued, and recognised woman as profoundly dangerous' (p.25). This, for Eva Figes, is the explanation of the equation of women's sexuality with sin, and of the male predilection for witch-hunting.

No analysis of patriarchal attitudes would be complete, however, without reference to the Judeo-Christian religion and the role it has played in constructing women's unworthiness and hence the justice of their subordination. Eva Figes' book gives some grim reminders of the contempt in which women have been held by male theologians. But there is a note of light relief when she quotes a *Guardian* (9 August 1968) report 'on a debate among Church dignitaries as to whether women should be allowed into the priesthood. "If the Church is to be thrown open to women," objected one archbishop, "it will be the death knell of the appeal of the Church for men" ' (p.56).

Perhaps because she sees that the pernicious influence of the Church has waned, and because she is aware of what women have gained, Eva Figes concludes that there has been progress:

> Change has come about, and a good deal of ground has been conceded, if only inch by inch and with a long hard struggle. The records show that the ground has not been conceded gracefully. Like all people who are privileged by birth and long tradition, the idea of sharing could only mean giving up. (p.20)

She does not delude herself about the extent of male self-interest and resistance, but she remains optimistic. Her overall framework is one in which women will continue to enter the fortresses of male power. For many feminists today, her thesis is one which continues to support the strategy of designating a particular area of male interest from which women are excluded, and of then conducting a campaign in order to be included. And her critique of male authority is as relevant today as it was when published in 1970. However, I remain sceptical and feel that there is much which she has left out. I do not think women's oppression is structured primarily by capitalism, although it obviously helps; nor that our oppression will end if women are represented in all offices of power and influence – even Prime Minister or President!

9. Can Men Qualify?:
Alice Rossi's political is personal

John Stuart Mill was a genius who wrote about liberty: John Stuart Mill wrote *The Subjection of Women* on women's lack of liberty and the injustice of this arrangement. In doing so he set up a contradiction: here was a male 'authority' arguing *against* the male view and *for* the emancipation of women. In the system of values which is consistent with male dominance – and which includes the precept that contradictions are to be resolved in the interest of *one* truth – how can sense be made of an authoritative male statement on women's right to liberty?

Perhaps the man wasn't such a genius after all: to establish this would certainly help to undermine his 'authority'. Or if he was to continue to be perceived as a genius then it would be rather convenient to forget that he ever wrote about liberty for women. Both would be useful strategies and, as Alice Rossi demonstrates in *John Stuart Mill and Harriet Taylor Mill: Essays on Sex Equality*, both were adopted in some measure. Considerable doubt has been cast on Mill's judgement in some instances, and in the more than 100 years since the publication of *The Subjection of Women* (1869), it has frequently been out of print and is seldom included by scholars in a consideration of his substantive work.

In many respects *The Subjection of Women* is an unusual book: it is one of the few[1] convincing justifications for women's liberation put forward by a man. For Elizabeth Cady Stanton who read it on its publication it was a remarkable experience: 'I lay the book down with a peace and joy I never felt before, for it is the first response from any man to show he is capable of seeing and feeling all the nice shades and degrees of woman's wrongs and the central point of her weakness and degradation' (Alma Lutz (1940), pp.171–2; quoted in Alice Rossi (1970), p.62).

Alice Rossi treats *The Subjection of Women* as an exceptional book and in her analysis of what it has to say she directly and indirectly raises a series of questions about the place of men in a world defined by women: Can men qualify as authorities on women's experience? Can men know what women know? By what *means* can men come to know what women know?

So far, in the feminist framework that has been outlined, much emphasis has been placed on woman's role as 'outsider' (the term used by Virginia Woolf): women have been seen as 'outside' the male reference system and it is the area of this discrepancy between men's official version of women's lives and women's *direct* experience of their lives, that has been considered the fertile field for feminist explanations. There have been suggestions that men cannot comprehend the essentials of women's cause, and accusations that they do not want to comprehend because of the loss it would represent to them – the loss of their hold on truth and the knowledge of their own supremacy. As Joan Roberts stated in 1976, 'Because of female exclusion from thought systems, the hardest thing for a man to know *is* what a woman thinks. But it is harder still for him to listen and to accept her thoughts because they are certain to shake the foundations of his beliefs' (p.19).

So when women are doing the explaining it is the man who is suspect, and this has implications for the credibility that can be accorded to a man's view of women's oppression. More than a conceptual issue is involved here, however. This is not an intellectual debate in a vacuum, but a problem with practical dimensions as well. When we want to know what will happen to women's authority *as feminists* if and when men are allowed validity in the feminist frame of reference, we have to keep in mind that we live in a society where a man's opinion *a priori* is considered to carry more weight than a woman's; that whenever a difference of opinion arises, it is systematically resolved in favour of males. Even when men enter what have traditionally been regarded as women's fields of expertise, men quickly become 'experts' – Dr Spock is no exception. By virtue of their sex men start with a distinct advantage and we should not be surprised when it is men and not women who reap the rewards. If it is in order disproportionately to promote the male pre-school teacher, the male nurse, the male lecturer in women's studies, on the various grounds that he has more authority, lends more prestige – or even provides 'balance' – then it is essential to ask what the consequences will be of accepting the authority of men in feminism.

Alice Rossi provides a very useful case-study by way of an answer. Although John Stuart Mill insisted that much of the material in *The Subjection of Women* originated with Harriet Taylor, he has subsequently been 'disproportionately promoted' over her, and over other women of the past whose comparable work was of at least equal significance and merit.

Practical issues aside, however, there are still the theoretical problems to contend with. If feminism is women's claim for full humanity in a society where full humanity is a male birthright, what does it *mean* when a man claims to be a feminist?[2] Is it a mark of merit when a man identifies with women's cause? Despite the fact that John Stuart Mill received harsh words from some of his male peers who preferred the case for women's liberty to remain unstated (see Sylvia Strauss, *'Traitors to the Masculine Cause' – The Men's Campaign for Women's Rights*, 1982), most of the women interested in women's rights then and since have accorded him a position of considerable prominence, and no small measure of gratitude. Knowing that it will carry more weight, among women and men, should feminists seek to have men espouse their cause? Is it the *same* cause?

The answers are varied: in some instances, John Stuart Mill's cause was *not* the same as Harriet Taylor Mill's and there are indications that while *she* sought women's liberty in the interest of *women*, *he* sought it in the interest of *men*. This is not surprising: feminists today can argue – as John Stuart Mill did – that men pay a price for their dominance, and it was therefore in men's interest for women to be liberated. Familiar too are the more subtle arguments that a liberated woman is a *better companion for a man*, an issue on which Harriet Taylor and John Stuart Mill parted company, with Harriet Taylor insisting that woman should be liberated for *herself*. In this context, even John Stuart Mill seemed to be unable to abandon the notion that a woman existed in relation to a man, although there were occasions when he explicitly repudiated this logic.

If it is not possible for either women or men to think in terms other than that of their own sex as a starting point, then the ideal state would seem to be one of coexistence. Perhaps women and men can *agree* on the desirability of women's liberation, even if they do so for different reasons or because it will signify different things in their lives. Under such circumstances each could be 'authorities' on their own sex, with the result that understandings of the world would be extended. Yet such coexistence presumes an end of male authority – a lynchpin in male supremacy, and one which feminists are determined to remove. Men won't cease to be exclusive authorities until women have authority – and women won't have authority until men cease to be the exclusive authorities. Full circle again.

What then is the relationship of John Stuart Mill and his contemporaries to women's liberation, and women's authority? Do we welcome such men as feminists, in the knowledge that men are disproportionately promoted even in women's fields, and that there is the possibility that men will become the authorities on feminism and define it in their terms? Or do we claim that this is the unique area of women's authority and that, while men can give support, can be pro-feminist, they are not the *real thing* – and this in the knowledge that we are defining *men as suspect*?

These are not speculative questions: they have practical implications on a day-to-day basis. Women are repeatedly placed in the predicament of trying to determine how much weight to attach to men's words, particularly when there is a difference of opinion. In essence, the issue is, by what authority do men hold such knowledge? What is the origin of male experience about women and women's liberation? How can they know what they do?

The crucial issue is whether it is necessary to have *direct* experience of a state or event in order to understand it, or to have an authentic view of it. In general, only a fraction of what we know originates in *direct* experience. Part of our power as a species comes from our ability to have access to experience outside our own immediate realm, to learn from the direct experience of others. We have a consciousness that allows us to comprehend what it would be like in other places, at other times, for other people whose circumstances are very different from our own. What is required is a willingness to learn – and here's the rub: it has been necessary for women to learn about men in the interest of their survival. There has been no such compulsion upon men to learn from women. And in a society predicated upon male authority there has been no *need* for men to learn from women.

When neither force nor necessity requires men to seek knowledge from women, it would be an unusual if not inexplicable act for a man to take a woman as his teacher. Yet to some extent this is what John Stuart Mill did, and he openly acknowledged that, in much of what he knew, it was Harriet Taylor who had been his guide. With the benefit of Alice

Rossi's research there is no mystery about the origins or authority of John Stuart Mill's work on women's liberty; nor is there any mystery about Harriet Taylor's convenient disappearance as mentor from the records. That she was later 'excised' from their work, so that it was he and not she who came to stand as a symbol for women's rights, does not detract from his willingness to learn. John Stuart Mill certainly did not try to engineer his prominence over Harriet: none the less this is what happened, and it raises the issue of a man's place in a feminist framework – an issue that is central to Alice Rossi's essay on John Stuart Mill and Harriet Taylor Mill.

Alice Rossi's contribution was distinctly different from the other contributions of 1970 that have been discussed, and did not arise from day-to-day personal politics. On the contrary, her starting point was in the public realm and her conclusion was that the *political is personal.* 1969 was the centenary of the publication of *The Subjection of Women* and Alice Rossi was asked to write an introductory essay for its reissue. Before she had got very far with her background reading, she realised that the figure of Harriet Taylor loomed so large and was so significant to any understanding of *The Subjection of Women* that it would be a gross distortion to present John Stuart Mill in isolation and to continue to eclipse Harriet Taylor (p.viii). She therefore decided that what she should be introducing was their joint work on equality between the sexes, an assessment of their relationship – public and private – and an explanation of why Harriet Taylor had been left out of scholarly commentary on the champions of women's liberty.

The volume she introduced was expanded to include *Early Essays on Marriage and Divorce* by John Stuart Mill and Harriet Taylor, *Enfranchisement of Women* by Harriet Taylor Mill, as well as *The Subjection of Women*, which, as Alice Rossi repeatedly points out, would have been very different without Harriet Taylor Mill. Alice Rossi is putting *in* what a male-dominated society leaves *out* – the resources of a woman. In doing so she not only integrates the private and public realm with her assessment of the relationship which generated these treatises, she also draws attention to the element of sexual politics in the public world which works to exclude women, to consign women and their work to invisibility.

Alice Rossi was fortunate in having access to the primary sources, and, when she went back to some of the original voices, she confronted no less a discrepancy between them and the 'official' version of history than Betty Friedan had when she listened to the voices of women and compared them with the 'official' version of their lives. Alice Rossi's sources might have been distanced by time, but they constituted a comparable problem.

One effect of Alice Rossi's contribution was to make way for a revision of history which took women's experience as its starting point.[3] I also think it was significant that it was a sociologist, interested in the sociology of the family and unapologetically sympathetic to women's struggle for liberation, who stepped out of the conventional framework of historical interpretation and helped to raise the issue of not just what we know now, what men know, and how we know, but also how what we know has come down to us from the past.

She also indicates that the women's movement of the time was acutely conscious of the limitations of heterosexual relationships, and yet it seemed there were few viable alternative models for women and men to turn to (pp.50-1). As a 'new vision of the relations between the sexes' was called for, Alice Rossi widened her sample when she looked more closely at the 'relationship of equals' that John Stuart Mill had described. Perhaps this was the type of relationship 'in which sex and intellect, family and work' were ideally blended and would therefore help to provide part of the answer for 'many young women searching for liberation in 1970' (p.7).

One of the difficulties she encountered immediately, however, was the place of sexual relations for, in the life of Harriet Taylor and John Stuart Mill, the equality was based on intellect: sex was very definitely subservient. But after the sexual revolution of the 1960s ('consumer sex' as Germaine Greer would label it), a heterosexual relationship in which sexual relations did not figure was unlikely to prove attractive as the ideal union. In her explanation of their relationship, Alice Rossi tends to make allowances for Victorian standards of morality. But she does provide us with a fairly detailed picture of the couple's life and work.

John Stuart Mill is presented as a man who in his own time was known as 'the logic machine', and who was primarily concerned with the questions of freedom and justice and the social organisation which would facilitate their development, for which his unusual and rigorous education had been designed. He was a man who, prior to meeting Harriet Taylor, had led an arid emotional life, and wasn't very happy. He was an expert at seeing through some of the circular arguments of his day – particularly those associated with justifications for power. He could see no case for the right to rule being confined to the aristocracy, and he had concluded – by extension – that there was no logical argument for confining the right to rule to men. In the circles in which he moved the tyranny of men was a topic of debate (p.21), and it was his stand on this issue which helped to draw him and Harriet Taylor together. His 'convictions' on women's rights 'were among the earliest results of the application of my mind to political subjects,' he wrote, 'and the strength with which I held them was, as I believe, more than anything else, the originating cause of the interest she felt in me' (Coss (1924), p.173; quoted in Rossi (1970), pp.20–1).

But there were complications. Harriet Taylor was a married woman with children. This did not prevent them from beginning their unusual intellectual partnership, which defied Victorian convention, persisted for twenty years until their eventual marriage (after the death of Harriet Taylor's husband), and which was, as Alice Rossi states, a relationship of spiritual intimacy 'which was the very core of their lives' (p.6). It also probably helps to account for their 1832 collaborative essay on marriage and divorce. For almost thirty years they were an intellectual team, and John Stuart Mill speaks glowingly of Harriet's role in the relationship. In fact, it is the 'exaggerated' and 'lavish' praise that he accorded her in their mutual intellectual endeavours that is the cause of much of the controversy about the part she played in producing some of his great works. When Mill insisted on the excellence of her intellect – as he often did – the verdict of some of his contemporaries and of many scholars since was that he must have been mistaken. As Alice Rossi comments: 'the hypothesis that a mere woman was the collaborator of so logical and intellectual a thinker as Mill, much less that she influenced the development of his thought, can be expected to meet resistance in the minds of men up to the 1970s' (p.36). The only time Harriet's influence is detected is when it is used to 'explain' ideas that subsequent theorists have not liked, or have regarded as a 'mistake' (p.45).

The means by which Mill's view of Harriet was judged to be wrong and hence her intellectual resources denied, are all too familiar today. Mill's publisher felt that in his assessment of Harriet's influence in their joint works, Mill 'outraged all credibility in his descriptions of Harriet's "matchless genius" '; his own view was that she 'intelligently contro-verted' Mill's ideas and did little more than provide him with a sounding board (p.32). Other prominent scholars have concluded that the influence of a highly intelligent woman cannot be discerned, and Mill must have been 'blinded by love' to think otherwise. That he was the only person the least impressed by her, that in fact she was stupid, unattractive and simply had a pretty knack of repeating what John had said, was the considered assessment of many of the noted scholars. Harriet's 'principled frigidity' was the explanation for the absence of a sexual relationship, according to one commentator, and another summed up the issue of Harriet's contribution as 'Harriet of the incomparable intellect . . . was largely a product of his imagination, an idealization according to his peculiar needs, of a clever, domineering, in some ways perverse and selfish, invalid woman' (Rossi, p.34). The *visible* woman is domineering, perverse and selfish: a powerful intellect is deemed not to exist.

But male scholars were not the only ones to malign her. Diana Trilling, writing appropriately in the *Partisan Review* (1952), borders on the vindictive in her evaluation of John Stuart Mill's assertion of Harriet Taylor's intelligence, as Alice Rossi points out, and raises another series of questions in the process. There are many explanations of why a woman should be more punitive to one of her sex who dares to step out of line – particularly if the woman feels that she herself is tempting fate, as Diana Trilling was doing as an 'intellectual' in a man's world; that women have to prove themselves in men's terms, that they are suspect and therefore must work harder to establish their credibility, are other possibilities. It can be very reassuring to a man to hear an 'intelligent' woman declare that intelligence is not an attribute of the 'normal' woman, and it can be very flattering for the same woman to believe that she is not representative of 'normal' (i.e. 'inferior') women. But whatever the explanation, what remains is that it was a woman who most savagely denied the possibility of intellect in another woman, and any feminist framework needs to take into account the extent to which some women are prepared to go – for all sorts of reasons – to uphold male values.

Nor did Alice Rossi ignore this issue. She made no simple equation of women are good, men are bad, but attempted a comprehensive outline of some of the complexities that are involved in the construction of women's inferiority, in a male-dominated world.

Alice Rossi makes it clear that Harriet Taylor was no 'clinging vine' but a strong and determined woman: her capacity to defy convention and to insist on her relationship with John Stuart Mill, while still preserving the social forms of life with her husband, is evidence of this independence of spirit. Despite the verdict of many of the scholars, she was also a very intelligent woman to whom the issue of women's rights was of passionate importance, and in *Enfranchisement of Women* (1851) she presented a perceptive and logical case for women's suffrage, which was found most impressive by the women in the United States who were similarly concerned.

Yet even those commentators who *do* concede Harriet Taylor's incomparable intellect are likely to be swayed by a predictable bias: they are much more inclined to emphasise the benefits that she derived from Mill's tutorship, rather than the benefits he derived from hers. The bias extends to the assessment of the *nature* of their individual contributions – especially his intellectual influence upon her, and her emotional and practical influence upon him.

To return to the question with which we began, however – can men qualify as feminists? – we need to dispense with this bias and examine not what John taught Harriet, but what she taught him: a much more provocative issue in a patriarchal society.

Alice Rossi had the task of analysing their joint works and deciding who wrote what. The name of the author was not a reliable guide, partly because it would have been embarrassing to have had Harriet Taylor's name displayed on the cover, thereby drawing attention to their relationship. Knowing what she does, the convention of attributing their joint work to Mill prompted Alice Rossi to remark, 'One can imagine Harriet chafing at the social conventions that required her to remain unknown and unacknowledged by the reading public' (p.41).

The criteria Alice Rossi used to make a decision about who contributed what might appear to some as quite a surprise. On the issue of women's liberty, Alice Rossi recognised that Harriet's position was far more radical than John's, particularly on the fundamental questions of women's education, work and pay. Harriet Taylor always held that a woman should be educated for herself and not to be the companion of man; Mill never departed from his position that while education for a woman was desirable, upon marriage it should be used in the service of husband and family. Therefore, trying to decide who wrote what was not such a difficult task as it may have at first seemed. And one of the reasons why Alice Rossi decided that Harriet Taylor wrote the major part of *Enfranchisement of Women* (1851) is because it is built upon the more radical position. Harriet Taylor advocated political rights, education, work and pay for women in the interests of women's autonomy: and this applied to married women as well: 'A woman who contributes materially to the support of the family, cannot be treated in the same contemptuously tyrannical manner as one who, however she may toil as a domestic drudge, is dependent on the man for subsistence' (Rossi, p.42).

There is little here of the distinction between 'private' and 'public': Harriet Taylor wanted women to have the same access to the public world as men, and for the same reasons. Although she does not express her ideas on childcare in *Enfranchisement of Women*, it is not unreasonable to suggest that her proposal of free access to the public world for women would be accompanied by increased access to the private world of home and children for men. Certainly her 1851 Charter for change still rings true, in many respects, and of course gives the lie to the assertion that the demands women are making today are something new.

It was the direct experience of dependency and all its ramifications that was Harriet Taylor's source of knowledge and she was able to pass much of it on to Mill. On his own initiative he had been able to conceptualise the social organisation in terms of power (he and Kate Millett would have much in common), and he had concluded that there was no rational basis for men to claim the right to rule over women, but this was a far cry from a rich understanding of the complexities of the interrelationships between the sexes. Mill knew that logic was not the primary motivating force behind human beings and that the most logical system of social organisation was not necessarily the one society sought. To his framework, Harriet Taylor added her own logic and much of the detail – the subtle implications of the prevailing arrangements, the evidence of a woman who knew from experience what male rule looked like to one who was ruled. It was a mark of her good teaching – and his willingness to learn – that he came to comprehend the range of experience that he did.

His efforts demonstrate that it is possible for men to learn and to appreciate the dimensions of women's experience: that is, their sex doesn't bar them from such comprehension nor does women's authority disallow their understanding or participation.

The Subjection of Women was written up and published after Harriet Taylor Mill's death and, of its composition, John Stuart Mill stated that 'As ultimately published it was enriched with some important ideas of my daughter's[4] and passages of her writing. But in what was of my own composition, all that is most striking and profound belongs to my wife; coming from the fund of thought which has been made common to us both, by our innumerable conversations and discussions on a topic which filled so large a place in our minds' (p.57). The book has its limitations – as do all our theses – but it remains a remarkable case for women's liberation. Alice Rossi attributes much of its current value to Harriet Taylor's input, but she also advances another reason, and one which appears in all the feminist publications of 1970 so far discussed.

The Subjection of Women continues to be relevant, she says, because 'it is not burdened with the dead weight of any of the social and psychological theories that have emerged during the 100 years separating us from Mill' (p.59), and she goes on to indict Darwin, Freud and Marx, among others, and the uses to which their theories have been put. Yet again, the social sciences are criticised at a fundamental level: far from assisting the development of our understandings, the last century of 'achievement' in the social sciences was, in the view of many women of 1970, one of the chief means of restricting and retarding our understandings.

With no comparable demand for an entirely new social science today, some explanation for the change is required. It could be that this is one of the feminist demands of 1970 that we have lost touch with: it could also be that feminism *is* the new social science. When Alice Rossi was writing her critique in 1970 and casting round for meaningful explanations there was no developed body of feminist research that she could turn to: fifteen years later there is a substantial body of knowledge which has generated an entire set of alternative meanings to Darwin, Freud and Marx, and many others.

If the feminist knowledge of today is partly a result of critiques like those of Alice Rossi, there are other areas too where her work has gained wide acceptance. By providing some of the historical background for the contemporary women's movement, she has helped to undermine the belief that there is something peculiar about the modern woman who is discontented with her lot. Her later publication, *The Feminist Papers: From Adams to De Beauvoir* (1974), was valuable in its revelation that women had been similarly discontented for a very long time, and that, far from being peculiar, modern women are reasonable to protest. The sense of power, the enrichment of resources that women can obtain from the recognition that there is a long tradition of honourable protest, should not be underestimated. Her recovery of Harriet Taylor and her indication of the potential of other such discoveries sets the contemporary women's movement on a particular and positive course.

Her pointing out of the discrepancy between what women of the past said themselves, and the way they have been represented since, not only suggests the possibilities that a women's history can be written, it also serves as a warning to contemporary women not to believe all they have been taught. A female figure from the past presented as domineering, selfish, frigid, stupid, of 'injured vanity, petty egoism and ambition' (Diana Trilling, quoted in Rossi, p.35), could well turn out to be an illuminating exponent of women's cause on closer inspection.

In her treatment of John Stuart Mill, Alice Rossi set out a framework for assessing the place of men, and in her assessment of Harriet Taylor Mill she reintroduced women's meanings to the issue of men's knowledge. She offered no easy solutions – and many of the problems she raised are still with us. But through her review of men's history she challenged male authority. This places her with the other feminist writers who helped to make 1970 such a good year.

10. A Lot to Learn:
Juliet Mitchell's theory

It was different after 1970. Not just because there had been a sudden eruption of feminist explanations which helped to reinforce each other and provided the evidence that the problem was *real*, although this was significant enough and helped to change reality. There was a more subtle difference as well, one that ties in with *how* we know (and how men know); yet this is rarely referred to.

The women of 1970 *made up* their descriptions and explanations of patriarchy, they *invented* their theses, and while this process has its compensations, it has its disadvantages as well. Among them are the *doubts*. None of the women who generated a feminist reality in 1970 would have been immune from the doubts. With the 'removal' of women from the mainstream of historical knowledge, they were not in a position to know that what they were saying had in substance been said by many women before. They believed that what they were saying was *new* (and in many respects it was), and one of the repercussions of this was the emergence of that haunting question, 'If this all seems so obvious to me, why hasn't someone said it before?' And while the answer could take many forms, few helped to bolster our confidence. Enormous doubts surface when anyone tries to project new ideas and realities which have little social currency, and these doubts can be intensified when the issue is sexual politics: numerous mechanisms are available to dismiss the discontented woman – and she knows them all. These doubts have to be overcome for a public stand to be taken.

Another disadvantage is the absence of known material which can be turned to for confirmation or inspiration. What is striking now about the 1970 publications is the very few references they contain to the work of other women. We have become accustomed to seeing that (growing) body of feminist knowledge in bibliographies – references which lend validity to our ideas, and work which serves to inform, challenge and extend our understandings. These sources did not exist for the writers of 1970.

But there are compensations in starting from scratch – the excitement, the exhilaration of discovery, the satisfaction of creatively forging new insights. There are the pleasures of reflecting on one's own experience and of making sense of it; there is the confidence that can come from beginning to trust one's own judgement and from shaping a new reality. In a society which has created a mystique around knowledge construction, which has reserved it as an activity for the few, and insisted on the pose of objectivity, we tend to forget that we can all have access to the construction of knowledge and that it can be an *emotionally* rewarding experience.

What the feminist writers of 1970 gave us was the beginning of a body of knowledge in a society in which there are conventions about knowledge and its transmission: in which knowledge is given a hierarchical order so that some forms of knowledge are deemed superior to others. And as we have been influenced by these conventions, the codification of feminist ideas, which 1970 produced, was accompanied by the traditional attitudes and values about knowledge. In 1984 it is no longer possible for us to know by the same means as the feminist writers of 1970; we have to know a body of knowledge as well as – or, perhaps, *instead* of – the knowledge forged from personal insights. Those who were 'in at the beginning' would have experienced some of the satisfaction of 'making up' the knowledge without the restrictions of paradigms; those who have since taken on feminist understandings may have done so via a very different route, required to *learn* what their sisters have *created*. This is not to suggest that we would be better off without a feminist body of knowledge: it is one of our major sources of strength and we need more of it, not less. But it is to suggest that we should be aware that before one can offer personal experience as knowledge there is an awful lot to *learn*.

In the late 1960s and early 1970s there was a virtual explosion of consciousness-raising groups, as women came together to *participate* in the process of generating some of the new feminist knowledge. This was a very active form of knowledge-making, with a collective dimension. It was also partly a response to the absence of the codified knowledge that women wanted from the books, articles and media of the time. Books such as *Sisterhood Is Powerful* represent the transition from personal knowledge to encoded knowledge and were necessary and valuable when it came to making women's knowledge more widely available. However, I suspect that there is a correlation between the decline in the dynamism of consciousness-raising and the increase in the number of codified sources. Books, of course, can still raise and change consciousness (as can other media) and they are a vital part of feminist knowledge, but coming to know through books - is a qualitatively different experience from coming to know through the collective and creative process of consciousness-raising. The existence of a body of knowledge invariably means that knowing feminism is not the same for the 'second generation' of women in the contemporary movement, who must first learn before they can introduce their personal insights, and for whom there is an increased chance that they will be 'wrong' in a way that would have been extremely rare for the 'first generation'.

Over fifteen years, feminist knowledge has acquired its own structures and conventions, particularly if it has become the substance of academic courses. Coming to know feminism in an institutionalised context brings with it its own complexities and diversities.

After the publication of all these books in 1970 (and there were many many more than have been referred to here), there was the basic outline of feminist descriptions and explanations. Subsequently, it was more a matter of describing and exploring *in depth*, for the surface had been surveyed: the 'problem' was real and there wasn't much doubt about its cause.

This was the starting point for Juliet Mitchell when, in 1971, *Woman's Estate* was published; this book helps to establish the continuity of feminist theory through its extensive coverage of the work of Kate Millett and Shulamith Firestone. But if strict chronological order were to be observed, Juliet Mitchell would have appeared directly after Betty Friedan – and would have been worlds removed. In 1966, her 'Women: The Longest Revolution' appeared in the *New Left Review* (40), and put one of the first and most forceful accounts of the systematic oppression of women.

The context in which the descriptions and explanations of Juliet Mitchell arose were substantially different from those that have appeared so far. Unlike Kate Millett and Germaine Greer, for example, it was not to literature that she turned for a primary source of evidence. Involved as she was in the Left movement of the 1960s in England, the main focus for her analysis was women in the workplace. Her concern was to explain the exploitation of women in the workforce and she linked their position with women's role in the family. Thus, the women whose world Juliet Mitchell began with were precisely the women who, in Betty Friedan's description, did not exist.

Theories which aimed to explain the exploitation of workers were an integral part of Juliet Mitchell's framework. But it was clear to her (as it had been to Shulamith Firestone) that while such theories may have been suitable for accounting for the exploitation of *men*, their failure to include any consideration of women's role in the family – and the contribution this made to women's exploitation at the workplace – meant that they were not adequate explanations for the oppression of *women*. Much more had to be taken into account, in Juliet Mitchell's view, if there was to be a satisfactory analysis of why and how women were oppressed, and she proceeded to identify the specific areas of women's experience which had been omitted from previous analyses of exploitation.

Her commitment to some of the existing theories – such as those of Marx and Freud – was not sufficiently challenged to require her to abandon them completely on the grounds that they were no longer relevant to the task that she was undertaking – a stand which was taken by many other feminists on the grounds that no matter how far you stretched Marxist or Freudian theory, they wouldn't begin to cover women. To qualify as a theory meant, in Juliet Mitchell's view, that there had to be a scientific methodology, an 'uncontaminated' means of making sense of the world, which was independent of the man who had formulated it. In other words, historical materialism and psychoanalysis were scientific *methods* for explaining the world, and they could be applied to women. In terms of the theory itself, it didn't matter that Marx and Engels had left out women, or that Freud hadn't liked them very much; as Juliet Mitchell stated, 'That Freud, personally, had a reactionary ideological attitude towards women in no way affects his science – it wouldn't be a science if it did' (p.167).

Given some of the definitions of 'science' (and of truth, proof and objectivity) which have been put forward in this book, the claim to be a 'science' doesn't carry a lot of weight. Attaching the label 'scientific' to a method doesn't put it beyond question: on the contrary, one of the issues that has been consistently raised is that of taking so-called 'scientific' and 'objective' knowledge out of the realm of the unquestionable, and showing that knowledge is the product of the knowledge-*maker*, and shows its affinity with him.

The 'other side' of Juliet Mitchell's view would be one like that put forward by Phillida Bunkle (1984):

> Men make knowledge. White, privileged men . . . . This ability to define reality, to tell us what is objective, rational and important, is their basic power. Knowledge is the most important thing men make. It is the power to declare that their view is the truth – the only truth. Such knowledge makes women or indigenous peoples invisible. We become deviants from the great white reasonable norm when we insist that what we do does count. (p.7)

Clearly, there wouldn't be much point in trying to persuade Phillida Bunkle that particular methods of explanation are free from the values of those who generate them and are therefore appropriate analytical tools for explaining women's oppression. It seems that one can *believe* that knowledge can be independent of those who construct it, or one can *believe* that it cannot be separated from its originator. There is evidence which supports *both* positions but Juliet Mitchell adopted the former and claimed the use of a tested method for exploring the specificity of women's oppression.

While appreciating the validity of much of the evidence provided by Kate Millett and Shulamith Firestone, whom she categorised as radical feminists, Juliet Mitchell none the less could not accept the validity of their analyses, and was critical of the circularity of their argument: the primacy of sexual politics, as far as Juliet Mitchell was concerned, was no more than an *assertion* without a theoretical context, and while it could well be accurate to describe sexual oppression as the basic form of oppression, it was hardly illuminating. She readily acknowledged that it wasn't easy to find the theoretical means of dealing with women, but she was convinced that radical feminism was not pursuing a plausible path: 'Radical feminism attempts to solve the problem of analysing the oppression of women by making it *the* problem' (p.99), she wrote, but this takes us no closer to understanding its origins or to developing strategies for changing it (p.90).

Juliet Mitchell did not dismiss the insights of radical feminism. Instead, she set herself the arduous and dual assignment of extending the framework of analysis of radical feminism so that it could readily lend itself to more of a cause-and-effect rationale. At the same time she attempted to extend the methodology of historical materialism so that it could account for the position of women. She makes a most forceful case when she lists, side by side, the explanations of both 'radical feminism' and 'abstract socialism' and concludes that 'Both positions are possibly right together, both are certainly wrong apart' (p.95). Unlike some feminists, however, who are prepared to live with contradictions, Juliet Mitchell was more concerned to integrate the two strands to provide a more comprehensive and cohesive explanation.

She took as her starting point that it was women's position in the family that was responsible for women's place in the labour force. The material conditions of having to provide domestic services, of having to socialise children, and of having to do it all for no remuneration, were what constrained women's entry to the workplace. The psychological conditions, the notions of women's proper place and fitting role, also played a part in determining what sort of work was considered appropriate for them. From these links of home and work, the private and public, Juliet Mitchell formulated a framework in which it would be possible to locate the oppression of women.

There were four fundamental structures which would have to be transformed, she reasoned, before women could be liberated: production, reproduction, sexuality and the socialisation of children (p.101). By conceptualising these areas and delineating the problems associated with them, Juliet Mitchell was able to pin-point the possibilities for change.

When it came to production there could be no dispute that, on any index, women were in a less favourable position than men: women were a reserve and cheap labour force, they were segregated into specific areas, and paid less than men. Juliet Mitchell wanted to know why this was so and what measures were necessary in order to transform these arrangements. One standard 'rationale' that she identified was that of tracing the division of labour back to women's physical weakness; this characteristic was then used to justify women's present weaker position in the labour force. There were numerous flaws in this argument, as Juliet Mitchell was quick to point out. First, the supposed lack of physical strength among women didn't preclude them from undertaking physically arduous work, and such a rationale did not account for existing divisions in the labour force, where nursing, for example, was much more physically demanding work than doctoring. Secondly, it was clear from cross-cultural evidence that women in different societies performed the entire range of physical work. And if there *was* a link between physical capacity and type of work, would this mean that women could be liberated, once physical strength was no longer a requirement for any sort of work? 'If it is just the biological incapacity for the hardest physical work that has determined the subordination of women,' she wrote, 'then the prospect of an advanced machine technology, abolishing the need for strenuous physical exertion, would seem to promise ... the liberation of women' (p.104).

This rationale of women's physical inferiority, entrenched and popular though it might have been as a justification for discrimination against women in the field of production, simply would not suffice. And Juliet Mitchell provides some excellent examples as illustrations of what lies behind the structuring of women's subordination. One, taken from the *Daily Herald* (23 July 1964), sums it up:

> Around 2,500 men went on strike yesterday because they fear a petticoat takeover at their factory. Strikers claimed that women – who earn £1.15.6d a week less than men – had been given men's jobs on two automated assembly lines.
>
> But the management of the works – Britain's biggest disc-brake factory – say that the jobs involved are women's work. 500 women disagreed and walked out with the strikers .... Mr Bryn Richards, an Amalgamated Engineering Union Official at the works, said: 'This could be the thin edge of the wedge. With automation some firms might say that the whole factory could be run by women. We do not dispute that these jobs can be done by women. But because automation makes a job easier, there is no reason to take it from a man who has sweated over it for years, and give it to a woman.'
>
> A statement by the firm said their proposals were in the employees' best interest because of the shortage of male labour. (p.127)

So the women – who are paid less – are given a job that the men concede that the women can do, but which has not been classified as women's work. Fearing that this might mean that they could be replaced by cheaper women, the men go on strike – and the women go with them. This is what requires explanation.

In Juliet Mitchell's frame of reference, the explanation lies in an economic system which pits individuals against each other, and which sets up a dynamic of divide and rule. By implication, a different economic system could eliminate the antagonism between workers and establish a commonality of interest, in which the divisions between women and men would no longer be meaningful. However, Juliet Mitchell fails to analyse why women should support men in their efforts to protect themselves – from women. In short, Juliet Mitchell's analysis leaves out the *sex*-consciousness in which this economic system – and others – originated. She demonstrates considerable skill in identifying some of the omissions of socialist theorists (pp.76–80) and presents a persuasive case against capitalism. But she does not make a focal point the fact that in essence the debate is an *internal* one – among men. Such an acknowledgement would not detract from her analysis, but would extend it.

Juliet Mitchell's discussion of production also extends to education and the way it prepares women for subordination in the workforce (pp.131–6). The female experience of education is one of devaluation, she claims. The more a girl aspires to break out of the restrictive mould, the more she is devalued (p.132): 'In academic subjects at secondary school and in institutions of higher education, a girl's career is a downhill struggle, a denial of her potentialities' (p.133). She is conceded to possess only one 'talent' – that of being a mother – and her education is designed to destine her for home and family, and to re-create the cycle by ensuring that she is qualified for little else. In consequence, 'women's role in reproduction . . . has become, in capitalist society at least, the "complement" of men's role in production' (p.106).

When it comes to reproduction, Juliet Mitchell finds women's subordination based on more tangible grounds: 'As long as reproduction remained a natural phenomenon, of course, women were effectively doomed to social exploitation. In any sense, they were not "masters" of a large part of their lives. They had no choice as to whether or how often they gave birth to children . . . their existence was essentially subject to biological pressures outside their control' (p.107). Under such circumstances, contraception must play a vital role in women's emancipation. However, anyone familiar with the history of the birth control movement in Britain and the United States in the nineteenth and early twentieth centuries could not fail to recognise the extent to which contraception was resisted, nor the supremely logical grounds for such opposition: if women could decide when and how many children to have, then men would forfeit their power over women.

Despite the fierce opposition and perverse obstruction, though, women managed to achieve their revolutionary demand. Earlier this century some women did gain access to birth control information – yet their subordination remained. The next breakthrough was the pill, with all the promises of liberation that it held – and women's subordination remained. The next move could be to artificial reproduction which, technically, could completely liberate woman from her biological ties, but I suspect that even under these conditions women's subordination will remain. (Others have suggested that artificial reproduction could bring with it an even more brutal form of oppression for women; see Rita Arditti *et al.*, 1984.) Accepting the premise that male power can allow men to derive advantage, no matter what the context; acknowledging that when women's material circumstances are changed – as they are with contraception – men can change the rules (and for many feminists this *is* a starting point), means that the crucial power lies in the power to generate the meanings: this source of power is not a central focus in Juliet Mitchell's analysis.

It would be unfair to imply that Juliet Mitchell's thesis is inadequate because while registering the need for a transformation in reproduction, she fails to outline any practicable means by which this could be achieved. No one, to my knowledge, has been able to come up with any solution. But I think it is fair to say that Juliet Mitchell's analysis, while focusing on reproduction and sexuality as sites for change, is neither as comprehensive nor as forceful as some of the theories put forward by radical feminists. She does state that one of the few resources women have is to 'sell' their bodies (p.55), but this recognition is subsumed under considerations of an exploitative and alienating *economic* system and is not directly linked with male power. Notable by its absence is any systematic analysis of heterosexuality – women's availablity to men, rape, violence and pornography.

The fourth dimension that Juliet Mitchell focuses on, and which is no closer to resolution now than when she first set out the problem, is that of women's role in the socialisation of children. Without question, children have to be socialised and this should not be considered part of society's 'dirty work'. The issue, however, is more a matter of the extent to which women's lives are circumscribed by this responsibility and its attendant guilt. Far from diminishing, the demands on women have increased over time. Juliet Mitchell points out that the socialisation of the young hasn't always been the time-consuming task it is today, but is related to the changes that have occurred in reproduction: as women have had fewer children they have been required to spend more time with them (p.119). (Shulamith Firestone would have seen this as part of the pattern of the oppression of children – once childhood is constructed so too is the need for supervision and for lessons about life from which children are segregated.) This can also be seen as another example of changing the rules, so that women continue to be constrained once the original need for constraint has been removed.

But as Juliet Mitchell makes clear, it isn't just the time factor which makes motherhood difficult: when women are urged to invest their energies and meanings in children and motherhood they are setting up 'a precarious venture on which to base a life' (p.109). If motherhood is woman's sole purpose in life, then she will continue having children as long as possible in order to have a purpose; sooner or later, though, this must cease – with its predictable trauma.

What then do we do about the socialisation of children? The only recommendation Juliet Mitchell makes for transforming social arrangements is contained in a brief reference to the absence of disadvantages and the possiblility of advantages in the kibbutzim in Israel (p.119).

Although Juliet Mitchell does not refer to Charlotte Perkins Gilman's socialist schemes for the organisation of housework and collective childcare, she does directly link the contemporary women's movement with former women's movements: 'It is sometimes necessary to shut women up,' she writes in relation to Christabel Pankhurst, 'but their political organizations are never to be taken too seriously' (p.12), and adds that the contemporary movement, despite its astonishing growth, can really claim little more than nuisance value: 'This raises many questions, not only about a society which sees women as always unserious, but perhaps more critically for the immediate future, about the nature of the movement itself' (p.13).

In her outline of the origins of the contemporary women's movement, Juliet Mitchell also takes into account the context of the 1960s and sees the emergence of the black movement, the student movement, the hippies and the women's movement as being closely linked, with the publication of *The Feminine Mystique* as the impetus for women. For although Betty Friedan's call to protest was directed exclusively at white, middle-class women, to Juliet Mitchell this was to be expected. There was no reason for women to apologise because it was more privileged women who were among the first to rebel; it was precisely because for these women 'the gap between the deprivation they suffered and glory they were supposed to enjoy was sufficiently startling for them to challenge both,' she writes. 'Seen from this perspective, the "middle-class" composition of Women's Liberation is not an unhappy fact, a source of anxiety and endless "mea culpas" but an intrinsic part of feminist awareness' (p.22). Of course, it would be a different matter if it were to be confined to a white, middle-class movement, and in some respects the development of a broader base still remains to be achieved: women of colour and working-class women are justifiably angered by concepts of the women's movement which remain where Betty Friedan began. And I am sure that it has escaped no one's notice that all the feminist theorists so far discussed have been white and middle class. If you accept, as I do, that theories arise from the theorist's own personal experience and material circumstances, and use this to explain the limitations of male theories, then the fact that these feminist theories have come from white middle-class women means that much is being left out.

The means by which *all* women could work towards liberation was for Juliet Mitchell to begin with the 'Politics of Experience' and she outlines the principles for its organisation. She deals directly with the need for an autonomous women's movement (particularly since some radical men have begun to endorse it) and makes many of the points Robin Morgan made and from the politicisation of her *own* experience:

At this stage it feels strange to have to 'justify' an all-women movement – but as it still does disturb a lot of people and as some Women's Liberation groups have men members – it seems a good idea to try. It is hard to recall the reasons we first gave, the fear and embarrassment we felt. Yet I do remember being surprised that it was 'all right' talking just to women. Many of us came out of predominantly male political movements, girlfriends belonged to childhood, women's coffee parties were not for us ... seriousness was men. (p.57)

And if I had to say what I believed to be one of the greatest gains of the women's liberation movement, I would focus on this: multitudes of women have made this same highly significant shift in consciousness with the result that sisterhood (perhaps like childhood) has become a reality and relationships among women have been transformed. There

129

is now a reference group of women (with women as authority) which was not there twenty years ago.

In all-women, small-group contexts, where principles of domination are challenged and collectivity is structured, Juliet Mitchell sees the potential of consciousness-raising as a means of enabling revolution:[1] 'Women come into the movement from the unspecified frustration of their own private lives,' she writes, and they 'find that what they thought was an individual dilemma is a social predicament and hence a political problem' (p.61).

High on the agenda of consciousness-raising is, of course, 'the problem of men', and here Juliet Mitchell distinguishes herself from radical feminists. In Juliet Mitchell's frame of reference, we live under an oppressive regime in which the male 'chauvinist' has internalised the domination of men. While radical feminists hold men responsible for their actions, Juliet Mitchell holds 'the system' responsible for structuring the tyranny of men and the subordination of women. In the end, however, it doesn't really matter which 'explanation' you offer, she states, for either way you are left with 'a man who takes up a position, either consciously or instinctively, of domination (and egotism) over and against women, by virtue merely of his status as a man' (p.64). It's the same *problem*, of course, but what one believes to be *the cause* will have significant implications for what one sees as *the solution*, and the strategies by which it can be achieved.

For Juliet Mitchell, the priority lies in changing the capitalist system which is predicated on exploitation, hierarchies and competition. She quite explicitly acknowledges that the introduction of socialism as it is practised will not automatically lead to a better deal for women. On the contrary, socialist theory has to be drastically reformed, she argues, if it is to take account of women. But it does constitute a different system which is not based on economic exploitation, and if women are not being exploited in the area of production, they are in a better position to achieve liberation.

Her analysis of women under capitalism adds a significant dimension to the feminist framework, partly because of her descriptions of women's place in production. One of the points that Juliet Mitchell makes which should constantly be kept in mind is that it is not so much that women do not have equal pay or equal work, but that women do not, as a rule, get *a living wage*. Any society organised on this basis is in need of transformation: that women systematically get the worst deal is one more reason for women to make the most revolutionary demands.

Yet even if the inequalities which prevail in production were to be eliminated, Juliet Mitchell emphasises that, for women, much of the problem would remain: it is woman's role within the family, and the very meanings of sex differences themselves, that lie at the root of the allocation of woman's place in society. Since the publication of *Woman's Estate*, in *Psychoanalysis and Feminism* (1975), and *Women: The Longest Revolution* (1984) Juliet Mitchell has primarily been concerned with understanding the origin and nature of these meanings in order to change them.

Much of her analysis is relevant today: the women's movement probably still has no more than 'nuisance value' in many areas, and it certainly hasn't helped to achieve a living wage for women. As has been stated earlier, women's poverty is getting worse (see Hilda Scott, 1984). The introduction of the Equal Pay Act has paid lip-service to the idea of women's right to equal remuneration, but the recession, in Britain at least, is challenging women's fundamental right to *paid* work. Men still see paid work as their prerogative, so that with high unemployment they start questioning the presence of women in the workforce. All the problems which Juliet Mitchell raised in this context clearly are still very much with us.

Since 1971, Juliet Mitchell has changed her focus. Her recent books are more concerned with meanings, more oriented towards understanding the human psyche, and it is possible that ultimately the questions of human liberation will need to be resolved in this domain. What are women to be liberated *for?* is part of Juliet Mitchell's framework (as it is Mary Daly's). The philosophical and psychological implications of women's liberation are still an essential and yet under-explored facet of women's knowledge.

11. Model Knowledge-making: Ann Oakley's research

When Ann Oakley wrote a 'New Introduction' for the republication of Hannah Gavron's 1966 *The Captive Wife*, in 1983, she acknowledged a personal debt to Hannah Gavron, and at the same time gave an account of the history of her own research in sociology. Her research represents a significant development in feminism because she was among the first to develop an appropriate feminist methodology for an exploration of women's existence. She went out and talked with women about their lives and not only provided some of the missing data – which could be used by women – but with her insistence on the inclusion of women, she challenged the fundamental structure of sociology itself.

But for Ann Oakley, much of it started with Hannah Gavron, who in the pre-feminist days of the early 1960s had unmasked in London some of the same problems that Betty Friedan had found among women in the USA. Working within the academic conventions of sociology, Hannah Gavron had noticed the absence of women in the literature of the family, and had elected to undertake for her PhD the seemingly simple task of interviewing women to add their reports to the reservoir of knowledge about the family. She interviewed 96 women to find out how they felt about their lives in the family: and ended up by asking whether the last 150 years of 'women's rights' had all been for nothing, for the women she interviewed were less than happy with their lot. Constrained by the rules of the academic discipline in which she was working – and by the demands of her *own* family circumstances – Hannah Gavron was caught in a web of contradictions that led her to chart, and to identify with, the problems of women, but which left her at a loss to explain them satisfactorily. As Ann Oakley says, she was suspended between the old explanations and the new evidence that she had uncovered (p.xii).

To obtain that new evidence, Hannah Gavron had had to take a radical 'leap' – to prefer grounding 'interpretations of the world on the unpretentious basis of the lives lived in it' (p.ix), for this was what talking with women and taking their reports seriously amounted to. Later, of course, this departure from accepted practice was to become a basis for feminist research and a methodology that Ann Oakley was to favour, but when Hannah Gavron set out there was little validation for her approach or her results. To have gone any further than she did in challenging the prevailing meanings and methods of the academic discipline in which she was working would have invited not just strong resistance, says Ann Oakley, but the possibility of being unacceptable, in an academic community, secure in its knowledge about the family, which had developed its own particular legitimate methods for the construction of knowledge, and which discouraged commitment and subjectivity among its researchers.

Ann Oakley is more surprised that Hannah Gavron got as far as she did, rather than disappointed at where she stops, for Ann Oakley has her own experience of this academic community:

> The entrenched hostility of sociologists to the social importance of women was the reason why, when I myself came to follow in Gavron's footsteps a decade later by carrying out a study of women's attitudes to housework ... I found it necessary to preface my main report of that study with a chapter on the invisibility of women in sociology. It was more than the intellectual context in which I worked; it was itself the obstacle to be overcome. The fact that I had enormous difficulty in 1969 in securing an academic supervisor for my work, who would be prepared to accept my definition of its subject (housework *as work*), suggested to me that Gavron's own path, some years before, had probably been rougher. (p.xi)

But before Ann Oakley followed in Hannah Gavron's footsteps and began to document women's reality – in particular, women's experience of housework, pregnancy and childbirth – she first embarked on another project: in the growing debate about what was women's proper role in the early 1970s, Ann Oakley set out to 'define the terms' of the debate in *Sex, Gender and Society* in 1972.

At the crux of many exchanges about the proper place of woman is the issue of precisely what about woman is changeable, and what is not. *Sex, Gender and Society* was written to distinguish between those aspects of woman that were immutable (sex), and those which were changeable (gender), and which varied according to context (society). Obviously, clarification was called for at the time, not least within academic circles where the knowledge-makers frequently conflated sex and gender, classified them as the *status quo*, and clung to their meanings tenaciously. Not that making clear what could be changed necessarily led to a climate for change, as Ann Oakley comments. Historically,

> The more justification there was in the argument that women were conditioned by society, the more reasonable seemed the fear that emancipation would change society. And the more people wanted to keep society as it was, the more they opposed feminism. (p.14)

According to Ann Oakley, things haven't changed much in the present.

To distinguish between *sex* and *gender*, Ann Oakley drew together a mass of data, primarily from a cross-cultural perspective, and so convincing was the evidence of the plasticity of human behaviour that the argument that it was *natural* for woman to be what she is in our society became increasingly difficult to sustain – show *one* example of women in another society which contradicted what was accepted in our own, and the whole notion of the *universal* nature of woman was called into question. And Ann Oakley produced *hundreds* of examples to demonstrate that, for every cherished characteristic of women believed to be natural in our own society, there was another where such a characteristic was unknown, or even quite the opposite. For example, on the question of women's physical weakness contrasted with men's as the reason why women were allocated certain work she wrote:

> a number of societies reverse our practice and give 'heavy' work to the women. Among the people of Bamenda, studied by Phyllis Karberry, the women do all the agricultural work. They carry the heavy loads and this is said to be because they have stronger foreheads than the men. (A similar situation was found by [Margaret] Mead among the Arapesh, who gave the same reason for it.) Karberry heard a group of men discussing a wifeless neighbour: 'He works hard, indeed he works almost as hard as a woman.' (p.55)

And again, 'In Bali, where males do little heavy work, males and females resemble each other in body size and shape. But Balinese men who work as dock coolies under European supervision develop the heavy musculature we think of as a male characteristic' (p.143).

Like Kate Millett, what Ann Oakley did in *Sex, Gender and Society* was to use what she had been taught against those who taught her. In retrospect, what is remarkable is that most of the evidence that she put together already existed within the male-dominated disciplines but had previously had little or no significance attached to it until Ann Oakley brought the information together to make a new and meaningful refutation of much of the received wisdom about sex and gender. She provided knowledge which was very much needed by women at the time. Many women knew that they had been *taught* to be feminine, but were unable to state just what those particular lessons were. For this reason, *Sex, Gender and Society* was not just a good manual for rebutting some of the accepted arguments, it was also a good consciousness-raising book, mapping those areas of our own behaviour which had been *acquired* rather than naturally allowed to emerge. (In my own case I could see how constantly I had been discouraged from developing strength in order to fit the stereotype of weak. *Sex, Gender and Society*, with its documentation of the enormous range of characteristics of women, opened up new areas of possibilities of what a woman could be.)

The book was very much a product of its time, though: the classification of lesbianism as deviancy says much about the values of sociology as a discipline. But as an early document on the 'facts of the matter', *Sex, Gender and Society* was a boost for many women and a practical handbook for assistance when it came to dealing with some of the daily put-downs used by men.

After defining the terms of the debate, Ann Oakley began to fill in some of the detail on the way women were made and the lives they were required to lead in our particular social context. Looking back to the early 1970s one of the most pressing issues in consciousness-raising groups was how to establish that housework was *real work*, and it was this problem that Ann Oakley set out to describe and explain within the academic context of sociology. Acknowledging that it was impossible to present her findings in a way that would be meaningful to both the academic community (which she wanted to reform) and the women (whose existence she wanted to validate), Ann Oakley published her findings in two books – *The Sociology of Housework* (1974) and *Housewife* (1974, 1976).

For her research on housework as *work,* Ann Oakley talked with women about this aspect of their lives and she unapologetically took with her her own experience of the same situation – and used it. She too discarded the 'grand theory' in preference for women's reality, but she had a much more developed theoretical framework than had some of her predecessors, and so was more confident about where to place her findings and decide what they meant. In Ann Oakley's research, some of the many strands of feminist knowledge-construction are brought together as she uses the personal approaches of Betty Friedan and Hannah Gavron, a comparable academic context to Kate Millett's, the meanings of Robin Morgan and the questions of Shulamith Firestone to forge a paradigm for feminist research.

Talking with women about their lives was a methodology quite consistent with the women's liberation movement strategy of consciousness-raising: for the researcher to acknowledge her own involvement and commitment to the research, expressly to include her own experience in the problem being analysed, to appreciate that the researcher can be changed by the research[1] not only eliminated the false claim of value-free research, but helped to break down the distinction between researcher and researched, and so made it possible for women to be the subject and not the object of the study. To accept the validity of women's reality, moreover, was not just to insist on the legitimacy of women's experience but was to have repercussions for some of the women who participated – many of the women Ann Oakley has talked with over the years would be the first to declare that those talks 'changed their lives'. (Ann Oakley would also be prepared to state that the research she undertook helped to change hers.)

In some respects, the methodology that Ann Oakley has used is similar to that employed by anthropologists – and is an indictment of the extent to which male experience has swamped the meanings of our own society when such techniques need to be used to map the dimensions of the existence of 52 per cent of our population.

For Ann Oakley this was the starting point in *The Sociology of Housework* (1974) which opens with a critique of sociology itself, its *political* assumptions and the biased nature of the knowledge it constructs. This indictment of a science, aggressively defended as value-free, was a direct challenge to male authority and to the right of this male-dominated discipline to speak with any authority at all – all nicely set out in their own territory and on their own terms.

Step by step, Ann Oakley went through the discipline and revealed the way it defined women out of existence and the means by which men ensured – in Jessie Bernard's appropriate words – that sociology was a male science of a male society (1973, 1974: 19). Men set the research agenda, determined the priorities, asked the questions, validated the methodologies, verified the results, handed out the degrees, and did so in a most convenient and highly circular fashion. For example, they began with the assumption that the male was more important, they defined as powerful the things that men do, they then studied the institutions of power – which, of course, consisted of studies of men – and so were able to 'prove' that the male was more important. How very little was known about women, and how very much was known about men was Ann Oakley's protest. For while men at the workplace were studied – and studied – what happened when a few studies were undertaken on the 36 per cent of women in the workforce?[2] Their presence there was treated as problematic: they were asked *why* they worked (p.19).

Another area where Ann Oakley took sociology to task was in its construction and use of stratification theory. The Elizabethans had prescribed a world view – the Great Chain of Being – which placed, in descending order, all creatures from God down to the smallest and humblest animals. Sociologists had similarly devised their stratification theory to divide the members of society into hierarchical order. The unit they used was the family and its status was determined by its head – the man. By this means, not only was the pre-eminence of the male created, but the educational, occupational and financial resources of women were completely denied. Academic training wasn't necessary to see that many women had very different resources from their husbands and were of a very different status, but sociologists none the less insisted on constructing a 'truth' which bore little resemblance to reality, and which denied the existence and resources of those whom they held to be subordinate and whom they clearly wished to remain so. Ann Oakley delivered one of the first systematic feminist critiques of a discipline from within the discipline and thoroughly discredited its claims for objectivity and value-free proof (pp.5–13).

If women were to have any place in sociological knowledge, then assuredly it should be in the family, reasoned Ann Oakley, because that's where women were supposed to belong. But an analysis of the literature of the family made it quite clear that, even here, women were not studied in their own right. When they were not a statistical entry they were generally referred to as being in a particular role and, where studied, the interest of sociologists was usually concerned with the *problems* that women in the family create – for men. 'Working wives' were studied not in terms of their lives, but in relation to the difficulties these created (p.17).

For Ann Oakley it was patently clear that there was no way of 'adding women on' to such a discipline: the discipline itself had to change many of its assumptions before women could be included. This was why her demand that sociology acknowledge that housework was *work* was a radical one, and one which was strongly resisted. Once it was admitted that women *worked* in the home, the way was open to discuss the appalling nature of their working conditions – arduous work, for long hours, in isolation, with little or no pay, no compensation, no pension, no relief, no time-off, no paid holidays, and no basis for negotiation for improved conditions – and, if women in the home were to be classified as workers, to expose men as exploitative *employers*. Sociologists could very well find themselves in the position of documenting gross injustices: this would be a deplorable political move, many of them argued, and the end of sociology as a science. Ann Oakley was well aware of the meanings of politics and science in this context and more than willing and able to change them.

Her documentation of women's lives as workers in the home provided the foundation of new knowledge about women. For centuries men had been encoding knowledge about themselves in which they and their concerns were central, which they took for granted as reliable knowledge, and which confirmed their existence and their supremacy in the world. Ann Oakley claimed for women the same right to encode their own knowledge to affirm their own existence, and then proceeded to construct it. In doing so she undermined male authority and supremacy with her challenge to the exclusivity of male knowledge-makers on male subjects.

Ann Oakley has continued in this tradition with her research on pregnancy and childbirth and has presented much the same challenge to the medical profession as she did to sociologists. In what has become virtually a hallmark of feminist research since the initial work of Betty Friedan, Ann Oakley locates the huge discrepancy between the official view of maternity and the reality for the women who experience it. She traces the origin of much of this problem to the makers of knowledge and meaning in this area: the medical men. 'The management of reproduction has been throughout most of history and in most cultures a female concern,' she writes in *Women Confined* (1980), but 'what is characteristic about childbirth in the western world is, conversely, its control by men' (p.11).

There is little speculation on Ann Oakley's part as to whether the more 'reforms' women gain, and the more freedoms they achieve, the more important it becomes for men to move closer to women's power base in their attempt to confine women, but this is an explanation that is quite consistent with the thesis of men changing the rules which has been discussed in earlier chapters. Ann Oakley is more concerned to describe and explain the daily realities of women who are being exploited (and more concerned to bring about improvements) than she is with the wider theoretical issues of how it came to be this way . She takes women's daily existence as the boundaries of her research, and undertakes her analysis within this framework. She presumes the ability of women to manage their own lives constructively when free from much of the interference of men – one of her most significant claims is that it is male intervention, from meanings to technology, which is responsible for some of the most serious problems for women, including post-natal depression. Her assessment of male management of reproduction is that it may not only be unsatisfactory politically, but it can cause more problems than it solves.

She directs her attention towards exposing and ending such male intervention by *information*, and her strategy depends on the ability of the medical profession to change many of its practices once confronted with their failure. While many feminists would have little faith in the capacity of the medical profession to respond, it is clear that the last few years have witnessed something of a reversal in Britain away from the technological (and pathological) model of childbirth. This would have been a most unlikely development without the evidence and protest *from women*. Ann Oakley helped to assemble the evidence and, with other feminists, helped to make that protest.

Using the experience of women she provides one classic example of discrepancy when she outlines the way medical men decree the authoritative meanings for women: the example is that of pain in childbirth. According to medical 'knowledge' such pain does not exist, and the women who declare that it does – and who tell other women about it – are trouble-makers who should be disciplined. Ann Oakley begins with quotes from medical knowledge:

> Another hidden anxiety is a fear of the pain of childbirth. All too often the young mother is told of the gruesome *imagined* experiences of older women. (Llewellyn-Jones, 1965: 65)

> An effort should be made to *restrain* or *rebuke* the parlous women who relate their unpleasant experiences to the unsuspecting primi-gravidae. (Matthews, 1961: 874)

> Why do women have to recount such stories to one another, especially when the majority of them are so blatantly untrue? . . . Probably more is done by *wicked women* with their *malicious lying tongues* to harm the confidence and happiness of pregnant women than by any other single factor . . . . Perhaps it is some form of *sadism*. (Bourne, 1975: 7)

> (Oakley, p.42; my emphasis)

This is more than a discrepancy, it amounts to a *conflict* between medical knowledge which denies pain and insists on 'contractions', and the direct knowledge of women who have given birth and, most decidedly, felt the pain. And, as is the case in the wider context of society, the example afforded by this institution reveals that male meanings can only persist while women can be prevented from pooling their own experience and from forging their own shared meanings and knowledge.

But this example also helps to explain why so many of the first time mothers Ann Oakley talked with felt that they had been deceived about motherhood. Like the women Betty Friedan had talked with almost twenty years before, Ann Oakley's subjects also felt that they had followed all the rules, had done what they were supposed to do, and yet it hadn't worked out the way they had been led to believe. There is a considerable gap 'between expectations and reality,' writes Ann Oakley, 'pregnancy, childbirth and motherhood are not the way most women expect them to be. On the whole they are more uncomfortable and less pleasant than anticipated' (pp.280-1). This is partly because the meanings of pregnancy, childbirth and motherhood as put forward not just by a male-dominated medical profession, but a male-dominated society, are as much a 'mystique' as the 'feminine' ever was and are constructed for much the same reasons.

The feeling that they had been misled though was not for Ann Oakley's subjects associated only with the discovery that childbirth hurt, or with the far greater level of technological intervention that they had anticipated: it was also because they believed they had *lost* something which they had not been prepared for either: 'What is characteristic of childbirth and becoming a mother today,' states Ann Oakley, summarising some of her work, 'is the tendency for women to feel they have lost something, rather than simply gained a child. What is lost may be one's job, one's life-style, an intact "couple" relationship, control over one's body or a sense of self' (p.280). Women feel they have given up something and if it is through reproduction and the social-isation of children that women are most exploited and oppressed, this response is not surprising, nor is the fact this was something the women were not prepared for.

But this brings Ann Oakley to the position that so many feminists arrive at sooner or later: if it is through our desire and capacity to be nurturers that women are most readily oppressed, should we cease to be nurturers? 'I have ended on the most apparently paradoxical and confused point of all,' concludes Ann Oakley in *Women Confined*, 'by saying that women are oppressed because they love children: or (alternatively put), that if they didn't have children, women would no longer be oppressed' (p.291). What requires acknowledgement, and what Ann Oakley is quick to add, is that there is nothing inherently oppressive about childbirth: what is oppressive is the social meaning and organisation which is built round reproduction, and which is directly linked with male dominance (and was the main reason Shulamith Firestone wanted to end women's association with repro-duction). Therefore it could just as easily be stated that while men have power, reproduction can be a source of oppression for women, and when framed in this way, we could conclude that this would not require us to abandon reproduction and nurturing, but to do away with male power. This is the conclusion that Ann Oakley reaches after her extensive research. It is no small task, she admits, but for reproduction to cease being oppressive to women it is necessary to have a society that authenticates female experience and a female point of view. 'Repro-duction is not just a handicap and a cause of second class status: it is an achievement, *the* authentic achievement of women' (p.291), a recog-nition of its status and significance should be central in feminist political programmes. In her view, the importance of reproduction can

141

be overlooked, a stand with which some more recent theorists concur, suggesting that this is one of the weaknesses in feminist theory.[3] What remains of paramount importance to Ann Oakley is that reproduction should be in the hands of women who are able to control its meanings and its organisation in their own interest. Reproduction, she insists, should be stripped of its male meanings and be designed and made meaningful by those who have authority in this area – women.

Her research, and its conclusions, constitute one of the first attempts to synthesise some of the old and the new methods of knowledge-making: hers is avowedly feminist and woman-centred research which manages to stay within the confines of convention even as it challenges those very conventions. While there are fundamental questions to be asked about research which is conducted within the traditional framework – who is it for, how useful will it be, are the 'researched' being exploited, can it be used against women? (see Liz Stanley and Sue Wise, 1983) – these issues are not problematic in relation to Ann Oakley's research; with her emphasis on constructing knowledge on the basis of women's *voices* she has helped to formulate a feminist research-model of enduring quality and credibility.

12. All Things Being Equal: Phyllis Chesler's superiority

Phyllis Chesler was to psychology, psychiatry and the medical establishment very much what Ann Oakley was to sociology (and the medical establishment), and again we have an in-depth analysis of a particular male institution and the damage that is done to women in its 'value-free' name. In *Women and Madness* (1972), Phyllis Chesler insisted that the rot had gone too far for there to be any hope of reforming the theories and practices associated with mental health. What was necessary, she argued, was a completely new way of describing and explaining mental health which was free from male politics, for in the hands of men the method had become nothing other than a blatant instrument of oppression used against women. Far from being designed to help women, she declared, psychiatry and the clinicians who practised it constituted a means of punishing women.

Women and Madness was no appeal to men to reform, but a call to women to make men reform as a matter of the greatest urgency. Phyllis Chesler was angry and it shows. She makes other women angry, which was her intention. Hers is an energising statement, partly because it presumes women as the audience and men as the target for criticism. She is no clinician hoping to be read by the psychiatric establishment, and bent on achieving recognition or respectability, but an 'insider' who is prepared to come out and tell the full story. It is a shocking story in which the shock is intensified by the stark realism of Phyllis Chesler's style. Again and again the most horrific evidence is presented in the most matter-of-fact tone, which serves to reinforce her argument that it is not the occasional exception she is describing and explaining, but the everyday practices, the routine details of the treatment of women in a male-dominated society and under a male-dominated institution.

The most fundamental and dramatic issue that Phyllis Chesler raised in *Women and Madness* was that, by definition, women are made, and this ensures their vulnerability as victims of the mental health weapon. She got straight to the crux of the belief-system which created a double-standard of mental health in the interest of men and male power. What society held to be a mentally sick man, she explained – someone who was dependent, passive, lacking in initiative and in need of support – was precisely the same as what society held to be a healthy woman, and vice versa. A sick woman was one who displayed some of the prized characteristics of the healthy male – self-reliance, confidence, independence. The superb convenience of this arrangement which allowed men to monopolise these human characteristics and to *punish* women who showed signs of possessing them was not lost on Phyllis Chesler who, in bald terms, exposed the blatant politics of mental health, and revealed how in a patriarchal society it is used to control and oppress women.

The values and belief-system of psychiatrists, she states, are very important, for 'Psychiatrists both medically and legally, decide *who* is insane and *why; what* should be done to or for such people; and *when* and if they should be released from treatment' (p.59). This is an enormous power to have over other human beings: an unaccountable power. It is power concentrated in the hands of a white, male élite and is used for the purpose of preserving that power and defending and explaining that élitism. It leads, according to Phyllis Chesler, to the edge of male reality in which male is the norm and woman is other, is deviant – is mad. Phyllis Chesler regards it as no coincidence that a patriarchal society has prided itself on *rationality* and claimed the realm of the rational as the prerogative of men. It is then 'rational' to allocate the irrational and the emotional to women, and with its basic definition of woman as mad, patriarchal society has one more means of placing women outside the cultural mainstream where the actions of women become inexplicable by rational, *male* standards. (p.32)

There is another example of men creating the meanings and the knowledge which structure the inferiority of women and help to justify the different treatment that women receive when male is the norm. The whole edifice is a cultural construction which originates in a male supremacist value-system and which has awful consequences for women. For what Phyllis Chesler is making clear is that *madness applies to all women*. One of her most startling findings is how little difference there is between women who constitute 'the problem' and women who are used as the 'control group' in any study of women's mental disability (p.90). In the context of male meanings, all women are defined as mad, or beyond normal explanations – when normality equals male – and women are required to be different: the ones who are directly penalised are arbitrary victims.

This is not new, says Phyllis Chesler, which she demonstrates (before Mary Daly's (1978) analysis of witch-hunting) by drawing parallels between the creation and treatment of witches in the past with the creation and treatment of mental illness in women in the present. In both cases woman was defined as suspect, as potentially a witch or mentally disturbed, and the ones who were singled out for treatment were unfortunate enough to attract notice and to warrant punishment. This is not the only feature the two have in common, she continues, extending the parallel: those who persecuted witches and those who practise psychiatry treat woman as a category in very much the same way – the major difference lying in the technology – for the purpose and the barbarism are still there today, but drugs and electric shock treatment have replaced witch-pricking and ducking-stools as a means of maintaining male control over females. The *threat* of punishment applies to *all* women and serves as intimidation and is quite sufficient to keep many women in their place.

More and more women are seeking psychiatric help, states Phyllis Chesler, and she tries to analyse some of the reasons for this development. It could be that increasing numbers of women are becoming 'difficult' and are in need of 'care', but she is quick to point out that while women are *used* by psychiatry, they are also in a position to *use* it. Madness, she says, can be a break from the many exhausting if not impossible demands of the female role. It can also be a definite protest, for women find it easier and much more in character to become depressed, rather than to engage in physical violence. The whole model of psychiatric help is 'in character' for women – one might even say it was designed for them – for while women are conditioned to find solutions in dependency then even greater dependence and self-abnegation can appear to be a plausible solution. There is also the distinct possibility that things are getting worse for women, states Phyllis Chesler, as more and more women find themselves 'out of work' when their children – or their husband – leave. Redundancy can well lead to depression, and she notes that 'Many newly useless women are emerging more publicly into insanity' (p.33). In terms of women's reality there could be good reason to be depressed; this could be a completely *rational* response to an untenable and seemingly unchangeable situation.

There are difficulties with the term *madness* for it is a general term and not sufficiently precise to distinguish between the range of behaviours it encompasses. There is the madness that men use against women, and the madness which is the other side of the coin – women's resistance to male power. That one of the most common indices of madness among women is to refuse to make themselves attractive or to do housework or other 'slave' tasks, certainly raises the question of whether women are on strike. This is a question which has also been raised in relation to the more recent epidemic of agoraphobia among women which effectively prevents them from fulfilling their service functions outside the home. If this does represent a *strike* on women's behalf and a demand for a fairer deal, it is a desperately high price to pay. Phyllis Chesler makes it clear that, while she acknowledges some of the constructs that create and coerce women's madness, as a form of resistance madness does not constitute a revolutionary force. 'It has never been my intention to romanticize madness or to confuse it with political or cultural revolution,' she states, partly because there is just too much pain involved in it. 'Most weeping, depressed women, most anxious and terrified women are neither about to seize the means of production and reproduction, nor are they more creatively involved with problems of cosmic powerlessness, evil and love than is the rest of the human race' (p.xxi).

Psychiatry, however, is held up as one of the products of a civilised society, it is the latest in scientific achievement applied to human understanding and, ostensibly, it holds out hope for mental disturbance for which in previous times there has been no cure. But to Phyllis Chesler this rationale is 'window dressing', for in her terms this is the institution which ranks among the most damaging for women and, for her, there is no mystery why it works this way, or how it came to be this way. Like every other feminist whose ideas have been discussed, she assigns much of the responsibility to Freud who set up a paradigm for treating women's reality – particularly of sexual abuse – as fantasy, finding it much more expedient to blame women than to cast a critical eye on male dominance, violence and sexual exploitation.[1] But there was no shortage of men to continue and expand the trade that Freud had started: as has been stated in earlier chapters his theory was timely, and eminently suited to control women in a period when they were beginning to enjoy more educational, occupational and financial freedoms.

It wasn't as if this 'new' treatment of women represented a radical departure from the traditions of a male-dominated society. As Phyllis Chesler points out, our history is replete with references to women who have been locked up (see Sandra Gilbert and Susan Gubar, *The Madwoman in the Attic*, 1980): in 1861 Susan B. Anthony and Elizabeth Cady Stanton had asked their own questions: 'Could the dark secrets of those insane asylums be brought to light,' wrote Elizabeth Cady Stanton in *History of Woman Suffrage*, 'we would be shocked to know the countless number of rebellious wives, sisters and daughters that are thus annually sacrificed to false customs and conventionalisms, and barbarous laws made by men for women' (1881, Vol.1, p.469). Freud, and the clinicians who followed, simply refined the practices and developed more sophisticated means of putting women in their place – literally and metaphorically.

Some of the insights presented by Phyllis Chesler, however, have little relevance outside the United States, because the majority of the world's population of woman, no matter what their problems, have no access to the male clinician who will define their reality for them, provide their meanings, encourage their adjustment and offer a personal solution based on the presumption of their own inadequacies, rather than those of society. But her thesis that mental health is a modern weapon used against women extends far beyond the confines of the United States. Phyllis Chesler constructs a principle which makes it possible for women to reorganise the evidence, to see some of the past and present brutality, which men have been prepared to perpetrate to preserve their dominion over women. This is part of the rule of force that Kate Millett refers to, and without which patriarchy would be inoperable as a system.

Identifying this principle and its systematic nature, recognising the brutality that it facilitates and acknowledging the culpability of all men, Phyllis Chesler paved the way for future theses which adopted and extended this framework. Susan Brownmiller's *Against Our Will* (1976) and Mary Daly's *Gyn/Ecology* (1978) both make the distinction between the capacities of *all* men and *all* women, and both analyse male dominance and violence against women within the tradition that

147

Phyllis Chesler helped to found.

This is not the only area where Phyllis Chesler lays some of the groundwork: *Women and Madness* also contains one of the first serious and non-pejorative assessments of women's sexuality and lesbianism. Explaining why male homosexuality has been far more visible than lesbianism she attributes this directly to the enhanced male image and states that a more 'glorious' tradition has been constructed for it: 'Historically . . '. many male homosexuals have waged "heroic" wars together, have headed governments, churches and industries, and created artistic and intellectual masterpieces' (p.174). Women, however, have a very different tradition: 'Lesbians do not have a gloriously extensive ancestry,'[2] she writes. 'Their mothers and grandmothers, like those of heterosexual women, lived with men and did not control the means of production. Lesbians are women: as such, most are traditionally more domestic, conventional and sexually monogamous than male homosexuals are – traits to which women are condemned, but for which they are not really valued' (p.175). If male homosexuality is more a part of society's reality, then this is simply a statement about which sex is valued, and it is a meaning which she turns back on male homosexuality:

> I must suggest that male homosexuality, *in patriarchal society*, is a basic and extreme expression of phallus worship, misogyny, and the colonization of certain female and/or 'feminine' functions. Male homosexuals, like male heterosexuals (and like heterosexual women), prefer men to women. It is as simple as that. (p.177)

Things are very different for women:

> In a sense, it is theoretically easier for women to love women than it is for men to love men. Our mothers were women and, Michelangelo aside, most object-models of sexual or aesthetic beauty in our culture are female. Also most women know how to be *tender* (not that they always are) with other people. Traditionally, most men, whether they are homosexual or heterosexual, know only seduction, rape and pillage – in bed and on the battlefield. (p.176)

In these circumstances, lesbianism is an eminently sensible and understandable choice.[3] And Phyllis Chesler links lesbianism with a passionate plea for a real sisterhood, with the revolutionary aim for

148

women to love and care for each other. It is her belief that women from birth are channelled into being nurturers and are themselves deprived of nurturance: one remedy for this is for women to nurture each other – an aim that is not always realised, even among feminists. But it is an aim that Phyllis Chesler would definitely like to see achieved, partly because of its revolutionary nature. When women's reference group is women (as is the case with *Women and Madness*), when women seek approval from each other and bypass the approval of men, much will have changed, for male centrality will have been undermined. This is another variation on Germaine Greer's theme of women taking back their resources which are within their power to reclaim.

Despite her idealised version of sisterhood, Phyllis Chesler does not idealise women's oppression. She raises an issue which I have only encountered in specific form once before.[4] During the nineteenth century it was not uncommon for feminists to insist on women's moral superiority and to imply that in their oppressed state women learnt a great deal that was valuable – compassion and nurturance, even spiritual values. To George Eliot this looked like dangerous ground indeed: if oppression produced noble souls, she argued, it was a good case for *more* oppression, not for ending it. Phyllis Chesler adopts a very similar line of reasoning: we have to be very careful of the claims we make for women in our oppressed state, she warns.

Obviously there is a fine line to tread. Phyllis Chesler makes it quite clear that men have power, but so too do women. It is not accurate, she states, to portray men as all-powerful and women as pathetic; even to move in this direction is to undermine the power that women do have, and to paralyse and pre-empt action among women. Nor is it accurate or helpful, she insists, to present a romanticised view of oppression which produces those warm and wonderful creatures – women. One example that she uses in this context is that of women's pacifism, a claim that is often made for women. If women are pacifists, she states, it is partly because violence is not a choice for them. If physical force was an option open to women but they elected not to use it, then we could hold up women's pacifism as a virtue. But while violence is not an option for women, 'Women are no more to be congratulated on their "pacifism" than men are to be congratulated for their "violence" ' (p.259).

Myths about women that are not useful to women are a constant target for elimination in Phyllis Chesler's book. (Myths that are useful are quite another thing – she is in the business of creating them, for it is not myths she is against, quite the contrary: it is the male meanings which she seeks to end.) Her defiant stance of exposing the utilitarian value of myths in a patriarchal society was one that she continued in her later book with Emily Jane Goodman, *Women, Money and Power* (1976). In the light of all the evidence today on women's poverty, it is difficult to remember the time when it was widely believed that women were secretly wealthy. But that was a myth that Phyllis Chesler helped to eliminate and, in doing so, she pointed in the direction of women's poverty.

Phyllis Chesler's attitude to men is also elaborated in a later book – *About Men* (1978) – but the basic meanings are all there in uncompromising fashion in *Women and Madness*. She classifies *all* men together as a social category and does not take males and male norms as her reference point – they have no redeeming features in her analysis. Nor is she writing for men or male approval. That all men are *not* equal is patently clear to Phyllis Chesler, and she points out that less powerful men are required to perform male rites of violence – 'Old, wealthy, white American men have not been dying in Vietnam' (p.271). Yet she is adamant that women do not exist for the purpose of looking after men: women have to begin to exist for themselves and to cease assuming responsibility for what men do to each other.

Her assessment of the way men will try to take over the topic of women's liberation and use it in their own interest is shrewd indeed, and she cites the way male clinicians can set out to discredit and destroy women's new-found (and to them threatening) reality, in order to preserve their own reality and, of course, their own dominance. Writing about how men take women's meanings out of sexual harassment, she states:

> Clinicians seem to dislike and pity the paranoia and anger of the feminists, . . . Slyly, confidently, they want to know why they are so 'nervous' about being found sexually attractive by 'poor' Tom, Dick or Harry. Why are they so angry at verbal abuse in the streets? . . . Don't these suddenly complaining women 'unconsciously' invite harassment or rape, and don't they 'unconsciously' enjoy it? (pp.228–9)

After the 'softening up' comes the takeover bid: 'Furthermore, isn't the point of women's liberation the liberation of men too, and not, heaven forbid, female power? Isn't capitalism the *real* enemy and feminism divisive and/or the "pouting" of spoiled, white, middle-class women" (p.229). This isn't new, of course, but these are the men who earn their living on the basis that they can solve women's problems; they are the men, Phyllis Chesler comments wryly, who are more concerned to talk about how sexism hurts men more than it hurts women (p.230). Even those who profess 'sympathy' frequently do so 'because they are sexually "attracted" to feminists, whom they see as more "interesting" and "sexually promiscuous" than their wives' (p.228).

No matter in what form women raise the topic, there is a tactic available to men which helps to take the threat out of it, and works to consign the topic – and women – to the realm of not-to-be-taken-seriously. This by no means surprises Phyllis Chesler, who sees power very much in terms of survival, and who regards the very concept of *female power* as a potent challenge to male survival, and she takes a remarkable but none the less reasonable stand on what women's aspirations should be. Equality is a spurious goal, and of no use to women: the only way women can protect themselves is if they *dominate* particular institutions and can use them to serve women's interests. Reproduction is a case in point. She also speculates on the realisation of equality and gives implicit credence to the explanation that women are intrinsically more powerful, which is the reason why males have found it necessary to create their compensatory culture. All things being equal, Phyllis Chesler remarks (almost casually), then women will be superior, and men know it – which is why there is a real fight going on as men seek to protect and preserve their power. But in present circumstances the only real alternative that Phyllis Chesler can see to man power is woman power.

The absence of any systematic discussion of consciousness and consciousness-raising in *Women and Madness* is perhaps surprising given its psychological framework. This does not mean that Phyllis Chesler does not take *talk* into account: on the contrary, her observations and analysis of talk between the sexes were amazingly astute and helped to provide the context for later interaction studies. But there is little discussion of what goes on in women's heads and the emphasis is on the practical and readily identifiable detail that serves to draw attention to the *politics* of the situation. Her categorical assertion that if women want to talk they had better talk to each other for they will get few if any opportunities to talk in the presence of men, provides a dramatic illustration of who has the power – and the right to talk (p.103).

Her commentary on the way men take over a topic and diminish and deny women's experience in the process, also reveals some of the political dimensions of day-to-day interaction between the sexes, and gives to women a helpful explanation of what is going on. Likewise, some of her descriptions of the exchanges between wives and husbands illuminate the dynamics of dealing with the oppressor, and release women from the conviction that somehow or other they are 'in the wrong'. 'The institutions of middle-class psychotherapy and marriage both encourage women to talk – often endlessly – rather than to act,' declares Phyllis Chesler. 'In marriage, the talking is usually of an indirect and rather inarticulate nature. Open expressions of rage are too dangerous and too ineffective for the isolated and economically dependent woman. Most often such "kitchen" declarations end in tears, self-blame, and in the husband graciously agreeing with his wife that she was "not herself" ' (p.103). It is virtually impossible for a woman to have a *real* conversation with a man – particularly if the man is her husband, a therapist or employer, who has *real*, direct power over her. For 'how is it possible to have a "real" conversation with those who directly profit from her oppression? She would be laughed at, viewed as silly or crazy and, if she persisted, removed from her job – as secretary or wife, perhaps even as private patient' (p.103).

Phyllis Chesler makes it clear that there is no point in turning to men. This is no solution but part of the problem. What women need to do is to turn to other women and to show some of the care and compassion for each other that for centuries women have lavished on men. (Thus echoing some of Robin Morgan's words in *Going Too Far*,1978.) Phyllis Chesler is distressed by our inability to live up to our own ideals of sisterhood and urges the greater effort and understanding necessary to a revolutionary goal. Woman power lies in woman support, she claims, and she baldly outlines the way women are deflected from achieving this goal, partly because of our own use of a double-standard. We too have one rule for men and one for women:

Thus in America Betty Friedan's or Gloria Steinem's or Kate Millett's 'contributions' to a particular women's cause are more actively expected and sought after than are Governor Rockefeller's, President Nixon's, the Ford Foundation's, the US Army's, General Motors' or the Vatican's, all institutions which have far greater resources than those of any individual woman or any individual woman's group. (Mommy is still safer to milk, blame and hate than Daddy is. Daddy is feared and addressed in 'good girl' tones, or not addressed at all.) (p.258)

I think it is still very much the case that feminists are harder on each other than on anyone else, an attribute which is hardly useful and is indeed even difficult to discuss. But there can be no doubt that if feminists direct their criticisms at feminists it will be revolutionary suicide and remove any necessity for men to develop their strategies for divide and rule. And given the extent to which women are excluded from the control of meanings in a patriarchal society, there can be no doubt either that feminist criticisms of feminists and feminism are a ready, ruthless and reliable weapon in the hands of men. Yet paradoxically, the possibilities for criticism within feminism have grown at the same rate as the growth of a feminist body of knowledge: the more knowledge is available the greater is the chance of being 'unknowledgeable', of being wrong.

Phyllis Chesler emphasises that there are more questions than answers for feminists, and that we really don't have a single solution or course of action that will lead us to our goal: 'How can women learn to survive – and learn to value survival?' she asks. 'How can women banish self-sacrifice, guilt, naiveté, helplessness, madness, sorrow from the female condition? How – or should – women sever their ties to child-bearing and rearing? Should women *stop* being compassionate? Should or can there be a single standard of behaviour for both sexes? Is there such a thing as a biologically rooted female culture that should remain separate from male culture, partly because it is "better" than male culture?' (p.276). It is significant that she concludes *Women and Madness* with 'Thirteen Questions' (pp.280–3) which are no less relevant and no closer to being answered today.

Women and Madness could not have been written without some of the publications that went before, because its framework is one that had already been outlined. It is an in-depth exploration of a particular and fundamentally important aspect of oppression which builds on some of the meanings previously established. Yet despite the way it readily fits into the feminist framework I think that this is one thesis which is no closer to cultural acceptance or accommodation than it was a decade ago. There has been a feminist response – the development of a feminist psychology and feminist therapy – but there has been no essential change in the ethics of mental health, partly because it is so inextricably interwoven with the concept of male-as-norm, a concept which shows few signs of being dislodged. To accept Phyllis Chesler's thesis that a male-dominated society defines women as mad is to challenge the foundations of our society; it is to challenge male power and to identify men as unqualified oppressors who have evolved a sophisticated and savage means of punishing women who step out of their place. This realisation would be too much for society to accept without its changing. I think it is highly significant that I have heard more criticisms of the Soviet Union's use of psychiatry for political purposes than I have ever heard of patriarchy's use of psychiatry for political purposes against women.

Women and Madness is too much: it is too bold, too bald, too bare. It strips patriarchy down to its essence and leaves little room for rationalisation. It paints a picture which is not at all pleasant: that is why I think many members of society prefer to look the other way.

13. The Knowledge Explosion: Woman as reference

Until about 1972 it would have been possible for some people to claim to have read *all* the contemporary feminist books: after 1972 such a claim would have become increasingly absurd. For while there was a steady increase in the publication of women's encoded knowledge in the first years of the 1970s, after this date there was a virtual explosion. Books, pamphlets, newsletters and courses flourished, and their very presence constitutes a feminist 'success story'. When the basis of much feminist theory was that a fundamental source of male power was the power of authority and the power to decree meanings, for feminists to have so quickly and so competently challenged the exclusive authority of men and to have created an alternative system of meanings was an enormous and radical achievement.

Suddenly there was a new reference group and an alternative authoritative voice which was constructing a very different interpretation of the world. And the authority of this new reference group departed from the traditional forms, for there was no leader, no official spokeswoman. Instead there was collective authority – the authority of participation and consensus – as women compared their version of experience with other women, and put forward the shared meanings of different groups. There were no proclamations from the top as to what women's version would or should be, but a much more free-flowing and cyclical process of exchange and discussion which served as the source of this new knowledge. Study groups read books, talked about them, modified them and wrote their own, which in turn were read and discussed by other groups. And at each stage the reference group grew bigger and the audience greater, the knowledge-base expanded and the range of meanings and explanations was elaborated. Because the very existence of such a group with its own set of different meanings undermined the right of men to determine how the world should be, the emergence of women as a reference group was an aspect of women taking back the power that men had appropriated. For women to speak for themselves, to dispute the meanings of males, and to validate the meanings of females, was a political act, and a very significant one.

This description of the growth of women's autonomous knowledge, however, does leave out much. It presumes the independence of women and makes little mention of the interaction between women and the (still) male-dominated society. A more comprehensive version of the development of women's knowledge would need to take account of the publishing industry (and profits!). Clearly, some publishers found a new market which they were quick to exploit – just as some educational institutions found a demand for women's studies courses which they were equally quick to exploit.[1] But the self-interest of publishers and educational institutions is not sufficient adequately to account for the emergence or the expansion of women's knowledge. Before either publishing or education could capitalise on women's knowledge, its reality and the demand for it had to exist among women, and this change in women's consciousness – which represents a shift in power – should not be minimised or overlooked.

Whether the construction of women's knowledge constitutes a permanent political achievement remains to be seen. My own research reveals that there are still male publishers, for example, who are convinced that the present popularity of women's books is a passing phase and that the *latest* book they have published 'on women' could well be the *last* book they will publish 'on women', because, any day now, the market will drop out of women's books and it will be back to normal again.[2] To suspect that women's books are *not* here to stay is to be pessimistic in the face of all the evidence of the continued increase in the production of women's books. It is my fervent hope that women's books *do* stay, because I have first-hand experience of that 'back-to-normal' state where there are no women's books, and know that feeling of ignorance and isolation it generates. But it is also because I know that women's books can be so subversive that I speculate about their future.

What I don't want to do is to contribute to a self-fulfilling prophecy and to assist in the decline of women's books. I don't want to take away any of the success that the growth in women's knowledge represents. In the early 1970s women did not have access to our resources and were often desperate for even the slightest knowledge that could shed light on women's lives. Those few pioneering books which made us acutely aware of our absence from codified knowledge merely whetted our appetites. We didn't wait for someone to provide us with knowledge – often it was the same women who were seeking knowledge who were creating it. And the same women who were going into print were also the women who were buying other women's printed words: women's culture was in the making.

Yet women of past generations have also known what it is like to be without women's knowledge and they also set out to produce it – in quantity – and to contribute to the creation of a women's culture. In 1911, for example, in England alone there were 21 regular women's periodicals (see Elizabeth Sarah, 1982). Admittedly, this was before radio and television, but even so it represents an enormous amount of literature. In 1920, after some women had gained the vote, *Time and Tide* was established. This was a weekly political periodical run by women with the express intention of causing such a fuss it could not fail to be noticed by men. Despite the extensive women's 'community' in England today, there is no counterpart to this radical paper.[3] In London there was the Woman's Press, and the Feminist Book Shop, as well as numerous organisations and societies which were avowedly femininst and were determined upon political change. So it simply is not accurate to suggest that we have established a literature and a culture that previous women's movements were unable to realise.

While there are similarities, however, there are also differences between the current women's movement and other movements of the past. For example, I do not think it was coincidence – or the mere expression of middle-class values – which sent contemporary feminists into the academic communities to demand knowledge about women, authenticated by women. This time, I think women have identified that bastion of male power – knowledge-making – and have attempted systematically to undermine it. Consciousness-raising was no fortuitous 'accident': it was a specific challenge to men's knowledge and a means of producing women's knowledge. It led to all sorts of questions about *why* women were left out, and to very pointed questions about why men were in charge of knowledge. Rebellion took the form of disregarding many of the sanctioned meanings of men, of displaying defiant disrespect for the knowledge-makers and their authority. I can find few historic parallels to this widespread resistance to 'truth'.

There have been individual protests of this nature in the past – hundreds of them,[4] but I know of no previous organised demand that the whole process of knowledge-making be drastically redefined. And this is one reason why I think the contemporary women's movement is different and why I think that its emphasis on the construction of knowledge is among its greatest strengths.

14. Necessary Diversity:
Variety and omission

So great and so varied has been the making of women's knowledge over the last decade that it represents a success to be obliged to admit to failure when trying to cover *all* the developments in feminist ideas. All that can be undertaken is a brief, partial and inadequate overview of some of the directions, and some of the omissions. But although feminist knowledge took off on many fronts – and significantly failed to make a start on a few – it was clear by 1972 that the feminist framework had a distinct identity: it was dynamic, multidimensional and cyclical; all conceptualisations which pose a challenge to the established male patterns of thinking and explaining. In 1973, Mary Daly effectively summed up women's way of interpreting the world in *Beyond God the Father.*

In a book that was basically a quest for the meaning of women's existence, she began with a critique of the great male fetish, *method*, and its followers. Method, as decreed by men, wouldn't help women much if they followed it, she claimed, because it demanded that so much be denied and ignored in the interest of preserving the centrality of men. The tyranny of method – methodaltry, as she called it, likening it to a cult practice and engaging in 'blasphemy' in the process – hinders new discoveries. 'It prevents us from raising questions never asked before and from being illumined by ideas that do not fit into pre-established boxes and forms.' And with total disrespect she describes the practices of the revered knowledge-makers. 'The worshippers of Method have an effective way of handling data that does [sic] not fit into the Respectable Categories of Questions and Answers. They simply classify it as non-data, thereby rendering it invisible' (p.11).

This has been women's fate – to be non-data. And if women are to change this, they will have to dispense with *method* and raise the questions that have not been asked, and see the evidence that has been invisible. This is what Mary Daly proposed to do, and she is quite unapologetic when she states that what she knows is neither 'objective' nor 'eternal truth'; and she is quite superb when she adds that what men know is neither objective nor eternally true either (p.7). In fact, this is the crux of her argument: men have passed off their half-truths as the whole truth. This is the problem.

She refers to this process as *naming*. This is the power that men have taken for themselves and the power that women must reclaim, she insists:

> it is necessary to grasp the fundamental fact that women have had the power of naming stolen from us. We have not been free to use our own power to name ourselves, the world, or God. Women are now realizing that the universal imposing of names by men has been false because partial. That is, inadequate words have been taken as adequate. (p.8)

Putting together language meanings and knowledge as a single entity – variously referred to as 'naming', 'the symbolic order' or 'making sense of the world' – Mary Daly argues, very persuasively, that the way to end male dominion and to generate woman power is through the reclamation of the right to name, through the formulation of ways of making sense of the world that are consistent with women's experience of the world: 'The liberation of language is rooted in the liberation of ourselves' (p.8).

Her repudiation of the male value-system which underpins the entire symbolic order is magnificent, and guaranteed to threaten male authority. She takes power by means of the challenge she presents and the method she employs: 'The method of liberation, then, involves a *castrating* of languages and images that reflect and perpetuate the structures of a sexist world.' There can be no mistaking her meaning:

> It castrates precisely in the sense of cutting away the phallocentric value-system imposed by patriarchy, in its subtle as well as its more manifest expressions. As aliens in a man's world who are now rising up to name – that is, to create – our own world, women are beginning to recognize that the value-system thrust upon us by the various

cultural institutions of patriarchy has amounted to a kind of gang rape of minds as well as bodies. (p.9)

There is no doubt for Mary Daly where the struggle for power is going to be waged – in the realm of meaning and knowledge. And while hers is a comprehensive – even a cosmic – analysis of the symbolic order, and an attempt to reclaim it for women, there were numerous other feminists at the time engaged in a similar process, even if they were confined to slightly narrower concerns.

One was Elaine Morgan who, in 1972, questioned the received evolutionary theory in *The Descent of Woman*. Only a man, obsessed with explaining the origin of man through the prism of man-the-hunter, could ever have come up with such distortions of the evidence, she argues. Her section on the evidence – and the way men account for it – borders on hilarious reading (pp.4–13). With the greatest disrespect she mocks the considered and absurd opinions of the authorities who, if they had thought of what *women* were doing – if they had thought of women as part of the species – could never have drawn such absurd conclusions. One can almost hear Elaine Morgan sigh as she states that

> A very high percentage of thinking on these topics is androcentric [male-centred] in the same way as pre-Copernican thinking was geocentric. It's just as hard for man to break the habit of thinking of himself as central to the species as it was to break the habit of thinking of himself as central to the universe. He sees himself quite unconsciously as the main line of evolution, with a female satellite revolving around him as the moon revolves around the universe. (p.3)

But as Elaine Morgan is about to produce some woman-centred knowledge, 'man as the centre' will be dislodged:

> The longer I went on reading his own books about himself, the more I longed to find a volume that would begin: 'When the first ancestor of the human race descended from the trees, she had not yet developed the mighty brain that was to distinguish her so sharply from all other species ... (p.3)

Thinking in terms of 'woman' instead of 'man' was the method that she followed. By taking woman as her reference point she was able to construct a very different explanation for the evolution of the species, an explanation which not only accounted for much that had formerly been inexplicable, but which exposed the distortions – and the ludicrousness – of much that men had put forward in their attempt to reconstruct the past on the premise that the human race was comprised entirely of brave, virile hunters.

At the same time Andrea Dworkin was trying to overcome the difficulties she was experiencing in finding ways to express her new meanings in *Woman Hating* (1974):

> I write . . . with a broken tool, with a language that is sexist and discriminatory to its core. I try to make the distinctions, not 'history' as the whole human story, not 'man' as the generic term for the species, not 'manhood' as the synonym for courage, dignity and strength. But I have not been successful in reinventing the language. (p.26)

And in an Afterword she gives some idea of the conflict she had with the publisher over her experiments with – punctuation. (He won.) However, despite her admission of the resistance of the language to the meanings she seeks to convey, *Woman Hating* makes a significant contribution to the reservoir of feminist ideas, partly through its linkage of fairy-tales with pornography and the mutilation of women, but partly too because it takes into account the diversity of women's experience and seeks to validate it all.

For Andrea Dworkin, 'One cannot be free, never, not ever, in an unfree world' (p.22), and she does not want to see the women's movement isolated from understandings of other forms of oppression. She rejects the concept of a single form of oppression and tries to outline some of its complexity by exposing the exploitative and discriminatory nature of class and race structures, asserting that middle-class women who are oppressed by men also oppress other women: 'our poor White sisters, our Black sisters, our Chicana sisters' (p.21). She surveys the social organisation of her country and states that 'This closely interwoven fabric of oppression which is the racist class structure of Amerika [sic] today, assured that wherever one stood, it was with at least one foot heavy on the belly of another human being' (p.21).

With good reason she was critical of some of the gaps in feminist theory and practice as they had evolved: 'The women's movement has not dealt with this bread and butter issue and that is its most awful failure. There has been little recognition that the destruction of a middle-class life-style is crucial to the development of decent community forms in which all people can be free and have dignity' (p.22).

While Andrea Dworkin wanted to acknowledge the shared oppression of women, she did not want to lose sight of the differences that existed among women and which had to be addressed, understood and, in many instances, changed. Nor did she want to set up a list of priorities with which all women had to agree in order to be 'proper feminists'. Her intention was to establish the common framework and to endorse the chosen actions of many women on many fronts. To expand an explanatory framework to take into account the many different priorities and strategies women could determine, and at the same time to preserve the bonds between women, was a feminist goal if not always a feminist achievement. It was a goal which Andrea Dworkin had in mind when she wrote:

> The analysis in this book applies to the life situations of all women, but all women are not necessarily in the state of primary emergency as women. As a Jew in Nazi Germany, I would be oppressed as a woman, but hunted, slaughtered as a Jew. As a native American, I would be oppressed as a squaw, but hunted, slaughtered as a native American. The first identity, the one that brings with it as part of its definition death, is the identity of primary emergency. This is an important recognition because it relieves us of a serious confusion. The fact, for instance, that many Black women (by no means all) experience primary emergency as Blacks in no way lessens the responsibility of Blacks to assimilate this and other analyses of sexism and to apply it to their own revolutionary work. (pp.23-4)

What is starkly obvious to me is the absence, even at this stage, of women of colour in the new codified knowledge of women. Every criticism that has so far been levelled at the restrictive and oppressive meanings generated by men as a result of their monopoly and in the interest of preserving their power, applies with equal force to white women's knowledge. It is accurate to state that white women have stolen the power of naming from their sisters of colour and reduced them to non-data. This is a terrible failure. I have gone over the reasons for this and none of them stand up to scrutiny, for they are the same reasons I have heard from men at various times to justify their own pre-eminence. I would not accept them then and I cannot accept them now, in relation to women.

I am the first to insist that it is not women's responsibility to put men's house in order. And I am equally certain that it is not the responsibility of women of colour to put the house of white women in order; white women have to do it for themselves as a matter of urgency and with the utmost commitment, for until the experience and reality of women of colour is an integral part of feminist reality, women's new knowledge no more accounts for the existence of women than does men's account for the existence of humanity.

When I began this book I had no knowledge of books of the early 1970s written by women of colour, but I have since found that this was not because they did not exist. In the United States women of colour were writing about sexism and racism – Toni Cade Bambara among them – but their books did not reach England or Australia. One of my reasons for writing this book was that I was concerned to establish that publication in itself is not enough, and that to preserve our women's heritage we must consciously and consistently re-state and remind ourselves in relation to the women – and the ideas – that constitute that heritage. Yet it is a white heritage that I am presenting here. For women of colour, publication is not sufficient: their voices must become an integral part of that restatement and that reminder, or feminism will continue to fail in the terms that Andrea Dworkin has set out.

This omission of the experience of women of colour was one of the issues that Andrea Dworkin was concerned to bring to the forefront, but equally determined that women's struggle should not be divorced from other struggles for liberation was Sheila Rowbotham, whose highly influential trilogy was published in Britain during the early 1970s: *Women, Resistance and Revolution* (1972); *Woman's Consciousness, Man's World* (1973); and *Hidden from History* (1974).[1]

Sheila Rowbotham was conscious of the very real predicament of women who wanted to ensure the liberation of all people from the oppression of class, race and sex, but who found themselves oppressed within the very movement for such liberation. What were the possibilities and priorities for women in this contradictory context? she asked, in *Women, Resistance and Revolution* (1972):

Women have come to revolutionary consciousness by means of ideas, actions and organizations which have been made predominantly by

164

men. We only know ourselves in societies in which masculine power and masculine culture dominate, and can only aspire to an alternative in a revolutionary movement which is male defined. [p.11]

For Sheila Rowbotham, language, meaning and the symbolic order were a crucial and constant problem when it came to working out what women should do: 'We are obscured in "brotherhood",' she wrote, 'and the liberation of "mankind". The language which makes us invisible to "history" is not coincidence, but part of our real situation in a society and in a movement we do not control' (1972: 11).

Yet for Sheila Rowbotham the choices which seemed available were not choices at all, for each represented a loss, an omission, a denial. Women could stay within the socialist movement, she reasoned, but the loss and the pain would be as great as women's newly awakened consciousness and reality would once more be denied, damaged, destroyed. The alternative, as she saw it, was for women to go it alone, to work *first* for women's liberation and to take up capitalism (and racism) *after* the women's revolution had been won. But this too was a distortion, a denial of the pain of others, and it would require women to isolate themselves from forms of oppression which still applied to women (1972: 12).

She continued to pursue the pathway of women's meanings more specifically in *Woman's Consciousness, Man's World* (1973), where she undertakes a systematic analysis of women's exclusion from the meanings and culture of a male-dominated society, and the implications this has for women's consciousness. 'We are not included in the notion now of what is human. Nor are we part of the alternatives made by men' (p.xi), she writes in the Introduction, and she warns against dismissing the entire framework in order to begin again, because as our consciousness as women is also confined to what we know, to the language we have available, we may simply reproduce the patterns of oppression in reverse. What we must do, she says, is to *transform* existing meanings, since 'The immediate response when you grasp this is to deny all culture, because everything that has been created, all universal values, all notions of what we are, have been made in a society in which men are dominant.' But this would be counter-productive, for the 'problem created by simply rejecting everything that is, and inverting existing male values to make a female culture out of everything not male, is that the distortions of oppression are perpetuated' (p.xi).

Reading Sheila Rowbotham it becomes increasingly apparent that some of the distinctions which have been made over the years between socialist feminism and radical feminism are based on little substance. Many of Mary Daly's concerns, for example, are echoed in Sheila Rowbotham, and many of Sheila Rowbotham's words would not look out of place in Mary Daly. 'There is also the question of language,' writes Sheila Rowbotham (1973). 'As soon as we learn words we find ourselves outside them . . . . Language conveys a certain power. It is one of the instruments of domination. It is carefully guarded by the superior people because it is one of the means through which they conserve their supremacy' (p.32). And where Mary Daly talks of 'recycling' existing words so that they are appropriate for our purposes, Sheila Rowbotham states that 'We can't just occupy existing words. We have to change the meanings of words even before we take them over' (p.33).

Sheila Rowbotham also returns to the concept of 'A man is in the right being a man, it is the woman who is in the wrong' (p.34), which was first put forward by Simone de Beauvoir and later elaborated by Kate Millett among others: 'Every time a woman describes to a man any experience which is specific to her as a woman, she confronts his recognition of his own experience as normal. More than this, his experience of how he sees the "norm" is reinforced by the dominant ideology which tells both him and the woman that he is right' (p.35). This is the experience of women being unable to find ourselves in existing culture as we experience ourselves, and this is a problem which is intensified by our own absence of history, of past, of a sense of where to locate ourselves.

It was the pressing need to find women's past in order to have meaning in the present which prompted the third of Sheila Rowbotham's trilogy, *Hidden from History: Three Hundred Years of Women's Oppression and the Fight Against It* (1974). Lost women, women who had been ignored, excluded, denied in our cultural heritage were reclaimed by Sheila Rowbotham in this positive re-creation of women's past. *Stella Browne: Socialist Feminist* (1977) is her biography of one such woman who asserted the right of women to control their own bodies against men's power of sexual ownership, and who also sought to transform the economic system. 'Her socialism and her feminism involved her in a continuing double struggle,' and 'It also made her search for connections which have been raised again by the contemporary women's movement' (p.7). Among the connections are those of male dominance with male knowledge. Regardless of the position held within feminism, the focus always turns to male authority at some stage as a principal and continuing source of women's oppression.

Two women who make this point superbly well with their documentation of the practical detail of male authority are Barbara Ehrenreich and Deirdre English in *For Her Own Good: One Hundred and Fifty Years of the Experts' Advice to Women* (1978, 1979). They too had begun to question the male-as-norm (particularly in relation to women's health) in two pamphlets first published in 1973, *Complaints and Disorders: The Sexual Politics of Sickness* and *Witches, Midwives and Nurses: A History of Women Healers*. These were the beginnings of an entirely new area of women's knowledge on women's health. Whereas Phyllis Chesler had pointed out that the ethic of mental health was male in our society, Barbara Ehrenreich and Deirdre English made it equally apparent in *Complaints and Disorders* that the ethic of health *per se* was male, and that this had enormous implications for the construction of women's illness.

Turning to the issue which makes its presence persistently felt throughout feminist theory, Barbara Ehrenreich and Deirdre English begin *Complaints and Disorders* with the statement that 'The medical system is strategic to women's liberation' because it is the guardian of reproductive technology and holds the promise of freedom from hundreds of unspoken fears and complaints. But, they add, 'the medical system is also strategic to women's oppression for medical science is a primary and powerful source of sexist ideology. Theories of male superiority ultimately rest on biology,' and male-dominated medical science generates many of the *meanings* of biological difference and constructs many of the justifications for male supremacy. While Shulamith Firestone elected to get rid of the biological distinctions so that such meanings of superior/inferior (and healthy/sick) could not be constructed, Barbara Ehrenreich and Deirdre English go further and propose getting rid of many of the members of the medical profession who continue to hold the values that determine that 'Medicine's prime contribution to sexist ideology has been to describe women as sick, and as potentially sickening to men' (p.9).

Medical practitioners may not have invented the belief that women are sick, they argue.[2] But then the medical profession didn't need to invent such a value-system: it was already encoded in a patriarchal society, and medical science, as a product of a male-dominated society,

167

invests science with the values of male dominance. Alongside the *normal* male, female *differences* can immediately be defined as strange, defective, pathological – and sick. Pregnancy and menopause can be treated as a disease, menstruation a chronic disorder; childbirth a surgical event. We only have to take the lesson provided by Gloria Steinem on how different it would be if men could menstruate to realise how the world would change if it was the 'superior' male who became pregnant and gave birth!

But along with the diagnosis of something wrong with women in a male-dominated society is the fear of contamination, argue Barbara Ehrenreich and Deirdre English:

> If woman is sick there is always the danger that she will infect men. Menstrual and *post partum* taboos, which serve to protect males from female 'impurity', are almost universal in human cultures . . . . Historically, medicine ratified the dangers of women by describing women as the source of venereal disease. Today, we are more likely to be viewed as mental health hazards – emasculating men and destructively dominating children. (p.10)

The development of the medical profession is the theme pursued in *Witches, Midwives and Nurses,* and it takes on a particular political significance given the fact that in other societies – and historically in our own – 'Women have always been healers' (p.19). Finding and presenting this crucial history of women as healers (which is conveniently excluded from men's version of their past), Barbara Ehrenreich and Deirdre English provide a new perspective on women's health and skills, and by undermining the male claim for 'authority', they start to generate a new confidence in women to control our own bodies. Women

> were the unlicensed doctors and anatomists of western history. They were abortionists, nurses and counsellors. They were pharmacists, cultivating healing herbs and exchanging the secrets of their uses. They were midwives, travelling from home to home and village to village. For centuries women were doctors without degrees, barred from books and lectures, learning from each other, and passing on experience from neighbor to neighbor and mother to daughter. (p.19)

Healing had been women's knowledge, based on women's meanings, and part of women's culture. And because it was women's knowledge, it was dangerous knowledge in a male-dominated world: it was the 'wise' women – the healers – who were frequently classified as witches by men threatened by women's knowledge.

How did women arrive at the present position of subservience,[3] from their former position of leadership? ask the authors. And in the answer lies a very grim tale: women's knowledge challenged male 'authority' so men annihilated it, often by getting rid of the women who possessed the knowledge itself. 'The stakes of the struggle were high,' declare Barbara Ehrenreich and Deirdre English. 'Political and economic monopolization of medicine meant control over its institutional organizations, its theory and practice, its profits and prestige. And the stakes are even higher today, when total control of medicine means potential power to determine who will live and who will die, who is fertile and who is sterile, who is "mad" and who is sane' (p.20).

The 1970s witnessed the birth of the women's health movement with many publications on the theory and practice of women's health (as well as many campaigns, and the establishment of numerous clinics). This growth of women's knowledge has had some impact on the medical profession itself: droves of women descending on doctors armed with *Our Bodies Ourselves* (1971) or some equivalent publication have forced the medical profession in some instances to revise a few of its practices.[4] Medical science has in a sense been demystified for women (that is, it has been denuded of its trappings of male authority) and alternative medical theories and practices have been widely developed (WEL – Woman Clinics being one such example in England). But while it is fair to state that some women have been able to regain part of their traditional knowledge and skill as healers – and are in a position to question male authority and its presumption of technological solutions – the majority of women still find themselves in the hands of the male medical profession, and for them there has been little qualitative change. A male-dominated medical profession continues to have control over the power to decide life and death, sterility and fertility, madness and sanity. The realisation that women's knowledge is a serious threat to the established power-base will probably be the same for us as it was for our foremothers – attempts will be made to outlaw our knowledge, to make women's efforts to be responsible for our own health appear immoral and dangerous, and to rule them illegal.

But from these beginnings of women defining women's bodies as normal (rather than as male with missing details, and mysterious parts that inexplicably malfunction) has come a whole range of understandings not just about women's bodies, but also about women's power. Such knowledge ranges from Mary O'Brien's *The Politics of Reproduction* (1981) to self-help manuals on artificial insemination, and includes information on abortion and birth control (*Woman's Body, Woman's Right,* Linda Gordon, 1977) and women's use of tranquillisers in a patriarchal society.

The way in which women's bodies are moulded to meet the needs and interests of the dominant sex – and the consequences this has for women – is explored in books like *Fat is a Feminist Issue* (Susie Orbach, 1978) and *Womansize: The Tyranny of Slenderness* (Kim Chernin, 1983) along with a range of books and reports on gynaecological mutilation. The concept of woman as whole and autonomous has also been a basis for developing understandings about women's sexuality: and with sexuality and heterosexuality come the knowledge from women's experience about pornography, violence and rape.

Against Our Will (1975, 1976) stands as the most shocking book I have ever read. Susan Brownmiller introduces it with 'A Personal Statement' in which she acknowledges that she is a woman who changed her mind about rape. I identify with her completely when she outlines what some of her ideas were about rape when she writes, 'That these attitudes might be antifemale never occurred to me. It also did not occur to me that acceptance of these attitudes gave me a feeling of security I needed: it can't happen here' (p.8). Rape was not something I had thought about seriously: a combination of hazardous surroundings, a 'deranged' mind and the crucial ingredient of the provocative woman. As I was careful, and not provocative, then there was little chance it would happen to me. . . . The simple assertion of Susan Brownmiller that rape is a conscious process of intimidation by which *all* men keep *all* women in a state of fear, not only fundamentally changed my view of the world but made me aware of the extent to which my understanding had been colonised by male meanings and had led me to deny my experience as a woman. The fear that I had concealed, the 'care' that I had taken, the daily habits of my life that were designed to dispel any signs of provocativeness, the pervasiveness of it all and in the cause of 'protection' were nothing but the habiliment of submission.

More than any other book, *Against Our Will* convinced me of the power of meaning, for I began reading it with the view that rape was avoidable and I followed that systematic and stark evidence of women's experience for page after page until just about every meaning I had required scrutiny, and change. At the end of that book I understood that if the evidence and reality of rape could be made so insignificant, if the pervasiveness of male intimidation could be made such a non-event, if women could even be held responsible for this violence against them, then truly it was possible to construct the sweetest of meanings from the foulest of events. After reading Susan Brownmiller's book, everything I knew was suspect for, having been so completely and crucially duped, how could I be sure that it would not happen again – or was not happening now – with another set of meanings?

Against Our Will stands as women's meaning in a male-dominated society: it is the other side of male power, the receiving-end, the reality outside male experience, the picture that patriarchy does *not* present.

The concept of men at the centre of the universe and with the rest of the world at their disposal to be mastered, exploited, used for their own purposes, is not confined to female human resources. The extension of this mind-set to the planet – the rape of nature – is one that has been developed by many feminists: Susan Griffin, *Woman and Nature* (1984), Carolyn Merchant, *The Death of Nature* (1982) and Leonie Caldecott and Stephanie Leland, *Reclaim the Earth* (1983). All reveal that women's experience of the world has helped to generate a different perspective on nature partly because – as Kate Millett pointed out – women are identified with nature in a patriarchal society as a means of curtailing their development. In the last decade an extensive feminist literature has emerged which takes some of its meanings from the 'natural' world and not only gives central significance to ecology but which sees an ecological world view with all its interlinking cycles as a more appropriate conceptual framework. While we know very little that can be relied upon, there is some justification for asserting that at least there is a pattern to the seasons, and a high degree of probability that, like other species, we shall all die. Instead of assiduously avoiding these insights it could be more profitable to base our understandings of the world on this ecological model. To adopt such a framework would make a significant difference to our explanations, even to our explanations of the women's movement, for example. Rather than judging the women's movement in the context of linear development in which we are beset by backlashes and takeovers, we could begin to see its cyclical changes in terms of the seasons and be confident that even with the onset of winter, it is more than likely that spring will follow.

The feminist criticism of the linear, cause-and-effect pattern (and of the arrogance of empiricism) has been extended to scientific method. Many books are appearing which question the authority of science and the limitations of its method. Evelyn Reed was among the first, in *Sexism and Science* (1978), to take up the point that scientific measurements were very much the product of the value-system of the scientific measurer.[5] Was it the maleness of the measurer that concluded from the presence of only one male in an animal pack that he was the leader, and not just a portable sperm bank?

More recently there have been a number of books which have put the scientific method under the microscope and found it wanting: Marian Lowe and Ruth Hubbard compiled an excellent critique in *Woman's Nature: Rationalizations of Inequality* (1983). This was followed by Ruth Bleir's *Science and Gender* (1984) and Louise Newman's *Men's Ideas: Women's Realities* (forthcoming). Joan Rothschild makes much the same criticism of technology as that outlined in relation to science in her *Machina Ex Dea: Feminist Perspectives on Technology* (1983), and with her book begun in the 1920s and published in 1983, *The Religion of the Machine Age*, Dora Russell reveals that there is little that is new about the male value-system and its manifestation in science and technology, and little that is new about women's reservations towards 'machines' as solutions. Only men, she insists, could ever have believed that machines were the sole answer to human problems and could have accordingly created a cult of machine-worship. From the worship of machines have come the terrifying machines of war; the drift towards the final and anti-human solution in Dora Russell's terms.

Her thesis has been given resonance by more recent publications such as Anna Gyorgy's *No Nukes* (1979) and Cynthia Enloe's *Does Khaki Become You? The Militarisation of Women's Lives* (1983). In stark contrast to the logic of war has come a range of women's understandings about the logic and necessity of peace. Following in the tradition of Virginia Woolf's *Three Guineas* (1938), there have been many books which link the male ideology of dominance with war,[6] and which suggest that an end to the threat of war will only be achieved with the end of the male ideology of dominance.[7] Even according to male ideology, less than half the human population has been designated as 'aggressive' and in need of 'conquests' and, on the grounds of majority rule, justice – and 'turn-taking' – there is a strong feminist argument for the desirablility of the introduction of cooperation and peace.

With the women's liberation movement's coming of age in the mid-1970s, there was also the emergence of knowledge on this new knowledge, as women began systematically to study and evaluate their own processes. Surprisingly, there has been no publication devoted to consciousness-raising and its significance, although Cheris Kramarae (1981) emphasises its importance in her book on language. There have, however, been books that are concerned with the way women cooperate and organise along non-hierarchical lines. In *The Politics of Women's Liberation* (1975), Jo Freeman raised the thorny question of when the equality of every member of the group can become 'the tyranny of structurelessness'. That there have been difficulties to overcome in relation to the development of processes and strategies which are consistent with feminist aims of non-exclusion and egalitarianism could never be disputed. There were few (if any) models which could be emulated and, themselves the products of patriarchal society, women had little (or no) practical experience of viable alternatives on which to draw. Of necessity, the attempt to formulate different means of operating in the world must be a matter of trial-and-error and it would be unrealistic to have expected women to find instant solutions. That different strategies have been tried, evaluated and modified is no indication that women have got it wrong: on the contrary, such self-analysis and evaluation as that provided by Jo Freeman is evidence of health and dynamism within the movement. It is the unwillingness to learn or to change that is suspect; the inability to entertain another point of view and to resort to dogma, which is open to criticism.

But the new knowledge on the new knowledge was not confined to self-questioning. There was also one book that was a celebration: *A Group Called Women: Sisterhood and Symbolism in the Feminist Movement* (1977) by Joan Cassell is an account of the value of the women's movement for the women who are in it. While it contains as many meanings for the movement as there are women who are part of it, there can be no doubt about the positive role it has played in so many women's lives.[8]

Part of the examination of the nature and structure of the women's movement were books which tried to explain the resurgence of the modern movement, such as Maren Lockwood-Carden, *The New*

Feminist Movement (1974), as well as those which tried to explain what happened to previous women's movements. Immense energy went into reclaiming women's past so that it could be used to illuminate women's present and provide a basis for women's future. And it wasn't just the more recent past which became the focus of historical research. Merlin Stone, for example, went right back as far as women could go in *The Paradise Papers: The Suppression of Women's Rites* (1977). Her aim was to establish the possibilities of woman power and to explain how and why it was taken over.

That the Judeo-Christian religion had much to answer for when it came to the oppression of women was an accusation that wasn't focused entirely on the distant past either: that patriarchal religions were still constructing, explaining and perpetuating women's inferiority was the thesis of numerous books, many of which advocated the validity of a female deity and sought a realm for the development of women's spirituality. With the unearthing of women's past came the evidence that much of the intellectual work that women were doing had already been done before. All the arguments against patriarchal religion, for example, had already been superbly put by two outstanding nineteenth-century American feminists, Matilda Joslyn Gage and Elizabeth Cady Stanton. Their books, *Woman, Church and State* (1873) and *The Woman's Bible* (1898), were reclaimed and reprinted, along with many other volumes which comprised women's heritage, and which had been suppressed (some would say *stolen* – Matilda Joslyn Gage among them).

The excitement, confidence – and anger – that women felt when they came to recognise women's past as one of persistent protest against patriarchy was sufficient proof that the dominant sex knew what it was doing when it omitted women from history. For it makes an enormous difference to women's consciousness to know that women have been resisting and rebelling against male authority for centuries. And it is precisely because it makes such a difference when women know about their revolutionary foremothers that there has been a systematic attempt to keep them from knowing.[9] Even women of past generations had identified this strategy at work, and their own 'disappearance' therefore has added ironic weight. The reclaiming of Margaret Fuller (Marie Mitchell Olesen Urbanski, 1980), of Matilda Joslyn Gage (Mary, Daly 1980; Sally Roesch Wagner, 1980) and Mary Ritter Beard (Ann Lane, 1977), who were all determined to preserve women's history, has directed the contemporary women's movement towards the contemp-

174

lation of its own fate. Will we too disappear, to be written up for future generations as mere reformers, committed to a single issue and really not worth bothering about when it comes to historical consideration? As yet, there is no book devoted to this topic, but research on women's history has helped to highlight it, and to place it at the forefront of our concerns.

The contributions to women's history are far too numerous to list but Gerda Lerner's research has done much to make women aware that they should not believe all they are taught. Her early publication *Black Women in White America: A Documentary History* (1973) represents one attempt to include the experience of black women. *The Grimké Sisters from South Carolina: Pioneers for Woman's Rights and Abolition* (1971) also helps to reveal some of the diversity among white women and to discredit the myth that *all* southern white women were accomplices in the institutionalisation of slavery and impervious to the sufferings of their black sisters.

A lesson that has been well learnt from the recognition of women's past is that experience in the world is most assuredly not the same for women as it is for men: for example, when women had *fewer* rights after the French Revolution than before it, there is little likelihood that women would label this period as one of 'liberation'. So even the conventional historical divisions and the significance attached to them have been inappropriate and unacceptable for women. It is not the simple task of adding on women's experience to the male records which confronts feminist historians. The very inclusion of women makes a nonsense of many of the male records, with the result that feminist historians have had to formulate a new framework which begins with women's experience. Such a framework leads to a very different version of the past. Historians such as Berenice Carroll (*Liberating Women's History: Theoretical and Critical Essays*, 1976) and Judith Walkowitz (*Prostitution and Victorian Society: Women, Class and the State*, 1980) have made a valuable contribution both in terms of content and theory.

In law, management, business studies and economics it has equally proved to be impossible just to add women to the picture, for the introduction of women changes the whole picture. Can we speak of fair and just laws, asks Ann Jones (1980), when a woman who finds herself in a fight with a man, finds herself at an immense disadvantage, and also finds that she will be severely punished for trying to make it a more equal contest? For a women who *does* try to equalise the struggle (by picking up a weapon, striking from the rear, or by premeditation to reduce the male advantage) is guilty of a crime in a way that no man – regardless of his advantages of size, strength or training – is ever guilty of in a conflict with a woman.

That women weren't suitable for management, that they had neither the necessary aptitude nor skills was a myth exploded by Rosabeth Moss Kanter (1977), who made it plain that if women weren't in management it was because men were there first, and determined to keep the place for themselves. And Lisa Leghorn and Katherine Parker started to ask some very awkward questions about economics in their book, *Woman's Worth* (1981): if men were so keen to measure in terms of production, they challenged, why didn't they include in their statistics the production by women of leisure for men? The world over, women were working harder to produce more leisure-time for men, and it was an absurdity not to include this in the GNP. Their book also helped to raise the issue of what leisure *is* for women, what places are allocated for it, what form it takes.

Most sporting complexes are the domain of men (with women permitted entry under certain circumstances) and today in Britain (and until recently in the United States) a breakdown of the expenditure on men's and women's sporting facilities in educational institutions serves as a stark reminder of our inequality. It has even been argued that if a fraction of the money spent on football and cricket pitches were spent on childcare facilities at universities, then perhaps women *would* have leisure-time – and the opportunity to avail themselves of the squash or tennis facilities.

The allocation of space to men has also been seriously questioned in relation to the arts. 'Why have there been no great women artists?' asked Linda Nochlin (1972). Her answer was far from the official one, which holds that women are not capable of reaching the standard of great art. Linda Nochlin's article was directed towards the standard-makers and raised the awkward and political issue of why men persisted in defining women's art as inferior. So that women could judge for themselves whether it was women who failed to be excellent artists or whether it was men who refused to admit women's excellence, Rozsika Parker and Griselda Pollock, in their book *Old Mistresses* (1981), included a range of women's excellent art which men had deemed unworthy of inclusion in art history, and had omitted from the record of great artists. (As with many literary works, when it was extremely difficult to deny the excellence, the artistic work of a woman was frequently attributed to a man. This practice – which was commented on by Aphra Behn in the seventeenth century – still persists in many places.)

Even the question of what constitutes art is relevant in the context in which men determine the definitions: it is no coincidence that they perceive men's traditional pursuits as 'art' and women's as 'handicraft'. However, a range of women's definitions of art is beginning to emerge and books such as Judy Chicago's *The Dinner Party: A Symbol of Our Heritage* (1977) help to create and define women's meanings, including the meaning of women's exclusion from man's culture.

Once more there is the evidence that those who are in charge of meanings and standards use their position to ensure that they continue to be in charge of meanings and standards. For contemporary feminism, then, pragmatics dictates that the issue is not so much one of *why* men originally attained control, but of *how* male dominion can be ended. Because, despite all the gains – the successful campaigns, the changes in the law, the proliferation of women's books – while men control the meanings and the standards, while men continue to define everything from health to art, they are able to decree that what men are and do, counts; and what women are and do, does not. So even if women were to be allowed the scope for equal achievement, in the end it would be valued as less than male achievement.

Nowhere is this tenet better illustrated than in literature. What few statistics we do have in relation to writing are drawn from education, where examination results lead us to believe that female students write more and that what they write is better. But when such good women students enter the world of work – when they begin to compete with men for jobs and for recognition – we find the pattern is dramatically changed. Women have never been more than 20 per cent of the published writers;[10] women comprise fewer than 7 per cent of the writers studied in literature courses in higher education in the USA (Joanna Russ, 1983) and probably fewer still in the UK (Dale Spender, 1984b); in England, women comprise fewer than 3 per cent of the writers prescribed for A-level courses; and over a six-month period in 1982, in a variety of review publications in Britain, less than 6 per cent of the column inches of review space was devoted to women's books (Dale Spender, 1984b).

Such figures make it quite clear that while women may be perfectly able to write as much and as well as – if not better than – men, because men control what is selected as good, worthy or publishable, then in every area where these judgements are made, women are excluded. Numerous feminist books and articles have set out the way in which men exercise their 'gatekeeping' function to keep women out of the class of writers who carry weight in our culture.[11] Joanna Russ (1983) and Lynne Spender (1983) have shown how women are eliminated at the first hurdle – that of publication. The second hurdle is that of evaluation, and again women are eliminated on a large scale by reviewers (who tend to provide no press coverage) and literary critics. Increased attention is being given to the systematic bias against women's writing and Annette Kolodny (1981) is among some of the many feminists who have challenged the partiality of the literary canon with its peculiar and patriarchal entry qualifications.

But *being* in print is not the final list of achievement: *staying* in print is also important. Many are the stories that today's women writers can tell about small print-runs, and out-of-print periods. The fact that Shulamith Firestone (among others) has been out of print for some time in the United States is not insignificant. That so many good women writers have been eliminated by being 'allowed' to go out of print by a male-dominated industry is startlingly illustrated by the Virago reprint series. (For some time now I have heard mutterings that soon the pile of 'forgotten' women writers must be exhausted, but the list continues to grow and the books continue to be good.) And while I am energised by the rediscovery of all these wonderful women writers, for me each reprint publication is also a reminder of the extent to which women of the past were not in charge of their own publishing fate, and nor are women in the present. The feminist publishing houses have made a valuable contribution – and a great difference – by removing some of the hurdles that men have set up for women, but feminist publishers also operate in a patriarchal world and it is absolutely fundamental that their political achievement is preserved.

Many contemporary feminists have reclaimed some of the women writers of the past: such publications are too numerous to mention but among them are Cora Kaplan's *Aurora Leigh and Other Poems* (1978) and Ellen Moers, *Literary Women: The Great Writers* (1978). In *A Literature of Their Own* (1977) Elaine Showalter reconstructs the 'lost' tradition of women writers who have been *sent* out of print, and questions the authenticity of the assertion that the novel is 'a woman's form'. If the novel is indeed where women are permitted to excel, why isn't women's fiction at the heart of our understandings of fiction? Elaine

Showalter indicates that the basis for this belief in the novel as a woman's form rests on the acceptance of a 'token' woman in the different literary periods and amounts to nothing other than a constant recycling of the 'famous five' – Jane Austen, Charlotte Brontë, George Eliot, Virginia Woolf and Doris Lessing.

I am by no means surprised to find that in the male frame of reference, the admission of five women to the select circle of the great is considered sufficiently threatening to the male monopoly to produce the defensive strategy of declaring the area overrun by women. In any space that a dominant group reserves as its right (and men of letters certainly see the pen as their prerogative; see Sandra Gilbert and Susan Gubar, 1979) the entry of even a few 'others' is perceived as too many. So 3 per cent of women in a non-traditional occupation, for example, can be construed as women taking over the occupation; 6 per cent of review space allocated to women can be seen as women having more than their share of column inches; more than 33 per cent of the talk done by women can be taken as evidence that women are domineering. Why not five great women novelists, and the novel as a woman's form?

Many women writers have understood the odds that are stacked against them when it comes to literary acceptance – Aphra Behn, Margaret Fuller, Elizabeth Barrett, Virginia Woolf, Tillie Olsen and Adrienne Rich, to name but a few. They have understood the requirement that they write for male acceptance because it is men who decide what is to be accepted. 'No male writer has written primarily or even largely for women, or with the sense of women's criticism as a consideration when he chooses his material, his theme, his language,' wrote Adrienne Rich in 1971. 'But to a lesser or greater extent, every woman writer has written for men even when, like Virginia Woolf, she was supposed to be addressing women' (Rich, 1980: 37–8).

And this brings me to a fundamental area, where I must confess to disappointment: education. While there have been numerous books on women and education, most have been well within the male framework with the emphasis on a better deal for girls within the prevailing system, rather than with any serious consideration of an alternative system. Taken completely for granted in many of the books on education that I have read is the validity of learning based on competition. Few are the feminists who have questioned the sanity of a system that is based on failure, where each year the number allowed to continue to learn is systematically (sometimes drastically) decreased in the interests of constructing the hierarchically organised order that we are asked to believe is natural. Few are the feminists who have questioned the justice of a system which decrees that those who are least capable of learning (a concept in itself with which I would quarrel) should be given the shortest time in which to learn. While we might have become quite sophisticated in our identification of the process whereby a male-dominated society constructs the female, we have barely scratched the surface of understandings of the means whereby that same society constructs the concept and reality of hierarchy. Yet if we didn't know about hierarchies, if our value-system was not founded on distinctions between superior and inferior, then we would have no way of perceiving male supremacy, and sex differences could well be meaningless. (An argument with which Shulamith Firestone would be most familiar.)

That feminist knowledge and women's studies have not progressed along this path is something of a puzzle, for not only were some of the early feminists (such as Kate Millett and Shulamith Firestone) scathing in their denunciations of education as a system, but the very process of consciousness-raising itself should have alerted women to the failures in the existing system and the potential alternatives for learning and knowing. How could one return to the sterile halls of academe and memorise abstract learning theories which bear not the slightest resemblance to the way one was learning in a consciousness-raising group? When a mixed-ability group of women who had passed no entry test, who had no 'teacher', no syllabus, grades, tests or journals all proved capable of learning some of the most life-shattering truths, what realities had to be denied to accept the educational dictum that some there are who can 'pass' but the rest must 'fail'? What contradictions have to be ignored in educational institutions where cooperation and the sharing of knowledge – the very heart and substance of con-sciousness-raising – has been called cheating, and been punished? When the very basis of educational knowledge has been found to be flawed and biased – found to be a political weapon that had been used against women – what accommodations have to be made so that women can work within the academy to produce knowledge on women by using many of the old, discredited methods?

In feminist circles today, I still hear the assertions that some work is not up to 'standard', but rarely do I hear discussion on the origin of standards. I know of no books (or courses) which are directed towards an analysis of the political dimensions of this concept. Yet if we made explicit what we already know – that the standards of our society are the standards of men and are used to exclude women – we could not continue to subscribe to the concept of standards. We would demand to know *whose* standards were being used to determine the value of a particular piece of work or of a particular person.

What does it mean to be scholarly when the methods of scholarship have been found so wanting? What does it mean to be 'objective' when objectivity has been exposed as a male name for unquestioned male authority? What does it mean to excel (or even to be accepted) in a domain such as the academy which continues to demonstrate its unmodified misogyny? Does it mean that women should stay *outside* the academy?

Virginia Woolf believed that it did. She would have nothing to do with formal education and its trappings of prestige (she refused to accept any honorary degrees). In *Three Guineas* (1938), she put forward the well-reasoned and well-documented argument that education, as it was then constructed, was based on competition and its inevitable outcome was hierarchies, dominance and war. So she urged women to be *outsiders*, to remain *outside* the halls of learning and to forge their own knowledge from their own frame of reference. Hers is the supreme rationale for independent women's studies courses.

To discredit and to disregard some of the sanctified values of the educational enterprise is not (necessarily) to throw away everything and to have nothing to put in its place. But if there are to be criteria of excellence and reliability, then surely we should form them ourselves from our own framework and invest them with our own (political) values. Surely it is possible for us to be aware of what we are doing. Perhaps we would still want standards, but we would be in a position to know who was setting them and why, and we could keep them under our own scrutiny and be prepared for constant revision. Perhaps we would still want 'objective' studies – although given the rapidity with which one 'objective' study is overturned by another which professes to be more 'objective' (but which is just as quickly overturned), I would want to go for something more reliable, enduring and helpful. Forming a basis for reliability is not such a difficult task. We didn't have much trouble accepting the reliability of women's evidence about their lives in consciousness-raising groups, although it was the same evidence that for decades social scientists had been rejecting as unreliable and non-data. And research which continues to express the voices of women (as does Ann Oakley's, for example) is reliable and remains reliable: it does not get overthrown by next weeks' dramatic discovery (or invention) of a new hormone.

At the very heart of feminist knowledge should be the critique of – and the alternatives to – knowledge (and learning), because it seems to me that at the very heart of the feminist endeavour to end the oppression of women is the necessity to end the male monopoly on knowledge- and meaning-making. For no matter what women achieve, no matter what gains are made, as Elizabeth Janeway states in *Powers of the Weak* (1980), while men remain in charge of the decisions about what is important and significant, they are able to decree women's achievement as unimportant and insignificant. And while they continue to do this, women continue to be oppressed.

I do not think it unreasonable to expect that these fundamental issues of knowledge and knowing should come well within the ambit of feminist educationalists, yet apart from some of the valuable work of Florence Howe and Charlotte Bunch, little reference has been made to these crucial issues. I appreciate that there is little within the discipline of education itself which would prepare or direct women towards consideration of the politics of knowledge, for it is the reiterated (but none the less erroneous) assertion of most educationalists that knowledge is free from the contaminating influence of politics (which is itself, of course, a highly political assertion). But somehow we have to break free from the mind-deadening belief that knowledge can exist apart from those who know it, and we have to take a highly critical look at the very people who are making up what we know.

Sexist images in children's books, biases against women in science and mathematics, neglect of female students in the classroom, partiality in grading and counselling women, and even a curriculum which is primarily about men and male achievements (Dale Spender, 1982b), are not the *root* problem of patriarchal education, but the manifestation of a patriarchal value-system. We may be able to remove some of the sexist images, allay some of the anxiety about mathematics, ensure that girls get equal access to the teacher's attention – and even to the computer – and introduce courses on women's literature and women's history; but unless we tackle the patriarchal value-system itself – a value-system which discounts women – then the sexism will be removed from one area, only to reappear in another. And then we shall have to start all over again.

This is what happened in the past. In the nineteenth century in Britain when it was Latin and Greek that was the entry qualification for positions of influence, it was widely established that women could not 'do' languages. Over the last few decades the entry qualifications have shifted to mathematics and science, and suddenly women are very good at languages – but are not competent at maths and science. Women educationalists have therefore put energy into establishing that women *can* do mathematics and science, if they are allowed to and are given equal treatment. I suspect that at the moment we are in a period of transition and that we are about to see that women are quite good at (old style) mathematics and science. But I don't think this means that the battle has been won – rather, that the power-base is shifting again, this time to 'high-tech'. And the evidence is already mounting that, in men's terms, women aren't very good at 'high-tech'. Should we start all over again, trying to establish that women can not only do languages, and maths and science, but 'high-tech' as well? Or should we see this as another example of men not only in charge of the rules, but prepared to change the rules when it suits them?

While most of this chapter has been concerned with the necessary diversity of women's knowledge and a consideration of the vast range of books that have been written, I have concluded with a consideration of books that have not been written yet. I have done so because I think that they are among the most crucial of books, the ones we need, for unless we are aware of the implications of male control of knowledge, and until we end that monopoly, feminist knowledge can all too readily be dismissed. We have created an enormous amount of knowledge but we also need to protect it and preserve it, and this means we must control it. At the moment we are no closer even to shared control than was Mary Wollstonecraft when she put forward a similar case in 1792.

15. Double Vision:
Adrienne Rich and Mary Daly

Given Adrienne Rich's early warning of the dangers of becoming a part of the university system, it is surprising that women's studies programmes and courses have not taken up this issue as a central research topic. In 1973–4, Adriennne Rich, in her essay 'Toward a Woman-centered University' (1980: 125–55), set out some of the pitfalls she expected women to encounter as feminist members of the academy, drawing on her own experience as well as that of women of previous generations such as Mary Ritter Beard, who had already outlined their reservations about women's membership. Drawing a direct link between her own concerns and those expressed by Virginia Woolf in *Three Guineas* (1938), Adrienne Rich analysed the role that universities played in a patriarchal society and suggested that unless they underwent drastic and fundamental change which oriented them more to social and human (and female) priorities, they would not be, and could not be, fit places for women.

She did not assume that the presence of more women in universities where knowledge was constructed would necessarily lead to the construction of more woman-centred knowledge. She did not assume that once women became members of the university club they would be free to do their own thing and to introduce their own priorities. On the contrary, she argued, the universities have their own rules for members of the club, and anyone who doesn't play by the rules doesn't stay a member for very long. This, she insisted, is why it is mistaken to believe that educational equality could ever consist of women's right of access to the institutions that men have set up for themselves and which they continue to control. Women's current educational rights amount to permission to sit in on men's education, she flatly declared.[1] Far from encouraging and assisting the growth and development of women's interests, what would have been astonishing would have been the capacity of such an educational system to begin to meet some of women's needs.

When men were educated and women were not, and when the justification for the male monopoly on positions of influence was that men were educated (and women were not), then there was no question that women should have demanded any education – let alone the same education as men – just to break the vicious circle, and to eliminate one of the artificially constructed sex differences which rationalised male supremacy. It was quite logical to argue (as Mary Wollstonecraft did) that when *both* sexes were educated, men would no longer be able to claim the exclusive right to power on the grounds that they were the educated sex.

But, remonstrates Adrienne Rich, those days have long since passed: now that women *do* have access to education, we must begin to ask what sort of education is appropriate for the female sex, and for society. We cannot afford unquestioningly to take our places in the system which men have established and which plays such a significant role in the oppression of women.

'As women have gradually and reluctantly been admitted into the mainstream of higher education,' writes Adrienne Rich, 'they have been made participants in a system that prepares men to take up roles of power in a man-centred society, that asks questions and teaches "facts" generated by a male intellectual tradition, and that both subtly and openly confirms men as the leaders and shapers of human destiny both within and outside academia' (p.127). If membership depends upon the ability to perform these feats, then we must ask what part women can play in the club. Adrienne Rich's answer, like that of Virginia Woolf and Mary Beard (and many other women before them), is that what women can do *as women* in universities isn't a lot. *Man* is the centre of gravity in higher education, states Adrienne Rich, and women are only tolerated in so far as they can fulfil *masculine* requirements – the cultivation of the competitive and hierarchical masculine skills that are taken as the symbols of success.

In order to be accredited, women must conduct themselves like men (become 'amateur' or 'honorary' men) and, of course, this pattern of behaviour brings with it its own peculiar problems. For it is patently obvious that no matter how hard women try – how good they get – they

185

can never be men: they fall short of 'the real thing', the norm, and are always suspect. And because they are suspect, women's behaviour can be even more carefully monitored and the evidence of their conformity to male standards more assiduously sought. This can lead to the distressing situation where women who may have joined the club with the express purpose of trying to change the rules to make it easier for future women members find instead that they have less scope than men for introducing changes. It's another example of the way women in positions of influence are constantly scrutinised to see whether they are showing favouritism to other women. What is omitted from this explanation is that patriarchy is founded on the principle of men showing favouritism to men. This is the *status quo*, the world-order that women could well disrupt if they were to hold positions of influence. The result is that many women are coerced into bestowing their patronage on men in order to demonstrate that they are being fair and showing no partiality for their own sex.

It's a pretty grim picture: universities are places which contribute to the oppression of women and yet, if women join them to try and bring about changes in the centre of gravity, as Adrienne Rich terms it, they can find themselves obliged to collude in women's oppression as a means of establishing their credentials for membership.

But if they do not establish their credentials for membership? Why, they can be classified as unscholarly, they can be accused of being biased or political, they can be judged as not up to standard – and their membership can be quickly revoked. This has been the fate of many feminists who have tried to bring women's values into the university which men control. Adrienne Rich wrote that 'only if the center of gravity can be shifted will women really be free to learn, to teach, to share strength, to explore, to criticize, and to convert knowledge to power' (p.128), but among the women who have tried to shift this centre of gravity there have been many academic casualties.

If universities in their present form are hostile to women's aspirations and development, and are resistant to change, what are women to do? If, in Adrienne Rich's words, 'a woman's integrity is likely to be undermined by the process of university education' (p.134), and if we have grave doubts as to 'whether this male-created, male-dominated structure is really capable of serving the humanism and freedom it professes' (p.133), what sort of educational institutions are women to seek? It is not an option to declare that knowledge does not matter, that we shall have

186

no part in it, because we have overwhelming evidence that the knowledge produced in universities plays a significant role in the oppression of women, and we must therefore tackle the issue of the construction of knowledge if we are to begin to deal with the oppression of women.

But where, and by what means, should women start to produce the much-needed, alternative, woman-centred knowledge? Should we stay out of universities altogether, remain outsiders, as Virginia Woolf urged? Should we develop 'women's universities-without-walls', as Mary Ritter Beard advocated? The consciousness-raising sessions of the early 1970s were steps in these directions, but over the last decade there has been an (unanalysed) drift back to the academy, and we have to ask ourselves whether this is where we want to go. I have no evidence that universities have put their house in order, yet we seem to be disregarding Adrienne Rich's warning when we turn to the university in the attempt to find a base for the construction of women's knowledge.

Another alternative – one that has been put forward for centuries by women and which is a possibility entertained by Adrienne Rich – is that of women's colleges. Institutions where women control the content and form of women's education are certainly an attractive proposition and they are not without precedents for, after all, men have taken it as their right to have a male-created and -controlled education for men, and it would be nothing other than genuine equality if women were to insist on the same right for themselves. Yet at the very time when women are weighing the advantages of women's colleges, many of the old and established women's colleges, which our foremothers worked so hard to set up, are disappearing. I do not think it is coincidence. I think it is another example of men changing the rules. In England, Bedford College, the first women's college, is being phased out, and Girton College at Cambridge University – the college that Emily Davies and Barbara Bodichon invested their energies in – is now coeducational and has recently had its first group of male graduates: there are no prizes for guessing which sex took out *all* the best degrees.

With the production of knowledge such a central feature of feminist analysis, women cannot afford to ignore the issue of the purpose and function of the university. It is precisely because universities have been so selective, protective, political and élitist that there is often among women resistance to the very idea of exploring the relationship between the university and feminism. When so many are excluded, it is

187

understandable that women should ask, 'What has the university to do with me?' – and shelve the issue in favour of one of more readily recognised relevance. Yet the influence of the university, as Adrienne Rich points out, is by no means confined to those who enter it. What goes on in universities can influence every member of society.

Universities are linked to the power structures, and so are able to influence the direction of society, the development of its values and priorities, the distribution of its resources. Universities do not undertake *all* possible research, but select areas for research, areas which are designed to attract sponsors, to produce knowledge which is needed by those in power, and which will lend status and prestige to their particular institution and personnel. Universities therefore are channelling us towards weaponry and war, towards aggression and competition, towards technology as an end rather than as a means.

Such universities are not for Adrienne Rich. She can see no place for women in institutions where, in the name of knowledge that will be beneficial to society, 'such distant and faceless masters as "the challenge of Sputnik", Cold War "channeling" or the Air Force' (p.152) are served. What she wants is universities which 'serve the needs of the human, visible community' (p.152). But for universities to do this they would, of course, have to reverse completely their present priorities and practices. Instead of selecting their research to cater for the needs of those who have power, they would select it on the basis of the needs of those who do not. Only then would universities be fit places for women: only then would they be able to produce knowledge which was directed towards liberating and not oppressive ends.

But such universities are no more likely now than they were ten years ago when Adrienne Rich listed her objections. Humane research which is concerned with qualitative improvements in society is rare, and where it does exist (within the academy), it is usually afforded low status and low priority and often regarded as being outside the mainstream of 'real' research. After more than a decade of demands from feminists, the blueprint for the university which Adrienne Rich set out – and in which childcare and community concerns are the central platform and where research is *for* individuals and not *on* them – is no closer to being realised.

Some women have begun to acknowledge the impossibility of university reform. Among them is the Norwegian Berit Ås, who has ceased to put her energies into trying to modify the prevailing system and has turned instead to the task of establishing a feminist university which will be open to all women, of all colours, all ages and all qualifications, and which will attempt to implement the ideas of Adrienne Rich, and those of the long line of feminist educationalists from Mary Astell, Mary Wollstonecraft, Frances Wright, Margaret Fuller and Virginia Woolf to Mary Ritter Beard.[2]

Had the university taken women's protest seriously we would now be witnessing fundamental changes in the curriculum and not the often begrudged provision of some small space (usually in the basement or at the furthest point from amenities) where women are given the most meagre financial assistance and permitted to get on with their 'eccentric' research, on condition that it does not disrupt the serious business of the university. The minimum demand made by Adrienne Rich was that the universities should study their *own* history and practice of woman-hating. As she wrote, 'Misogyny should itself become a central subject of inquiry rather than continue as a desperate clinging to old destructive fears and privileges.' She had her own speculations about university reform: 'It will be interesting to see how many men are prepared to give more than rhetorical support today to the sex from which they have, for centuries, demanded and accepted so much' (p.154). And, indeed, it is interesting to examine what men have done in the face of challenge to their power: there are fewer women in tenured positions in universities in the United States now than there were when Adrienne Rich wrote her article.[3]

Adrienne Rich recognised the *politics* of an institution which professed to produce objective, 'pure' and irrefutable knowledge about the human condition, and which in practice produced knowledge which enhanced the position of one sex and diminished that of the other. With such huge political bias at the core, how could these universities be taken seriously? she asked. When *human* means *male*, a society is blinded and headed on a self-destructive path:

> Outside of women's studies, though liberal male professors may introduce material about women into their courses, we live with textbooks, research studies, scholarly sources, and lectures that treat women as a subspecies, mentioned only as peripheral to the history of men. In every discipline where we *are* considered, women are perceived as the objects rather than the originators of inquiry, thus primarily through male eyes, thus as a special category. That the true

business of civilization has been in the hands of men is the lesson absorbed by every student of the traditional sources. How this came to be and the process that kept it so, may well be the most important question for the self-understanding and survival of the human species; but the extent to which civilization has been built on the bodies and services of women – unacknowledged, unpaid and unprotested in the main – is a subject apparently unfit for scholarly decency. (p.135)

An economics that does not address itself to the *non*-payment of human beings for their work, which does not examine exploitation and the ethics of the rich getting richer and the poor getting poorer? A technology that refuses to count the costs? A psychology permeated with one patriarch's opinion that women must learn to be cheerfully fulfilled in the debased role men have decreed for them? A history that makes no reference to the centuries of male tyranny, which ignores the witch persecutions, although they represent 'one of the great historical struggles – a class struggle and a struggle for knowledge – between the illiterate but practised female healer and the beginnings of an aristocratic *nouveau science*, between the powerful patriarchal church and enormous numbers of peasant women, between the pragmatic experience of the wisewoman and the superstitious practices of the early medical profession' (p.135)? It is no free and open inquiry that universities are engaged in, argues Adrienne Rich; they are in the propaganda business, producing the rationalisations that the white, male masters need.

The phenomena of woman-fear and woman-hatred illuminated by those centuries of gynocide [i.e. the witch hunts] are with us still; certainly a history of psychology or a history of science that was not hopelessly one-sided would have to confront and examine this period and its consequences. Like the history of slave revolts, the history of women's resistance to domination awaits discovery by the offspring of the dominated. (p.135)

And such a discovery is a mammoth task and requires not just material resources:

As the hitherto 'invisible' and marginal agent in culture – whose

190

native culture has been effectively denied, women need a reorganization of knowledge, of perspectives and analytical tools that can help us know our foremothers, evaluate our present historical, political and personal situation, and take ourselves seriously as agents in the creation of a more balanced culture. (p.141)

But universities are unlikely to provide women – or any other 'out-of-power' group – with these resources, for the very good reason that to do so would be effectively to give away their power. To establish a woman-centred university would represent a loss in patriarchal terms, because it would mean the end of a male-centred university and the end of the current links between universities and the prevailing bases of power.

Fortunately for feminism, however, universities have not proved to be indispensable for the production of knowledge. A great deal of feminist research has been conducted – and written up – *outside* the university, in a manner in which women like Frances Wright (who set up the Hall of Free Enquiry) and Margaret Fuller (who set up 'Conversations' for women) would no doubt approve. Admittedly, there are difficulties in being outsiders, but the disadvantages can be offset by the advantages of being able to ask and explore the questions which originate in women's experience of the world, and for which the university has so little tolerance. Just checking through some of the research which I have found most useful and most credible (and, indeed, checking off the authors whose research and writing has been the substance of this book), it has been salutary to note just how little of this feminist research has had the benefit of university backing.

What is becoming increasingly clear is that the knowledge women want and need is not necessarily produced by the model favoured by the universities – the large-scale, expensive, empirical model in which every attempt has been made to eliminate or control the contaminating variables. Much feminist knowledge, like that produced by Adrienne Rich, originates in the experience of women, and is directly concerned with assessing and reassessing those very variables which the objective approach outlaws. It is concerned with the exploration of values and not with the defensive political stance of being value-free (and therefore supposedly beyond question). Research which is *for* human beings calls on skills of sharing, listening and reflecting, and demands an emotional commitment to the development of a better world. It is hardly surprising that such skills and commitment are more likely to flourish in the university-*without*-walls.

Certainly, much of the research that Adrienne Rich has undertaken and which has proved invaluable to many women (and which is crucial for society) would not have been warmly welcomed within the university. Her exposure of racism and her analysis of compulsory heterosexuality are not among the issues the university seeks to scrutinise. Who would be the sponsors of such research? Which section of the white population with sufficient resources would want to *pay* to be informed of how deeply unjust and unjustifiable is the white value-system? Who among the wealthy men would want to *pay* to learn how appalling has been their treatment of women and how systematic has been their coercion which ensures that women are obliged to align themselves with men? Yet this knowledge – which I count among the most valuable, and the most credible – has been produced by Adrienne Rich.

Until questions were raised about who would want and who would pay for particular research, it seemed astonishing that there was virtually no knowledge in our society about motherhood as it is experienced by women, before Adrienne Rich's remarkable book *Of Woman Born: Motherhood as Experience and Institution* (1977). But, of course, the picture of motherhood which she represents and which originates in the lived experience of women, is so far removed from the official version of motherhood (decreed and preferred by men) that it is not at all surprising that men should not have wanted to 'encourage' the construction of such knowledge. Not only does it fail to portray them in a flattering (and superior) light, but it points to the ways in which men have used, exploited and controlled women through institutionalised motherhood – and if such oppression is to continue unproblematically it is best not to draw attention to its operation. This is precisely why Adrienne Rich *did* draw attention to this aspect of male control, and why such knowledge plays a vital part in making the oppression of women problematic.

Probably one of the most awkward questions that Adrienne Rich has raised is why – if heterosexuality is so natural – it has been necessary to set up so many penalties in order to keep women on the heterosexual path. Why should 'such violent structures . . . be found necessary to enforce women's total emotional, erotic loyalty, and subservience to men' if women are innately oriented to behave like this anyway? she

asks in *Compulsory Heterosexuality and the Lesbian Existence* (1981: 9).
And she makes use of the inventory provided by Kathleen Gough (1975)
to outline the awful dimensions of these strictures.[4] Is it that there are
good grounds for suspecting that women might want to relate to
women, and that the system of patriarchy has been devised to make
men central and to redirect women to relate to men? Outside the values
of our male-dominated society it would be perfectly feasible to
speculate in an open way on the possibility that women might prefer to
identify with women; but within the patriarchal framework such an
hypothesis is *loaded*. To suggest that it might make sense for women to
relate to each other as *equals*, rather than to make themselves
vulnerable to their oppressors, borders on the outrageous. It is no
accident, argues Adrienne Rich, that 'there is a taboo against questioning
heterosexuality', while all the focus of the problematic centres on those
who do not conform . 'Yet the failure to examine heterosexuality is like
failing to admit that the economic system called capitalism or the caste
system of racism is maintained by a variety of forces, including both
physical violence and false consciousness' (p.20).

That men have been in charge of the organisation and meanings of
society cannot be disputed, and the organisation and meanings they
have established allocate resources to men, with the result that women
are required to 'trade' themselves to men in return for (limited) access to
these resources. Women who protest that this is not a system to which
they are partial frequently find the full force of the establishment
unleashed upon them. To suggest that it might be a better arrangement
if women were allowed their own resources to utilise in their own way is
to utter a subversive statement in a male-dominated society, and would
spell the beginning of the end of male domination.

And what would men do then? This is no facile question. Admittedly,
the whole of society is constrained by its pattern of thinking in
hierarchical orders, and we can slip into the line of reasoning that once
men are no longer at the top then there is no place for them to go. But
there is also the niggling doubt – openly and fully expressed in a recent
publication, *The Redundant Male* (Cherfas and Gribbin, 1984) – that if
men are no longer made centrally significant in women's lives, men may
have little significance. It is another version of Evelyn Reed's interpretation of one male in the troop: he could be the master of a harem; or
he could merely function as a portable sperm bank. From their present
position, it would be quite a come-down for men to see their function

193

solely in terms of the providers of sperm: it is not a prospect to be relished, as Phyllis Chesler indicated and as Adrienne Rich points out. What men really fear, she writes, is that if the arrangement of compulsory heterosexuality is overturned, 'women could be indifferent to them altogether, that men could be allowed sexual and emotional – therefore economic – access to women *only* on women's terms, otherwise being left on the periphery of the matrix' (p.15).

The other side of requiring women to align themselves with men is the steps that must be taken to prevent women from aligning with women, and it is a painful story that Adrienne Rich tells as she documents the patriarchal measures that have been taken against the woman-identified woman. Once more we are made aware of the massive censorship that has operated to prevent women from knowing the historical (and contemporary) reality of women's relationships to women. We are swamped with a literature of 'male-bonding', but when we seek documentation of 'female-bonding' we encounter only a silence, an absence. This is not because women have not had satisfying and enriching relationships with women, but because the knowledge of this positive aspect of women's lives has been excised from the knowledge of society. When experience is unknown, it is so much more difficult to conceptualise its reality and meaning, so much easier to be led to believe that all that *is* known, is *all* that there is. This is why Adrienne Rich has written that 'The destruction of records and memorabilia and letters documenting the realities of lesbian existence must be taken very seriously as a means of keeping heterosexuality compulsory for women, since what has been kept from our knowledge is joy, sensuality, courage and community, as well as guilt, self-betrayal and pain' (p.21).

But as so many feminists have discovered, it is no simple matter to find woman-centred terminology which can convey what women mean, when for so long men have been in charge of the language. So Adrienne Rich defines her terms of 'lesbian existence' and the 'lesbian continuum' in a way that helps to account for the range of relationships that women have with women. She seeks to avoid the patriarchal connotations of 'sex' – connotations that originate in male consciousness and that have been grossly commercialised. It is no mean feat to dissociate intimate relationships from the mind-set of 'sex' as a rationale for viewing other human beings as a resource available for use. But, at the same time, Adrienne Rich does not want to deny (as patriarchy has done) that there have always been women who have experienced the sensuality of women: hence her use of two terms to embrace the diversity of women's relationships to women.

'*Lesbian existence,*' she writes,' suggests both the fact of the historical presence of lesbians and our continued creation of the meaning of that existence. I mean *lesbian continuum* to include a range – through each woman's life and throughout history – of woman-identified experience' (p.20). If we expand our meanings beyond 'genital sexual experience', she adds, we come closer to understanding the dimensions of women's existence, dimensions that encompass the many 'forms of primary intensity between and among women, including the sharing of a rich inner life, the bonding against male tyranny, the giving and receiving of practical and political support' (p.21).

Adrienne Rich is also concerned that lesbian existence and lesbian continuum should not be seen as *reaction*. If we think that women turn to women simply out of hatred for men, then we have not moved from the premise that the world begins with men. Of course, women can identify with women as a reaction to men, and this reaction is not without its political overtones; but to imply that this is *all* that is embodied in women's relationships with women is to reinforce the idea of woman as secondary. It is absurd to suggest that if only men were to mend their ways all women would cease to register their 'protest' and return to the fold. This is but another denial of women's autonomy, another manifestation of the belief that heterosexuality is the one, real, genuine sexual relationship.

Adrienne Rich focuses on the fundamental feminist insight of the interlinked nature of beliefs and reality, and reveals the way that compulsory heterosexuality depends on the centrality of the male, which in turn depends on compulsory heterosexuality. She also makes it clear that the notion that either one or the other can be separately challenged is difficult to sustain.

This is not the only either/or dichotomy that Adrienne Rich finds inappropriate. It is important to emphasise that she does not set up a either a heterosexual or a lesbian existence: she does not exchange the heterosexual norm against which lesbian existence is measured as deviant for a lesbian norm against which heterosexuality is measured as deviant. What is at issue in her analysis is not heterosexuality *per se*, but the *compulsory* nature of heterosexuality in our society. Until lesbian existence ceases to be problematic and punished and is as viable as heterosexuality, women are without a choice: they are channelled into heterosexuality and become part of the perpetuation of men having access to resources and women having to gain access to men. And, of course, once women do have a genuine choice, the present structured centrality of men will no longer apply. It will be no mere matter of a choice of 'sexual preference' or 'life-style' (terms which, like 'stereotype', take out all the political and emotional meaning); it will be a matter of women being autonomous. In control of their own resources, women may choose lesbian existence or heterosexuality, but they will do so on their own terms, and their actions will not support a system of male dominance.

Adrienne Rich has the remarkable power to tease out and clarify some of the tangled and often painful threads within feminism. Without excluding any group of women, without devaluing or denying significant aspects of women's experience, she is able to formulate an explanation which not only takes account of the great diversity of women's sexual experience, but which actually takes our understandings forward. Her careful and caring analysis is affirming and illuminating: it has integrity and can be trusted (which is much more than can be said of most traditional research).

Because I have such great respect for her interpretations, I take her warnings very seriously. 'I believe large numbers of men could, in fact, undertake childcare on a large scale without radically altering the balance of male power in a male-identified society' (1981: 10), she writes, ominously. Like many other of her ideas, this understanding questions certain strands of feminist thinking. That to involve men in childcare will of itself modify the male power-base is not an uncommon hope among feminists – and where it is happening it is sometimes even taken as evidence of substantial change. But, as Adrienne Rich points out, there may be few grounds for such optimistic assessments. While the rules remain the same it is not unreasonable to suggest that men's involvement in childcare could result in a shift of power, but this does not allow for the possibility that men could change the rules. What if childcare were redefined as a creative, worthy, responsible and high-status activity? (As well it should be and no doubt would be, if sufficient men were involved in it.) Like the developments in reproductive technology, it could be but a short matter of time before men were asserting that they were better at it than women. We now have such convincing evidence that when men move in they take over,[5] that we should at least take this into consideration. Even the involvement of fathers in birthing is beginning to give rise to some doubts. Dr Michael Odent, a pioneer of the active birth movement in France, and among the first in the medical establishment to encourage the involvement of fathers, has changed his mind: 'If I were a woman in the feminist movement,' he concludes, 'I would fear that participation of men in birth is just another stage in the control of childbirth by men' (*Sunday Times*, 29 July 1984).

Because of the patterns of thinking in which we have been reared, it is necessary to point out that Adrienne Rich is not suggesting that men should be categorically excluded from childcare or childbirth. What she is doing is highlighting the complexity of the issues of male power. In her framework (and it is one I subscribe to) there is no simple or single strategy which will lead to satisfactorily significant change. Despite the fact that many of our foremothers – as well as our contemporaries – have identified a specific platform of male power and have sought to change it, the position of women in relation to men remains much the same. There is no one truth but many aspects of truth, and there is no *one* sure way of proceeding towards it. Yes, women are better off now that they can be educated, own property, get divorced, obtain contraception, vote, establish women's health centres and get feminist knowledge published; but yes, too, men still retain the power. And if that power is to be eroded, then women must work on *many* fronts. There is a vast range of contributions that can be made and feminist theory has to be flexible enough to encompass and validate them all. A feminist theory that is based on a simple cause-and-effect model, which maps out a straight line as the path to be followed and labels as 'incorrect' any departures, is not consistent with women's experience and values.

The value of Adrienne Rich's framework is that it pushes us beyond the limitations of our unthinking thinking-patterns. She is ever mindful that we are *all* constrained by what we know and how we think, and she emphasises that as feminists we have a responsibility continually to reflect on our own values and politics, and to ensure that in articulating our own objections to being dehumanised in a patriarchal world we do not follow the patriarchal pattern of structuring a class of 'others' for dehumanisation. Nowhere are her own value-system and politics more explicit or more careful than in her analysis of racism.

Racism – like sexism – can be dealt with as an intellectual and abstract problem. *Both* can have the power-base taken out of them and even become an issue of 'attitudes' which can ostensibly be changed with the adoption of a particular educational programme. It is under-standable that white males who have power might want to deflect attention from considerations of power, remove the 'emotional' and political implications of the problems (remove the dimensions of suffering and anguish) and reduce racism and sexism to the simplistic level of the proposition that some human beings have learnt the 'wrong' things but that all will be well when they have learnt the 'right' things. We have certainly been reared with the model of treating human problems in this intellectualised fashion, and we have been asked to believe that it embodies a superior form of reasoning: 'emotion', because it is supposedly a contaminant, is to be avoided and kept out of the descriptions and analyses. But to remove 'emotion' is to remove the human element, the people who experience the heavy penalties extracted by those in power, and this is the last variable Adrienne Rich wants to exclude from her analysis of racism and its consequences.

In terms of power, white women stand in relation to black women in much the same way as men stand in relation to women; there are social structures which support the power and privilege of men, and of whites. Whether or not men elect to make use of that power and privilege in their daily life, there is no man who does not derive benefit from the structures of male supremacy; and whether or not a white woman chooses to make use of the power and privilege of being white in her daily life, there is no white woman who does not derive benefit from the structures of white supremacy. And because of the all-pervasiveness of racism, because of its presence within feminism, and because of the human toll it takes, Adrienne Rich appeals to women to grapple with the issue in all its many forms.

On occasion, states Adrienne Rich in her harrowing essay 'Disloyal to Civilization: Feminism, Racism, Gynephobia' (1980: 275–310), the issue of racism has been raised within feminism, but too frequently in terms of those who have access to power and at the expense of those who have that power exercised against them.

Even where racism is acknowledged in feminist writings, courses, conferences, it is too often out of a desire to 'grasp' it as an intellectual or theoretical concept: we move too fast, as men so often do, in the effort to stay 'on top' of a painful and bewildering condition, and so we lose touch with the feelings that black women are trying to describe to us, their lived experience *as* women. It is far easier, especially for

198

academically trained white women, to get an intellectual/political 'fix' on the *idea* of racism, than to identify with black female experience: to explore it emotionally as part of our own. (p.281)

What Adrienne Rich is *not* doing is holding white women responsible for originating racism: what she *is* doing is holding them responsible for any participation in and perpetuation of its practices. Racism is one form of civilisation to which women are bound to be disloyal, she states: 'Women did not create this relationship' of white to colour, 'but in the history of American slavery and racism white women have been impressed into its service' (p.282). Feminists cannot collude in this structure, and to demonstrate that this is another area of male power which historically women have resisted, she quotes examples of women of the past who have defied the law of unjust and immoral rule.

Her account is bruising. Yet it is vitally necessary: 'The mutual history of black and white women in this country is a realm so painful, resonant and forbidden that it has barely been touched by writers either of political "science" or of imaginative literature. Yet until that history is known, that silence broken, we will all go on struggling in a state of deprivation and ignorance' (p.281). We cannot risk separation and silence, she states, but must *together* expand our understandings: we must overcome the obstacles which divide and defeat.

Women have used racism, but women are used by racism, as Adrienne Rich points out. Any means can be used in a patriarchal society to obstruct the bonding of women, and racism has clearly been utilised to this end. 'Identification with women *as women*, not as persons similar in class or race or cultural behaviour, is still profoundly problematic,' she writes.

The constraints that have demanded of white women that to keep our respectability or advantages we must deny our sisters (and our sisters in ourselves) have also seemed to require black women to deny either their sex or their race in political alignments. The charge of deviance, always leveled at women who bond together, especially across racial and class lines, has been used against black and white feminists alike. (p.287)

In her analysis of the invidious nature of racism, Adrienne Rich moves beyond the confines of patriarchal thinking which predispose us to arrange the world in hierarchical order. She does not lend credence to a classification system which ranks suffering, which, in her words, 'diverts energy into the ludicrous and fruitless game of "hierarchies of oppression", which has the savor of medieval theology' (p.289). Nor will she structure scapegoats and *blame* those who have had no control:

> An analysis that places the guilt for active domination, physical and institutional violence, and the justifications embedded in myth and language on white women, not only compounds false consciousness: it allows us to deny or neglect the charged connections among black and white women from the historical conditions of slavery on; and it impedes any real discussion of women's instrumentality in a system which oppresses all women, and in which hatred of women is also embedded in myth, folklore, and language. (p.301)

To apportion blame or to inculcate guilt within feminism is not to address the problem: to identify the deep-seated racism which all feminists have a responsiblility to eradicate, *is* to begin to address the problem. 'If black and white feminists are going to speak of account-ability,' she states with passion, 'I believe the word *racism* must be seized, grasped in our bare hands, ripped up out of the sterile or defensive consciousness in which it so often grows and transplanted so that it can yield new insights for our lives and our movement' (p.301).

With all the charged connotations of racism, and all the opportunities discussion of the problem affords for misrepresentation, Adrienne Rich showed great courage and compassion when she ventured into this morass of multiple and mined meanings. Writing at a crossroads of pain and anger, she was concerned that her words did not 'lend themselves to distortion or expropriation, either by apologists for a shallow and trivial notion of feminism, or by exponents of a racial politics that denies the fundamental nature of sexual politics and gender oppression' (p.279). What she sought to do – and did do – was to make way for the dialogue among women which could clarify the complex of connections between women, and forge the framework for the understanding of differences. Only when this was achieved would it be possible for women to move towards the 'profound transformation of world society and of human relationships' (p.279). Feminist theory is enormously indebted to Adrienne Rich's heartfelt explanations and analysis.

She made from silence an issue that was *speakable*. She pointed to ignorance, prejudice and fear and emphasised the necessity and importance of women's knowledge. What was, and still is, required in her terms is women's knowledge of racism, predicated on women's experience *of* it (in contrast to patriarchal pronouncements *on* it). It is abundantly clear that we cannot generate such knowledge if we conceive of it as adding on the experience of black women to that of white women. As is the case with men's knowledge, the full recognition of women's lives cannot be accomplished merely by adding on women to the categories already defined by men, because the inclusion of women changes the categories that men have set up. So it is with the knowledge of women of colour which has been systematically devalued and denied in a white context. The experience of women who have been oppressed by racism is not *additional*: it engages with and transforms what has been defined in white terms. It cannot be a matter of white women allocating space to women of colour (as patriarchal institutions have allocated space to women), but must be a researching, relearning, regenerative process which reshapes the whole, and reformulates what is known.

What women know and men do not is enormously significant, and much of the thesis of this book has been that the reluctance or inability of men to hear what women are saying is part of the structure of women's oppression. If and when men can hear what women are saying – and can expand their comprehension to incorporate what women know as part of their own knowledge of humanity – then part of that structure of oppression will have been overthrown, and to that extent, society and human relationships will have been transformed. There are parallels here with racism within the women's movement. If and when white women can incorporate the knowledge of women of colour as part of their own knowledge as women, then the racist structures of oppression will be weakened; if not, if the knowledge of women of colour continues to be excluded, denied or devalued, then racist structures will remain intact. But if white women – and Christian women, and women from English-speaking countries or wealthy nations – comprehend what is being described by black women, Jewish women, Islamic women, Philippino women, Indian women (to name but a few groupings of women whose knowledge has too often been excluded from overall feminist understandings), then a start will have been made in dismantling some of the structures of racist oppression.

Audre Lorde's powerful meanings of the workings of power are part of the reality of all women as they are expressed in *Zami: A New Spelling of My Name* (1982), and *Sister Outsider* (1984). And it isn't the additional information that Alice Walker provides about a black woman's experience of racism which makes *In Search of Our Mothers' Gardens* (1984) invaluable: it is the shift in focus in her explorations of the relationship of life and art, of community and individualism, of pain and joy – and of her understanding that, as women, 'Something is always wrong with us' (p.288) – which enriches our woman knowledge. Alice Walker amplifies the intricacies of so many of the contradictions of women's existence, and because of her own commitment to 'non-exclusion' she pushes at our boundaries of limited comprehension.

The mosaic of what we can know as women is given form and detail by some of the more recent publications in Black Women's Studies: *This Bridge Called My Back* (Cherrie Moraga and Gloria Anzaldua, 1981), *But Some of Us are Brave* (Gloria Hull, Patricia Bell Scott and Barbara Smith, 1982) and *Home Girls* (Barbara Smith, 1983) are helping to change the pattern of feminist knowledge, but we still have a long way to go before the charge of tokenism is completely without basis. Yet some difficulties are already emerging with the little knowledge of black women which is being validated because most of it originates in the United States, and much of it is in English – and not a translation! This is not unproblematic: again there are many women of colour who do not necessarily want to be added on to the existing knowledge of the realms of black experience that are culturally specific to the United States. There are many women who want to define their own terms (and, in turn, help to expand the understandings of North American feminists): *In Search of Answers: Indian Women's Voices from 'Manushi'* (edited by Madhu Kishwar and Ruth Vanita, 1984) brings yet another perspective which mixes with and changes feminist meanings.

None of us is free from the disposition to assume that our experience is *the* experience, and that what we know represents the limits of the knowable. None of us has a true analysis, a correct line, a monopoly on the right meanings. And if we want to see the end of one group defining the world of another group, on the grounds that this constitutes oppression, then all of us have a responsibility to strive to extend our horizons, to encompass and validate women's experience that is different from our own. All of us have to be vigilant about what we are leaving out of our explanations – and why!

Feminism is not, however, value-free liberalism which 'tolerates' each and every view (the implication of 'tolerance' is that other views are permitted to exist without meeting with or modifying one's own). Feminism is based on values, on values of self-identity, responsibility, autonomy, equality and the absence of dominance, coercion and oppression. Understandings which do not respect these values, no matter from whom they emanate, are not tolerated. And yet it is not so simple as it sounds, for within each of us is (at least) the propensity to insist on our own terms at the expense of someone else's self-identity, responsibility, autonomy, at the risk of structuring inequality and of paving the way for a form of dominance. Perhaps this propensity is a product of the patriarchal pattern of thinking in which we have been reared; perhaps as we challenge the values of patriarchy we shall begin to release ourselves from the hold that hierarchy and exclusion have over our minds. Meanwhile, we must be concerned to change ourselves as we try to change the world. Feminism is about 'double vision', about focusing on 'in here' as well as 'out there'.

There are other reasons too for entitling this chapter 'Double Vision'. It is a term used by both Mary Daly and Adrienne Rich as a mode for feminism (which they juxtapose against the 'tunnel-vision' of dominance), and as these two superlative theorists together constitute a double vision of feminist ideas, it seemed fitting to conclude with a joint review of their work, and an indication that feminist theory is not a single focus.

But to attempt to plumb the contents of Mary Daly's work is to attempt the impossible. This is primarily because, to her, feminism is a process, a process of *lucid cerebration*,[6] a way of thinking, rather than a body of knowledge. Throughout this book, the issues of meaning, of the limitations of understanding, and the role played by language and myth, have been returned to again and again as problems for feminism. No matter what the origin of the writers, they have all met with resistance to feminist ideas, of our means of making sense of the world. And this is precisely the area where Mary Daly thinks and writes. But whereas most feminist theorists who have recognised the obstructions posed by the patriarchal symbolic order have despaired of ever being able to break the mind-set of male dominance, and have acknowledged their own inadequacy when it comes to changing the shape and substance of what we know, Mary Daly breaks through these barriers and conceptualises a meta-patriarchal reality. By so doing, she energises and enspirits women and helps to realise women's positive, creative force.

Here is, of course, one vision of post-patriarchy, and she is aware of its idiosyncrasies and the possibility of omissions, for while she accepts that women have a common realm of meaning, they are all profoundly different from one another. 'Not only are there ethnic, national, class and racial differences that shape our perspectives,' she writes in *Pure Lust* (1984), 'but there are also individual and cross-cultural differences of temperament, virtue, talent, taste, and of conditions within which these can or cannot find expression. There is, then, an extremely rich, complex diversity among women and within each individual. But there is also above, beyond, beneath all this a Cosmic Commonality, a tapestry of connectedness which women as Websters/Fates[7] are constantly weaving. The weaving of this tapestry is the realizing of a dream, which Adrienne Rich has named "The Dream of a Common Language"' (pp.26–7). But the issue with Mary Daly's work is not where it fails to go, but how far it does go, for while much will remain unrevealed to one journeyer, that it is possible to journey is the crux of her contribution. Her thesis is that 'Breaking the bonds/bars of phallocracy requires breaking through to radiant powers of words, so that by releasing words, we can release our Selves' (1984: 4), and in her own thinking and writing she puts this theory into practice.

Mary Daly's view of patriarchy is that it is an all-pervasive and woman-destroying system which has taken over women's minds and bodies; and her reasoning – which in places parallels that of Germaine Greer (although I might well be the only one who sees it this way) – is that women can reclaim their power, their right to their own minds and bodies and to existence on their own terms. Women are locked into the misogynist, 'male-centered, monodimensional' meanings, where 'deception is embedded in the very texture of the words we use' (*Gyn/Ecology*, 1978: 3), but we *can* 'find our way back to reality by destroying the false perceptions inflicted on us by the language and myths' of men that have distorted and denied us (p.4). So instead of stating the case for the necessity of a new set of uncontaminated meanings which structure an authentic and autonomous reality for women, Mary Daly engages in the creative process of generating those meanings and reality, partly through the exhilarating process of making us 'word-conscious', and by beginning to make us aware of the origins of and obstacles to our knowing and thinking. She pushes us to deliberate on our own mental processes so that we become conscious of how much we have unthinkingly taken for granted about the way the world works, how much we have let our minds move along patriarchal tracks without questioning the journey, or the destination. She urges us to 'cerebrate', to examine what we know, and to identify the destructive forces within the language, myths and thinking-patterns we are daily making use of. 'The Amazon Voyager can be anti-academic', she declares, but 'Only at her greatest peril can she be anti-intellectual' (p.xiii).

To classify Mary Daly's thesis pejoratively as psychological (with the implications that it is monodimensional and disregards the realm of the material – see Carol Anne Douglas, 1984), as I have sometimes heard critics do, is to evaluate her work against patriarchal standards and to find – not surprisingly – that she 'fails' (refuses) to meet them. She makes it abundantly clear that she has absolutely no intention of structuring something which is meaningful within the patriarchal frame of reference, because her entire thesis is based on the premise that such a frame of reference is soul-destroying. Much of her strength lies in her defiance of patriarchal order and her determined derision of it (again, I see similarities with Germaine Greer, who counselled comparable strategies). In *Beyond God the Father* (1973) she exposed the limitations of *method* and indicated that the sanctioned methods of knowledge-making in a male-dominated society produced knowledge which supported male dominance:[8] If the avowed aim is *not* to support but to dislodge male-dominated reality, then the existing methods of knowledge-construction are most definitely not the ones to be used. In many ways she reclaims women's 'wrongness'. Deviance from the norm can become positive when the norm is so devastatingly discredited, and by insisting on the strength and value of women's departure from what makes sense and meets with approval in patriarchal terms, she helps to weaken that patriarchal reality which deems women to be 'wrong'. If women, as outsiders, declare themselves to be a legitimate source of reality and therefore central, who then is outside of what? By such persuasive reasoning Mary Daly reveals some of the workings of reality and raises the fundamental issue – expressed throughout this book – of the extent to which patriarchal reality will persist if women refuse to acknowledge its existence. Would men be content to agree among themselves that they are dominant, if women gave no credence to such male belief? Would the male of the troop see himself as the leader of the harem if the females structured the reality that his presence would be acceptable only while he continued to make a contribution?

These theoretical considerations are given substance by Mary Daly when she repudiates the patriarchal conventions of scholarship, reveals them to be arbitrary, and insists on her own women's standards. Of *Gyn/Ecology* (1978) she states that 'the pedantic can expect to perceive it as unscholarly. Since it *confronts* old molds/models of question-asking by being itself an Other way of thinking/speaking, it will be invisible to those who fetishize old questions – who drone that it does not "deal with" *their* questions' (p.xiii). She is just as explicit in *Pure Lust* (1984), where she pursues her policy of 'killing off' method ('methodicide'): 'In keeping with the tradition of Methodicide, this book is a work of studied errata.[9] From the patriarchal perspective, therefore, it is quite simply and entirely a Mistake' (p.30).

There is a price demanded, however, from the women who refuse to submit to patriarchal standards, part of which is to brand their work as anti-male, beyond the pale. Again, Mary Daly redefines *anti-male*, beginning with women's premises. We must recognise that it is not a matter of *degree*, she argues, for 'even the most cautious and circum-spect feminist writings are described' as anti-male: it is more a matter of *kind*, and it is used as a ploy to prevent any hearing of criticism of patriarchy. For what does it mean to be anti-male in a society which is so perversely and pervasively anti-female, where there is such over-whelming evidence of the rape of women, of 'the actual rapist behavior of professionals, from soldiers to gynecologists'? (1978: 27–8). Mary Daly lists some of the systematic atrocities men have committed against women – all of which are known – and asks why the women who condemn this behaviour are so quickly condemned by those who engage in such behaviour.

The custom of widow-burning [*suttee*] in India, the Chinese ritual of footbinding, the genital mutilation of young girls in Africa (still practised in parts of twenty-six countries in Africa), the massacre of women as witches in 'Renaissance' Europe, gynocide under the guise of American gynecology and psychotherapy are all documented facts accessible in the tomes and tombs (libraries) of patriarchal scholar-ship. The contemporary facts of brutal gang rape, of wife beating, of overt and subliminal psychic lobotomizing – all are available. (p.28)

But as Adrienne Rich and so many other feminists have pointed out, these 'anti-male' topics deserve no scholarly attention, warrant no examination. 'What then can the label *anti-male* possibly mean when applied to works that expose these facts, and invite women to free our selves?' asks Mary Daly.

The fact is that the labelers do not intend to convey a rational meaning, nor to elicit a thinking process, but rather to block thinking. They do intend the label to carry a deep emotive message, triggering implanted fears of all the fathers and sons, freezing our minds. For to write an 'anti-male' book is to utter the ultimate blasphemy. (p.28)

What is meaning? What do we mean? Why are we here and what for? Is there a real meaning or is all meaning a random product of our mental processes? These are the questions pursued by Mary Daly, and fundamental to her framework is the understanding of the links between symbols – our language, our myths – and what we can know and make meaningful. Meaning is not something 'out there' waiting for us to discover it, but something which human beings project onto the world in relation to the meanings they have already acquired. And the meanings that a male-dominated society has projected onto the world, the sense that patriarchy has provided, is harmful and destructive to women, society and the planet.

This brings us back full-circle to the thorny issue, the 'Catch 22': we cannot make sense of the world until we have a system of meaning, and yet once we have acquired a system of meaning it constrains what sense we can make of the world. So, as each generation – female and male – learns to see the world in patriarchal terms, we become the victims of our own limited inheritance which we, in turn, bequeath to the next generation – unless we glimpse what lies outside.

Central to Mary Daly's analysis is the way in which human beings are constrained by systems of meaning, the way in which we can be drawn into meanings which conceal, deceive and distort. It is the ability of a set of meanings to lead us away from ourselves and to accept a reality which is so far removed from any that we could have generated for ourselves, that is her prime concern. Although she documents the range from the stark (the barbaric treatment of women) to the silly, Mary Daly's fundamental question is how we can come to accept such distortions, how we can be schooled to see them as unproblematic.

Are we 'programmed', destined to follow unthinkingly the patterns into which we have been initiated, when the slightest departure from the programme would reveal the absurdity, the cruelty and the destructiveness of thinking which presents as reasonable and sensible, rape, violence, nuclear war? Or can we reject the 'programme' and simply devise a new symbolic system which allows us to see the world in a different way and make sense by different means? Or is it that either/or is a false division, a product of our ever-prevailing programme of monodimensional reality, and the more appropriate explanation is that we are *both* – both constrained by the symbolic order we know, and free to modify it? That we are both governed by the patriarchal system but able to get outside it is Mary Daly's stance.

Clearly, her emphasis is on 'cerebration', and not on particular campaigns. Clearly, she concentrates on *why* the world is as it is, and why and how it can be different. But hers is no abstract philosophy, it is a theoretical action for, by revealing how and why we see as we do, she simultaneously changes the how and why. This is a form of activism in the real world. 'Although I am concerned with all forms of pollution in phallotechnic society,' she writes in *Gyn/Ecology*,

> this book is primarily concerned with the mind/spirit/body pollution inflicted through patriarchal myth and language on all levels. These levels range from styles of grammar to styles of glamor, from religious myth to dirty jokes, from theological hymns honoring the 'Real Thing', from dogmatic doctrines about the 'Divine Host' to doctored ingredient-labeling of Hostess Cupcakes, from subliminal ads to 'sublime' art. Phallic myth and language generate, legitimate, and mask the material pollution that threatens to terminate all sentient life on this planet. (p.9)

This is why, in her terms, women must know the 'deep' structure of meaning if we are to formulate our strategies for the 'surface' structure of life; this is why women must reclaim the right to name, for 'the liberation of language is rooted in the liberation of ourselves' (p.8).

I do not pretend to follow Mary Daly all the way, but I do have some appreciation of her meanings because they are part of my own experience. They are the meanings which confront feminists as we try to bend the language to make it meet our needs, and they are the meanings which have become clear to us because we have changed them. When I confronted Susan Brownmiller's meanings of rape, I was devastated in part by the recognition of the horror of rape; but part of my shock was also that I could ever have been led to believe the anti-female meanings of rape that were my reality at that time. How we are led to believe in such a pernicious reality is Mary Daly's contribution. How we can begin to believe in a more positive reality is her achievement.

This book began with assumptions, with an analysis of what they are and how they work. It will tie up some of the loose ends if I conclude with a consideration of assumptions – those of Mary Daly, for she assumes the meaningfulness of existence. Hers may not be the meaningfulness that we are accustomed to, but she assumes an ultimate order, as distinct from flux, randomness and chaos.

At each stage, as she delves into our symbolic system and finds the presence of patriarchal pollutants, she is prepared to go still further in her journey for phallocratic-free meanings. For example, she quotes Virginia Woolf's lament that 'As a woman I have no country' and her leap to the declaration that 'As a woman I want no country. My country is the whole world' (1938, 1966: 109). Mary Daly writes, 'there is something poignant about this brave assertion, for "the whole world" is groaning under phallic rule'. So Mary Daly too goes further, takes a leap in the light of this evidence of patriarchal pervasiveness. 'It must be, then, that it is in some other dimension that "the whole world" is the country, the homeland of the Race of Women' (1984: 6).

I think she thinks that if we can only strip away the perverse patriarchal meanings which are our mental baggage we shall get to that new dimension and ultimately arrive at that nugget of pure meaning, the beginning, the first, the uncontaminated essence – the cause.

I think, I think, I am not so sure.

16. Account Rendered:
Writers' response to writing

We have all conspired in matricide. We are all mistrustful of our own daughters. We commit sororicide daily . . .

These words have made their mark on me. They are written by Phyllis Chesler but they symbolise the feelings of most of the women who responded to the questionnaire I sent them. Until I received their feedback, I had not fully appreciated the extent to which most feminist writers have been deeply and harmfully hurt by some of the responses to their work. This new knowledge chills me.

As the letters and comments have come through my post – and as I have waited for some replies in vain – I have had to consider my own stand in relation to evaluating the writing of other women. I think it was because my work (and, by implication, my self) has on occasion been 'misinterpreted' (to state the case euphemistically), that I was sensitive to the dangers inherent in representing other women's ideas. I have often wanted a right of reply, and so it seemed only fair that I should provide for others what I had often required for myself. But I did not realise that providing 'fair play' for others would make a significant difference to my own contribution. I had recognised, of course, that allowing the women I wrote about to have their say would mean some extra planning and work (contracts, time-schedules, etc.); and I understood that it would make a difference to the structure of the book. What I did not realise was that it would make a crucial difference to me and my writing.

In retrospect, I have to confront the fact that when I decided to send my version of their work to the various women involved, *I took great care*; I read, re-read, revised; I substantiated every statement; I was wary about imposing my own interpretation; cautious about possible mis-constructions. My purpose in writing the book had predisposed me towards positive evaluations. It was not my aim to discredit the ideas of any one woman, but to discuss them and to outline the contribution they had made to the overall feminist framework. I was looking for the omissions, but I was also looking for the inputs into feminist theory, so it was part of my task to seek out what I saw as the valuable elements in their work which had helped to form feminist theory. Even so, this was not enough to explain my diligence and *care*. And the question which started to haunt me was, why do I not always adopt this careful approach? I knew that my reading of feminist texts and my writing on them were qualitatively different from any that I had undertaken before, and I was uncomfortable with the idea that this was a one-off exercise, a process that wouldn't be repeated. I did not like some of the answers to my own questions. Would I have been so careful if I had *not* extended the right of reply?

When the replies started to come back, my doubts intensified, as it became clear that many feminist theorists who have, with the greatest integrity, 'come out' with their ideas and explanations, designed to increase and enhance our understandings, have made themselves vulnerable doing so, only to be scorned for their efforts. One thing, then, that I have learnt from the women who have made use of the right of reply is that, at the most basic and crude level, we simply cannot afford to hit so hard at our sisters so that they withdraw, and determine not to risk themselves again. This approach is nothing short of destructive of some of our most valuable resources. What painful irony if we perceive our different interpretations as more in need of condemnation than those huge differences which divide us from patriarchal understandings. I am reminded of an old saying among Australian feminists: 'The patriarchy won't have to raise a finger to eliminate feminism if we keep attacking each other so effectively; we can readily eliminate ourselves.'

So I am enormously grateful to the women who have replied; grateful for the time they have taken, grateful for the quality of their replies, and grateful for the lesson they have once more reminded me of. I have learnt much from their work, and much from their responses. I have learnt that it is possible to analyse the ideas of other women critically but not destructively; that it is possible to engage in a dialogue and not end in a dismissal. I have learnt that we can pool our insights and build on them; borrow from one another and blend and refine our ideas in a way that is strengthening and illuminating. I have learnt that while we can be culturally coerced into putting forward our own views as *the* 'correct line', dismissing all others; while we can be conditioned to put our own case at the expense of all others, we don't have to behave in this way. It is possible to break the pattern and to recognise that an *exchange* can enrich us all. What we need is more care, surely not such an unreasonable or unattainable goal for feminists who have valued the caring of women?

Finding that it is possible to share ideas has been a positive experience for me. I have long been distressed at some of the barriers which prevent women from sharing knowledge with other women. Our history, in many respects, is the history of one generation of women being cut off from another, of one group of women being cut off from another. I thought that this was a major obstacle to the growth and development of women's culture and liberation. But given some of the replies that I have received, I now believe that obstacle to be surmountable.

Alice Rossi has taught me much. Of all the women whose work I reviewed, I took the most liberty with hers. I 'used' her ideas on Harriet Taylor and John Stuart Mill to raise the question of whether a man could be a feminist. I drew conclusions with which I thought she would disagree. I was careful, but I still recognised that she could well be astonished to find her work used in this way. But her response was considered and *generous*. For while not subscribing to my interpretation, she readily granted it validity. I certainly benefited from our exchange of views.

The following women were initially contacted and asked whether they would be willing to participate: Mary Daly, Andrea Dworkin, Phyllis Chesler, Eva Figes, Shulamith Firestone, Germaine Greer, Ruth Hubbard, Kate Millett, Juliet Mitchell, Elaine Morgan, Robin Morgan, Ann Oakley, Adrienne Rich, Alice Rossi, Sheila Rowbotham and Micheline Wandor. Because of the pressure of space I was not able to include an extensive coverage of all their work, so while Andrea Dworkin, Ruth Hubbard, Elaine Morgan and Micheline Wandor all generously agreed to be involved, I had no extended analysis to send them. Sheila Rowbotham did not want to participate, and at this stage (and with no more time) replies have not come from Mary Daly, Kate Millett or Juliet Mitchell. Adrienne Rich, for personal reasons, was unable to meet the response deadline, but wishes the book well. The responses which follow tell their own story. The fact that there are only minor matters of misinterpretation is, I think, of great significance. The care with which I read and reviewed their work has paid dividends. I hope I have learnt a lesson I shall not forget.

Phyllis Chesler

Reading Dale Spender's essay on my work brought tears to my eyes, and joy. Spender's perception of me as a theoretician is rare and I bless her for it. Most often, I am (merely) praised for 'critiquing' patriarchal institutions, and not perceived as a theory-maker at all.

My major themes, first sounded in *Women and Madness*, unfold in each subsequent book: *Women, Money and Power*, 1976; *About Men*, 1978; *With Child*, 1979, as well as in other feminist literature. For example, in *Women and Madness* (1972) I wrote about what it means to be 'mothered' – and not to be 'mothered'. I described the psychological consequences of women's enforced separation; and how psychologically disfigured daughters and mothers later surface in adult life, and within feminist groups.

In *Women and Madness* (in addition to analysing the mistreatment of madness and the sexism of mental health care), I wrote about the essentially incestuous model of all male–female relations, including those of marriage, romantic love, employment and psychotherapy. I wrote about the meaning, presence and persecution of Amazons, Great Mothers, witches – both in the context of psychological history and of female psychology. I discussed the dangers of forgetting, romanticising, misusing or re-creating such figures in ourselves.

I finished *About Men* in 1976; it was delayed for publication until 1978. I described how fathers kill sons – literally and symbolically; and how male rage and anguish about not being loved and protected by other men is displaced onto women and children. I wrote about male conformity and bonding; and about male uterus envy in its psychological, economic, religious and technological manifestations. I explored brotherhood, fratricide, and the non-incestuous mother–son bond. I related these themes to the patriarchal worship of death.

In *With Child*, I chose a literary approach for sounding the great existential themes of pregnancy, childbirth, and newborn motherhood. Any patriarchal hero can be a woman in labour, labouring; or a child being born. In *With Child*, I explored the ways in which a mother's emotions deepen, become whole, and how this very wholeness is devalued by everyone, including the mother herself.

Most of the views that Spender attributes to me, based on her excellent reading of *Women and Madness*, are still my views. Some are not. For example, I have re-evaluated the dangers of test-tube babies in terms of a feminist future. I am probably more of a feminist–anarchist than ever before; more mistrustful of the organisation of power into large bureaucratic states than I once was.

I am just completing a work on *Women and Custody*. The custody issue is, in a sense, the abortion controversy – after birth. History is also the story of mothers and children lost to each other too soon, and in ways not chosen. What mother chooses to lose her child at birth or to the plagues of war, disease and accident that level each century into orphans and grieving mothers?

What mother freely hands her young over to blood-strangers – to be enslaved, legally adopted, even 'battered' by their mother's conqueror; to be taught to forget her; to be punished for who she is – small hostage of her misfortune, bone of her bone, apple of her eye?

What library holds the first-person accounts, of what *all* women felt over a 10,000-year period, about not having, or about having and losing their children; about being forced to bear children, without the health, the time, the peace of mind or the resources to enjoy and protect them? Death separates us soon enough. Why are there so many unnatural mother–child separations? Who and what is more heartless than Death?

This book explores why mothers are unnaturally separated from their children. I also study how mothers under custodial siege fight. They do so in heroically non-violent ways. Mothers and women, including feminists, are, however, violent to each other.

For a number of years (my whole life?), I have been working on a book entitled *Female Inhumanity to Women*. The egg, the origin, of this book is also contained in *Women and Madness*. Spender notes my concern with an absence of sisterhood among feminists and among women. At some level we are all Electra; certainly we are Electra's daughters. We have all conspired in matricide. We are all mistrustful of our own daughters. We commit sororicide daily, unconsciously, consciously, to survive, to express our frustration; to save our children. Sometimes we do so in the name of ideology.

Over the years I (along with many other naive intellectuals) have been mystified to find how little of my theory-making is mentioned (agreed or disagreed with) in the works of feminist academics; and in the works of feminist anti-academics. So many of us – not just intellectuals – feel unnamed, forgotten, unappreciated, not fully credited by *those who mean the most to us.*

Why do feminists (like other ideologues) recognise our intellectual foremothers so selectively? Why latch on to a 'saviour' one year – and then dethrone or behead her the next, embracing a new saviour for the year? Why so little independent or autonomous thinking in this regard?

Why do so many feminists recognise personal friends – and forget their 'enemies' or competitors? Why recognise those whose favour is being courted rather than all who deserve it? Why debase the very herstory we are making by rewriting it as it is being made?

Why is it easier for feminists to remember a dead foremother rather than a living one; a 'minor' rather than a 'major' one? Why such amnesia – if not in the service of psychological matricide?

Dale Spender is writing about many of us in our time, while we are alive. Her book of essays on contemporary feminist theorists is a goddess-send. I eagerly await more from her and from others.

This brief essay was literally 'dashed off' in the midst of meeting my *Custody* book deadline. It is in no way considered or comprehensive. I felt Spender's request for feedback deserved to be met and I did the best I could.

Eva Figes

Dear Dale Spender,
Let me deal with your treatment of *Patriarchal Attitudes* first of all.

I think you have overstated my concern with capitalism. I am not a Marxist, never have been, and I certainly do not regard capitalism as the root cause of women's oppression, as you imply. I do think capitalism effected a separation between work and the home which caused women to lose out economically. The male wage-packet is after all a direct result of capitalism.

Secondly, you have left out other aspects of my analysis which I regard as very important. For instance, I emphasise that achievement is tied in with expectations and motivation. If women are not expected to achieve in a particular sphere, most of them will not try to do so. I also regard the reasons why men have wanted to control women as of key importance. (Odd how few women bother to think about this at all!) In my book I gave the reason as a wish to control female fertility, as the only way of ensuring that one's children, and hence one's heirs, really were one's own. The ability to control fertility has meant an enormous change for men and women, and for the relationship between them. Frankly, I regard the pill as more important in the development of the modern women's movement than any amount of political literature. Until women could effectively control their fertility, their interest in making use of opportunities in the 'outside' world was necessarily limited, which is why there was so little agitation for equal opportunities before the 1960s. My argument is borne out by the fact that recently disillusionment with the pill has led to some remarkable back-tracking by feminists, notably Germaine Greer.

Which brings me rather neatly to my last point. You mention that I did not participate in consciousness-raising whilst writing my book. Well, no, during the late 1960s, when I was writing *Patriarchal Attitudes*, it was not going on, and books like mine made that activity a possibility. Frankly, I think you are muddling cause and effect, and consciousness-raising has never been more than a side-effect of social change, and a rather unproductive one at that. I do not believe that women are passive, as you suggest, but I do think we are all part of an historical process, and that our ability to think and act freely is limited by that process. In that sense my book is also part of the process.

You ask me what I would add or change now. As far as analysis or objectives are concerned, nothing. But the book was written at an optimistic time, and takes no account of the clouds that have darkened our horizon since – mass unemployment, environmental pollution, and the growing possibility of nuclear war. I think my book has withstood these changes rather better than most, and it is, of course, true that even if I could have seen into the future, it was not part of my brief to deal with them. But I cannot conceive of myself writing a feminist polemic now without taking such factors into account.

Yours sincerely,
Eva Figes

Germaine Greer

I wouldn't want to quarrel with your interpretation; I think you should be able to give it freely. But it is refreshing to see that you perceive *Sex and Destiny* as a development rather than a contradiction in my work. A lot of my ideas have changed in the crucible which has been spending time in other cultures, but the changes have been developments, not changes in direction. You might have made a bit too much out of the interview on rape, but still, it is a point worth considering. And I think maybe your chapter is a bit too long. But I certainly don't quarrel with your interpretation.

Robin Morgan

I'm grateful for Dale Spender's thoughtful analysis in the chapter, 'The Living Evidence'; what any honourable writer (or thinker, or political activist, for that matter) most desires - far more than approval or praise - is *understanding*, even where the understanding may take issue with some of one's own arguments. I do feel that Spender has comprehended one of the most basic themes in my work: *interconnections*. That she has located this theme as early as the Introduction I wrote for my anthology *Sisterhood Is Powerful* is especially gratifying, since that attitude and politics on my part persisted and intensified not only in my subsequent prose books but in my three books of poems as well, culminating and expanding in *The Anatomy of Freedom* (prose) recently, and in the new anthology *Sisterhood Is Global* (1984). The end of 'either/or' thinking - and its replacement with what I term 'both/and' inclusive and integrative thinking and action seems more than ever, to me, to be at the heart of truly profound radical feminist perception. To settle for less seems a failure of both nerve and vision. As for future directions I envisage for feminism, one is surely the further growth and strengthening of global feminism in all its celebratory diversity and with no sacrifice of complexity in its solidarity. As for other trends and details, I trust that I, along with other women writers (and, one hopes, some men of conscience), will be exploring, experimenting, and daring in works - on paper *and* in the legislatures, *and* through the streets - for years to come.

Ann Oakley

Dear Dale,

I'll go through the chapter and give you my response bit by bit. There are a few items I don't quite agree with.

1. You state that I challenged the 'structure' of sociology; I think I challenged the *status quo*, content, orientation. And then the bit about talking to women – maybe some people have always talked to women, the problem being that of getting other people to listen to the results of their conversations.

2. Researchers – even in the male mechanical world – are supposed to be 'committed'; I think it's about the type of commitment, professional versus personal.

3. By the way, *Sex Gender and Society* grew out of the Housework project. I found I couldn't make sense of either the contemporary or the historical material on the division of labour without going back to the beginning; that is, to the nature versus nurture debate.

4. Spelling mistakes!

5. All our books are products of their time. In fact, quite soon after *Sex Gender and Society*, I wrote (in *Conditions of Illusion*) some criticisms of it; including some things picked up from reviews – one pointed out that the graphs in the book had the heavy black line for males and the thin broken one for females. I think one of the most useful functions of *Sex Gender and Society* was as a teaching text.

6. When I started the Sociology of Housework study I didn't know anything about CR groups. Rather the idea for the study (I describe it in *Taking it like a Woman*) came directly out of a sort of inner clash between my past training as a sociologist and my then current immersion in housework.

7. Men read my books too and I know have (occasionally) had their attitudes altered by them.

8. I think you should take out the bit about women having their lives changed from talking to me. If their lives only could be changed by something so simple. It denies the social and economic conditions of their lives.[1]

9. My methodology was a bit more complex than you have represented it. I used 'straight' interviewing and definitely not anthropological techniques. But obviously, women doing academic research do have a sense, often, of being outsiders and of needing to study or

describe what to insiders are obvious dimensions of their world.

10. I do not claim it is male intervention that is responsible for some of women's most serious problems in childbirth. The male–female divide is important but 'men' are not coterminous with intervention or with the approval of it. There are some difficult issues here – such as who wants technology in childbirth, for example. I would prefer to locate this issue within the debate about the social control of technology, generally.

11. The post-natal depression research showed that difficult social conditions (class, not gender inequalities) were also associated with depression.

12. The medical profession has responded, but the question is whether the response is sufficient. (Even when it is demonstrated to doctors that what they are doing is ineffective, there is still evidence that doctors are reluctant to change their practices.)

13. I don't think the technological model of childbirth is less dominant; it's more dominant. Some procedures (e.g. induction of labour) have become less common, but others have become more so – especially those relating to pregnancy, rather than to labour and delivery.

14. There are some women who don't feel pain when they have a baby. I find it difficult to believe, but I have met them.

15. I think it's clear from developments in the field of artificial reproduction that if it were possible to have reproduction without women, women would still be kept in their place – with males owning the means of production, *and* reproduction.

And thanks for the last paragraph.

Ann

Alice Rossi

Dear Dale,
Your letter and the pages of your book that deal with my analysis of John and Harriet Taylor and a bit on the Feminist Papers arrived at a point when I have been under great pressure from other deadlines. But I did squeeze in an hour or so this morning to read over the section of your book. I am handicapped in doing so in not knowing better the larger context of these pages; hence I may have missed some

points that help to illuminate what you are about in this section.

First of all, you pose the question of whether men can 'qualify' as authorities on women's experience. We have all had much experience in being 'misunderstood' by men, and men report the same sense of not being understood by women. What gives us special pleasure, *is* the experience of feeling 'here is a man who understands women as I do'. The great writers of fiction sometimes have this, both male and female, though god knows the bulk of western past literature does a better job of getting inside the skins of men than of women. Even today, with more androgynous writers of both sexes abroad in the world, I find myself impatient and disinterested in most fiction written by men, simply because the issues of concern to them are different from those of concern to women writers.

I know many feminists today are of the persuasion (which suits them politically and personally) that men cannot understand women, and should be excluded from feminist circles so that only women speak for women on women. I do not subscribe to this view, for a simple reason: I see no hope for the world without an overlap of deep emotional significance between men and women. There are things blacks can best say about blacks, but what they say about whites is of equal importance and the same is true of whites *vis-à-vis* blacks. What hope of an integrated world in terms of race or sex if we did not hold this view?

In sum, I am an 'integrationist', and believe that we as feminists should be encouraging, not excluding men, to make efforts to understand women. The efforts may miss on many points, there is bound to be only a 'partial' view, but those efforts pave the way for a future in which one hopes for some blending of understandings.

Whether the future will mean no distinction in perspective between men and women is a debatable question. Those who subscribe to the view that all is culturally and politically determined may hold such an expectation. I do not, for the simple reason that I believe we carry characteristics as an evolved species, that differentiate between the sexes. There are good evolutionary reasons for women to have evolved with a finer sense of 'relationship dependencies' than men, and the array of physical senses in which women are different from men (higher voice, more rhythmic appreciation of tonality, finer finger dexterity, greater responsiveness to faces and facial expressions of emotion) are not simply a consequence of the victims having to be alert to nuance from their 'rulers', as some feminists would argue, but because we have the species' responsibility to bear and rear human infants, while men's reproductive strategy has centred on maximal impregnation rather than tending to, caring for dependent young. From that core in our evolutionary heritage, much follows that we today experience as 'uniquely' female, and why sisterhood is a special and necessary complement to any heterosexual bonding we have. Were this *not* true, then all that holds women together would be an oppressed class huddling against their oppressors. I don't for a moment think this is the case: we are strongly drawn to those who share our own kind of intimate experience of our kind of bodies, body functions, all the things that go with being 'female sex'. Gender is another story, partly infused with sex, partly with what the culture defines as appropriate to one sex and not the other. (I'll enclose a copy of my presidential address on these matters so you can see where my head has moved to since the work of the early 1970s on historical issues.) All this is very threatening to many of my feminist friends, who hold to an erroneous view that biology can be separated off and neglected while we wage our compaign for equality in economic and political domains.

This may seem wide of the mark as a response to your query, but necessary as establishing my own 'context' within which I respond to your specific queries of my reaction to what you did with my analysis of the Mills.

You ask if my analysis was fairly represented. While you write in a more 'breezy' style than I, I see no misrepresentation as that is usually construed. You caught the highlights of my effort to disentangle truth from mythology in previous works on the Mill book and Harriet's role in his work. There has been more scholarship on both of them since I wrote that essay in 1970. I think my central 'sociological' observation was the best part of the essay – to show that those thinkers/writers over the past 100 years who accepted Harriet's role were those whose own politics was more radical, while the conservatives tended to reject her and see her influence on Mill as an aberration on his part from what is lasting about his contributions, which exclude in their view the *Subjection of Women* book.

You ask, do I still hold the views I expressed in that book? Yes, for the most part. I think, from what I have read of others' work on Harriet Taylor and Mill in the decade since, that I would be somewhat more 'psychological' in my treatment of them. She was a complex, difficult woman, and Mill a sad case of a man emotionally crippled by his father's stern education. There was probably a 'neurotic contract' between them.

But we don't have to 'like' the people we find 'admirable' in what they produce and contribute to the world. I think, in retrospect, I gave more attention to the search for 'models' for today's young women, than I would today. I have come to the view that there is some 'passive dependency' in searching for models that we should be aware of. There is no reason why we can't construct our own models for emulation – a bit of this from person X, other qualities from person Y, etc. And in selecting those attributes from others we need not draw just from one sex either, but from a composite. I take that to be the essential meaning of androgyny – that there are socially desirable attributes of what has been viewed as traditional masculinity that women need, and some attributes equally desirable that have been viewed as traditional femininity that men need. So our models should also be composites – strength, tenderness, assertiveness, empathy, independence, yielding – a whole array of attributes to call upon as situations require one or another skill. The pity is that we are as a species so far from this – men fear intimacy, women fear impersonality, as Carol Gilligan has shown in her research. But what a half-world that is for both men and women when a sizeable proportion of both sexes are deprived of the other sex's attributes. By the same token, it will be harder to rear males in a way that encourages intimate relational skills and harder to rear females in a way that encourages genuine ease in impersonal situations, but try we must.

I am not sure how to respond to your last query, on what direction feminist ideas should go in future. Because I do not believe in sex-segregation, I am of the persuasion that feminist ideas should not be segregated, nor women scholars working off by themselves in a self-imposed intellectual ghetto – that's as bad as having been in a ghetto imposed on women by men in the past. Hence I wish to see feminist ideas infused into mainstream theories in the academic disciplines, and feminist values infused into the family system, the workplace, and the polity. My current focus has returned to old concerns for family and kinship, and to understand the direction of changes taking place in this institution where gender is concerned. This takes me out of the main areas of current feminist work here in the States. Also, my own controversial views on the physiological foundations for some sex dimorphism make it difficult to accept some of the current directions of feminist thinking of a more 'radical' persuasion, so I am not in close

222

touch. It may shock you, but I do not even believe in 'women's studies' as a specialty, because it is too turned inwards to a narrow world of women alone. I want *men* in my classes, because they need far more educating than women on the issues I teach about – sexuality, fertility, parenting, adult development. There are very few such men even in courses *not* offered under a 'women's studies' label, but there are *no* men in the latter.

In any event, I must close now, and turn to other matters. I wish you well in your new venture. Please feel free to edit and use anything that is germane to your enterprise from this letter, or my enclosed paper.

Cordially,
Alice

Alice S. Rossi
Professor of Sociology

Notes

Introduction (pp. 1–6)

1. For further discussion see Dale Spender (1984b).

Chapter 1 (pp. 7–18)

1. An assertion many would contradict, and one which Betty Friedan herself undermines when she describes some of the financial barriers women face when it comes to education.

Chapter 3 (pp. 27–30)

1. The documentation of the development of man-made reality is centuries old, with women like 'Sophia' (1739) launching an all-out attack on the limitations of male 'logic'. More recent accounts are provided by Dora Russell (1983) and Dorothy Smith (1978).

Chapter 4 (pp. 31–47)

1. In 1946 Viola Klein wrote *The Feminine Character: History of an Ideology*, a scathing critique of the origin of authority and truth about women (for further discussion see Dale Spender, 1982a, pp.502–6). And what happened to Simone de Beauvoir? Why was her work not better known and turned to more quickly during the 1960s? In less than twenty years her monumental work had faded, while Jean-Paul

Sartre continued to be at the forefront of contemporary thinking.

2. This is not unlike the explanation offered by Azizah-al Hibri at the US National Women's Studies Convention, 1981, where she suggested that in the early stages of human existence, women were considered magic: they bled – in time with the moon – and did not die; they reproduced themselves and fed their offspring from their own bodies; men felt superfluous and so set up their own 'games' designed to make them feel important!

3. For a society so disposed to construct 'causes' it is surprising that as yet no one seems to have made the women's movement 'the cause' of women's poverty.

Chapter 5 (pp. 48–68)

1. The women who sought to establish that nothing would change, and that men could safely acquiesce, were not the suffragettes, they were the suffragists. The militant suffragettes (or the militants, as the members of the Congressional Union were called in the United States) vowed that the world would change once women had some power. In fact, the philosophy of the militants, with its emphasis on action and audacity, was very close to that of Germaine Greer's.

2. For further discussion see Dale Spender (1982a), particularly pp.52–63.

3. Apart from the modern adherents of the school of irreverency for the masters, Rebecca West has been among those who have had the most to say (and do) on this subject. In her view, part of the problem was that women took men at their word and treated them seriously and with respect: women would be better served by seeing men as silly, she frequently observed (Spender, 1983b: 46).

As evidence she has cited examples from the suffragettes, having been one of them for a time. When men were insisting that women were by nature passive and polite, women changed reality and found freedom in the process, she argued, by persisting with the demonstration of their (natural) capacity for resistance and rudeness. When men decreed that women be modest and make no mention of the not-so-niceties of sexual intercourse, Christabel Pankhurst, in raising the topic of venereal disease repeatedly and rowdily, and in the worst possible taste, 'did an immense service to the world, by shattering as nothing else would, as not the mere cries of intention towards independence had ever done, the romantic conception of women' (see Spender, 1984a).

Men, declared Rebecca West, were not nearly so impressive a foe once women were able to laugh at them, as distinct from being intimidated by them; and in the interest of deflating male power and of empowering women she advocated that women follow her example and laugh loudly and frequently at the men who tried to claim superiority, and that women do this preferably in public. Germaine Greer, while not using quite the same rationale, stands firmly within this tradition of rebellion.

4. It has to be acknowledged that her solution does rather beg the question of children, and the responsibility for them, an issue Germaine Greer has since taken up in her more recent book, *Sex and Destiny*.

5. There have undoubtedly been changes when it comes to domestic work, but those who assert that men now assume equal responsibility or even do their fair share are likely to be mistaken. This is the classic example of misperception where frequently the man who helps in any way at all can be seen to be doing his 'share', for which the woman is expected to be grateful – which entails more work!

Chapter 6 (pp. 69–80)

1. For further discussion see Dale Spender (1982a), pp. 373–80.

Chapter 7 (pp. 81–96)

1. I realise the risk of misrepresentation that is involved here: it is inaccurate to suggest that Shulamith Firestone merely followed. But having arbitrarily chosen Kate Millett, Germaine Greer and Robin Morgan to represent the dimensions of feminist analysis, Shulamith Firestone fits into the framework, as distinct from significantly extending it.

2. In my research, 'full of women' can sometimes mean that women comprise less than 10 per cent of the numbers.

3. For further discussion of feminist theorists during the period from the

earlier women's movement until the renaissance of the 1960s, see Dale Spender (1982a), pp. 435–518.

4. This book attempts to view feminism in its three- and even four-dimensional character, as the holograph I believe it is . . . . One cannot understand a holograph by settling down to view it: on the contrary a willingness to shift perspectives repeatedly is necessary for such understanding. That in turn requires of us that we relinquish our position as passive observers and instead become active participants: we must move around the holograph to see its different sides, to discern its multi-faceted realities, to understand its depths' (Robin Morgan, 1982: xiv).

5. Shulamith Firestone presents a systematic and extensive critique of the academy and its construction of knowledge. Her 1970 analysis is very close to my current view of the pervasive male bias which persists across the entire spectrum of the pursuit of knowledge within the academic community and which, as *the politics of knowledge*, is a substantial and significant topic which should concern us all (see Dale Spender, 1981, Introduction in *Men's Studies Modified: The Impact of Feminism on the Academic Disciplines*). Why is it, I wonder, that the issue of what we can know and how we can come to know it, is not of overriding importance in feminist research today? For surely this is of primary concern to those of us who are trying to know different meanings and in different ways from the patriarchal ones we have been presented with. It is possible that we have had to pay a high price for our insistence on having women's studies in the academic community, for no matter what the advantages or how sound the reasons, in the last analysis we have entered a men's institution, on men's terms, and we are subject to the conditions that men have set (see Gloria Bowles and Renate Duelli Klein, 1983). This has been readily acknowledged by Berit Ås (forthcoming), who sees the only solution as an autonomous women's institution devoted to the construction of knowledge on women's terms. Perhaps this will be the place where we return to some of the serious questions that Shulamith Firestone raised. From my present vantage-point, it certainly seems as though we have lost some of that open challenge to the process of the codification of knowledge. Shulamith Firestone's contention, for example, that psychology, education and the social sciences in general are far from being endeavours of free inquiry and are far closer to being agents of social control which help to explain and legitimate existing inequalities, is a

view that I wholeheartedly endorse, but it is not one that currently attracts great interest among feminist researchers. More popular is the research which works within the confines of the paradigms of various disciplines – paradigms which originate in the male view of the world, which are resistant to women's meanings, which perpetuate all the political stratagems of objectivity, proof, scholarship and standards, and which – regardless of the direction it takes or the energy which goes into it – is research that will ultimately lead us full circle with male experience being *proven* (by objective and scholarly standards) to be more authoritative and significant than that of the female.

6. This ideology was later exposed by Adrienne Rich (1977) and is currently being re-questioned within the reproductive rights movement. See Rita Arditti *et al.* (1984).

7. Nancy Henley, *Body Politics: Power, Sex and Non-verbal Communication* (1977) is a notable exception; see also Sally Cline and Dale Spender, *Reflecting Men* (forthcoming) for elaboration on Virginia Woolf's statement that for centuries women have been serving as looking, glasses for men, reflecting them at twice their normal size.

8. Two examples come to mind: in many African societies women are considered stronger than men; in our own they are considered weaker. There is also the example of the male voice 'breaking' at puberty; this is unknown in some societies and frequently doesn't occur in our own when the male has been deaf from birth. See Dale Spender, *Man Made Language* (1980).

Chapter 8 (pp. 97–106)

1. See Virginia Woolf, *A Room of One's Own* (1928, 1974), p. 29.

2. As Adrienne Rich (1980) has alleged, labelling their own subjectivity as objectivity is another example of the limitations of male logic. That men are frequently seen by women to be constrained by their pattern of thinking has given rise to the suggestion that men suffer from tunnel-vision (Spender, 1980: 99–102). It has also given rise to the question of whether, if women's experience is the norm, men's experience is deficient.

3. I would suggest that we all end up with circular arguments – feminists included – that being the only way we *can* think. The difference in my value-system is that feminists can acknowledge the limitations of logic and the human intellect, which depend upon a value-system and a set of assumptions, and this is a long way from a declaration that we are in possession of the truth.

4. I have noted that on the 'blurb' of *Patriarchal Attitudes* it is stated – by way of a compliment – that this book is 'intelligent' and 'unhysterical': this is an achievement for a woman, and we are expected to be suitably surprised. My thesis in *Women of Ideas – And What Men Have Done to Them* (1982a) is that this patterned discrediting of women's writing is a form of sexual harassment where a woman is judged on the basis of her sex and not her work, with the intention of keeping woman in her subordinate and not very competent place.

5. Margaret Mead was beginning to figure in feminist explanations by this time.

6. In the area of sociobiology, critiques of the recurring male supremacist bias have been consistent from Antoinette Brown Blackwell (1875) to Ruth Herschberger (1948), Elaine Morgan (1972), Evelyn Reed (1978) and Ruth Bleir (1984). The omission of the social sciences from such critiques and the concentration on the meeting place between social science and science seems somewhat strange.

7. She had come to believe that men's case rested on their ability to reserve education for themselves. Because they were educated they could claim to be more intelligent and, in good circular fashion, they could then explain women's *lack* of intelligence in terms of their failure to be educated. Mary Wollstonecraft decided that the way to break this vicious circle was to ensure that women had the *same* education as men. Then, she reasoned, men would no longer be able to substantiate their claim for greater intelligence. *A Vindication of The Rights of Woman* is in the main the case for equal education as a means of ending male supremacy. Among the men of her time, Mary Wollstonecraft's argument was considered valid, she was seen to be making a revolutionary demand – which is why men resisted. It took another 150 years of campaigning in England for women to become full members of Cambridge University, and was only successful, according to Rita McWilliams-Tullberg (1975), when the power enjoyed by full members

of the university had shifted.

8. Different studies at different times have captured this process in operation when subjects of both sexes are given for assessment the same articles, reports, transcripts etc., which are arbitrarily attributed to males or females. The result is that the supposed 'male' contributions are perceived to be more impressive than the 'female' ones, despite the fact that it is the same material (see Dale Spender, forthcoming). This is not a new understanding; and explains why women writers have frequently resorted to male pseudonyms.

Chapter 9 (pp. 107–118)

1. The only other book I do know like it is William Thompson's *Appeal* . . (1825), and in it the author insists that the insights it contains come from a woman, Anna Wheeler.

2. I am indebted to Renate Duelli Klein for our many hours of debate on this topic: this question is primarily hers.

3. I was greatly influenced by her work – not just *Essays on Sex Equality*, but *The Feminist Papers* which appeared in 1974 and which led me eventually to *Women of Ideas – And What Men Have Done to Them*.

4. Helen Taylor, Harriet's daughter and John's stepdaughter.

Chapter 10 (pp. 119–131)

1. Many other feminists – Germaine Greer among them – would see this *as revolution*, not as a preliminary to it.

Chapter 11 (pp. 132–142)

1. As Liz Stanley and Sue Wise (1983) asserted.

2. Even the percentage of women in the workforce is misleading for it is always set against the assumption that 100 per cent of men are in the workforce, which, of course, is not the case. Figures on the percentage of

men in the workforce are hard to come by – particularly in Britain – but the difference between the percentage of women and the percentage of men in the workforce is probably not very great. It could even be reversing.

3. Some have suggested that this is one of the weaknesses of feminist theory. In the reproductive rights movement there has even been a discussion that, with the advent of widespread artificial reproduction, women could be in the position of looking back to the time when they were 'allowed' to have babies, and were able to maintain a 'power-base'. See Arditti *et al.* (1984) and Andrea Dworkin (1983).

Chapter 12 (pp. 143–154)

1. I have noted that many feminists have made the point that Freud based his theories on the belief that women's experience was 'unreal', but this seems to have generally gone unnoticed: since a *man* has come out and made a similar allegation, there has been uproar. See Florence Rush (1984).

2. Lillian Faderman has since provided some redress with *Surpassing the Love of Men* (1981).

3. This is not to suggest that lesbian existence has its source in a reaction to men: it can be the autonomous choice of women without any reference to men. For further discussion see the chapter on Adrienne Rich, p.184

4. In the writing of George Eliot. This is a reference to her article 'Margaret Fuller and Mary Wollstonecraft', first published in 1855 and not reprinted (not surprisingly) until 1963. For further discussion, see Dale Spender (1982a), pp. 172–7.

Chapter 13 (pp. 155–158)

1. Many women's studies courses brought in new students so that more teachers were required to provide their services 'voluntarily', and were given few if any resources.

2. See Dale Spender (1984b), and panel discussion, 'Who Reviews Women's Books?' at First International Feminist Book Fair, London, June 1984. One male publisher there stated that he was damned if his publishing house would become known as a women's publisher: it was time to turn back the tide.

3. For discussion and reprints see Dale Spender, *Time and Tide Wait for No Man* (1984).

4. Three in particular which come to mind are Matilda Joslyn Gage, *Woman, Church and State: The Original Exposé of Male Collaboration Against the Female Sex* (1873); Charlotte Perkins Gilman, *The Man-made World or Our Androcentric Culture* (1911); and Elizabeth Robins, *Ancilla's Share* (1924).

Chapter 14 (pp. 159–183)

1. Sheila Rowbotham had earlier written *Women's Liberation and the New Politics* (1969).

2. Women as 'defective versions of men' is as old as Eden and this belief has been aided by the additions of various authorities who have pronounced women as anything from misbegotten to incomplete – with notions of 'perpetual infirmity' on the way.

3. They quote statistics in the US at the time when 93 per cent of doctors were men and when virtually all influential positions in the profession were held by men.

4. Not uncommon, at least in Britain, is the complaint from some doctors about this new knowledge and confident aggression among women: 'Who is giving them all this information?' is not an unusual question, and the implication is that it is not appropriate for women to have this knowledge which is, rightly, the province of the professional man.

5. For example, Evelyn Reed looked more closely at the 'objective rationale' that males were dominant because, in the animal world, there might be only one male in a troop, his presence being construed as that of the leader of the harem. Why not an alternative measurement that the females only needed one male, and his presence was tolerated for purposes of reproduction only?

6. Among some of the British publications are *Breaching the Peace* (1984); Wilmette Brown, *Black Women and the Peace Movement* (1983); Cambridge Women's Peace Collective, *My Country is the Whole World* (1983); A. Cook and G. Kirk, *Greenham Women Everywhere* (1983); Barbara Harford and Sarah Hopkins, *Greenham Common: Women at the Wire* (1984); Lynne Jones, *Keeping the Peace* (1983); and Dorothy Thompson, *Over Our Dead Bodies* (1983).

7. A forthcoming publication on this topic which has been my pleasure and privilege to read is that of Birgit Brock-Utne.

8. I cannot overlook the fact that for me and many other women of my generation, the emergence of the women's movement was in many senses a form of liberation in itself, as it transferred the responsibility of our restrictions from ourselves to our societies. Far from being embittered and unhappy (the standard media portrayal of feminists), I was a very happy women's-libber when I began to realise that it wasn't inadequacy (or envy) on my part that led me to protest about the injustice of housework, the intolerableness of sexual harassment, the inequalities at the workplace, and the iniquities of male power. Yet we have constructed few records of the pleasure of feminism: perhaps we are enmeshed in the media belief that *good* news is not good *news*.

9. For further discussion, see Dale Spender (1982a).

10. Publishing is tightly controlled by men – see Lynne Spender (1983) and Kay Symons (1984).

11. See *Women's Studies International Forum* (1983), Vol. 6, no. 5, 'Gatekeeping: The denial dismissal and distortion of women'.

Chapter 15 (pp. 184–209)

1. Dorothy Smith (1978) pointed out in Canada and Eileen Byrne (1978) pointed out in England that the educational system in which so many of us had placed so much faith, and which for so long women had struggled to enter, was a system devised by men with the avowed purpose of providing the best preparation for a manly life. See Dale Spender (1982b).

2. For further discussion of the educational philosophies of these women, see Dale Spender (1982a).

3. In her article, 'Assimilation or Integration: The Woman Student, Women's Studies and the Transmission of a Women's World View' (1984), Joan Roberts states that for women in higher education in the United States there has been 'a decline in top-level administrators and in the proportion of tenured faculty women', as well as 'an increase in salary differentials'. And there has been a decrease in the number of women's colleges, from 298 in 1960 to 146 in 1975 (p. 7). The issue, she says, is to *maintain* what has been achieved.

4. These are: 'men's ability to deny women sexuality or to enforce it upon them; to command or exploit their labor to control their produce; to control or rob them of their children; to confine them physically and prevent their movement; to use them as objects in male transactions; to cramp their creativeness; or to withhold from them large areas of society's knowledge and cultural attainments' (Gough (1975), pp. 69–70; quoted in Rich (1981), p. 10). 'These are some of the methods by which male power is manifested and maintained,' writes Adrienne Rich, and 'what surely impresses itself is the fact that we are confronting not a simple maintenance of inequality and property possession, but a pervasive cluster of forces, ranging from physical brutality to control of consciousness, which suggests that an enormous counterforce is having to be restrained' (1981: 12).

5. 'The histories of education, social work, librarianship, and even home economics [and I would add nursing and pre-schooling] all point to the fact that the inclusion of men into these disciplines [and areas] has led to the problem of male domination over what was once a woman's domain' (Joan Roberts, 1984, p. 12).

6. '. . . the free play of intuition in our own space, giving rise to thinking that is vigorous, informed, multi-dimensional, independent, creative, tough' (1978: 23).

7. 'Websters' and 'Fates' are examples of Mary Daly's names for women's existence. 'Webster' once meant a female weaver (p. 13) and 'Fates' are the threads of life that spin 'Stamina' (1984: 11).

8. See pp.159-160 for further discussion.

9. '*Errata*, of course, is the plural of *erratum*, the archaic meaning of which is "an error" (as a mis-statement or misprint) in something published or written' (fn., p. xi).

234

1. I take Ann Oakley's point. But apart from the fact that it is too late to alter the typeset text, I think I also want to stand by the statement that there is a difference, a change, when women can talk to women; even the recognition that they are not alone can be a significant change in the lives of many women. This was what I meant, not that their material conditions were dramatically altered.

References

References are to the most recent editions. Dates of original publication appear in the texts.

Acker, Sandra, and Piper, David Warren, eds. *Is Higher Education Fair to Women?* Slough: SRHE/NFER, 1984

Arditti, Rita, Brennan, Pat, and Cavrack, Steve, eds. *Science and Liberation.* Montreal: Black Rose, 1980.

Arditti, Rita, Duelli Klein, Renate, and Minden, Shelley, eds. *Test Tube Women.* London: Pandora Press, 1984.

Ariés, Philippe. *Centuries of Childhood: A Social History of Family Life.* New York: Vintage Books, 1962.

Ås, Berit. 'The Feminist University'. *Women's Studies International Forum,* forthcoming.

Astell, Mary. 'A Serious Proposal to the Ladies', reprinted in Rogers, 1979, below.

Atkinson, Ti-Grace. 'Interview: Amazon Continues Odyssey.' *Off Our Backs* (December 1979).

Barrett Browning, Elizabeth. *Aurora Leigh and Other Poems.* London: The Women's Press, 1978.

Beard, Mary Ritter. *Woman as a Force in History.* New York: Macmillan, 1946.

Beauman, Nicola. *A Very Great Profession: The Woman's Novel, 1914–39.* London: Virago, 1983.

Beck, Evelyn Torton, ed. *Nice Jewish Girls: A Lesbian Anthology.* New York: The Crossing Press, 1984.

Bernard, Jessie. *The Future of Marriage.* New York: World Publishing, 1972.

— 'My Four Revolutions'. *American Journal of Sociology,* 78, 4 (January 1973) and in Huber, ed., 1974, below.

Blackwell, Antoinette Brown. *The Sexes Throughout Nature.* New York: G. P. Putnam's Sons, 1875.

Bleir, Ruth. *Science and Gender: A Critique of Biology and Its Theories of Women.* New York and Oxford: Athene Series, Pergamon Press, 1984.

Boston Women's Health Collective. *Our Bodies Ourselves.* New York: Simon and Schuster, 1971.

Bowles, Gloria, and Duelli Klein, Renate, eds. *Theories of Women's Studies.* London: Routledge & Kegan Paul, 1983.

Breaching the Peace: A Collection of Radical Feminist Papers. London: Onlywomen Press, 1984.

Brock-Utne, Birgit. *Peace Begins in the Minds of Women.* New York and Oxford: Athene Series, Pergamon Press, forthcoming.

Brown, Wilmette. *Black Women and the Peace Movement.* London: King's Cross Women's Centre, 1983.

Brownmiller, Susan. *Against Our Will: Men, Women and Rape.* Harmondsworth: Penguin, 1976.

Bunch, Charlotte. 'Feminist Theory and Education', in Bunch and Pollack, eds., 1983, below.

—, and Pollack, Sandra, eds. *Learning Our Way: Essays in Feminist Education.* New York: The Crossing Press, 1983.

Bunkle, Phillida. 'Encyclopaedic Blunders'. *Broadsheet*, New Zealand (April 1984).

Byrne, Eileen. *Women and Education.* London: Tavistock, 1978.

Caldecott, Leonie, and Leland, Stephanie, eds. *Reclaim the Earth: Women Speak Out for Life on Earth.* London: The Women's Press, 1983.

Cambridge Women's Peace Collective. *My Country Is the Whole World.* London: Pandora Press, 1983.

Carroll, Berenice A., ed. *Liberating Women's History: Theoretical and Critical Essays.* Urbana: University of Illinois Press, 1976.

Cassell, Joan. *A Group Called Women: Sisterhood and Symbolism in the Feminist Movement.* New York: David McKay Co., 1977.

Cherfas, Jeremy, and Gribbin, John. *The Redundant Male.* London: The Bodley Head, 1984.

Chernin, Kim. *Womansize: The Tyranny of Slenderness.* London: The Women's Press, 1983.

Chesler, Phyllis. *Women and Madness.* London: Allen Lane, 1972.

— *About Men.* London: The Women's Press, 1978.

Chesler, Phyllis, and Goodman, Emily Jane. *Women, Money and Power.* New York: William Morrow, 1976.

Chicago, Judy. *The Dinner Party: A Symbol of Our Heritage.* New York:

Anchor Press, Doubleday, 1977.

Cline, Sally, and Spender, Dale. *Reflecting Men*. London: André Deutsch, forthcoming.

Cook, Alice, and Kirk, Gwen. *Greenham Women Everywhere*. London: Pluto, 1983.

Coote, Anna, and Campbell, Beatrix. *Sweet Freedom: The Struggle for Women's Liberation*. London: Pan Books, 1982.

Coss, John Jacob, ed. *Autobiography of John Stuart Mill*. New York: Columbia University Press, 1924.

Daly, Mary. *Beyond God the Father: Towards a Philosophy of Women's Liberation*. Boston: Beacon Press, 1973.

— *Gyn/Ecology: The Metaethics of Radical Feminism*. London: The Women's Press, 1978.

— *Pure Lust: Elemental Feminist Philosophy*. London: The Women's Press, 1984.

— 'Foreword', in Gage, 1980, below.

De Beauvoir, Simone. *The Second Sex*. Harmondsworth, Penguin, 1972.

Douglas, Carol Anne. 'Feminism: Socialist? Liberal? Radical?' *Off Our Backs*, Vol. 14, no. 7 (July 1984).

Dworkin, Andrea. *Woman Hating*. New York: E. P. Dutton & Co., 1974.

— *Pornography: Men Possessing Women*. London: The Women's Press, 1981.

— *Our Blood: Prophecies and Discourses on Sexual Politics*. London: The Women's Press, 1982.

— *Right-wing Women: Politics of Domesticated Females*. London: The Women's Press, 1983.

Dyhouse, Carol. 'Good Wives and Little Mothers: Social Anxieties and the School Girls' Curriculum'. *Oxford Review of Education*, Vol. 3, no. 1 (1977).

Ehrenreich, Barbara, and English, Deirdre. *Complaints and Disorders: The Sexual Politics of Sickness*. London: Writers and Readers Publishing Co-operative, 1973a.

— *Witches, Midwives and Nurses: A History of Women Healers*. London: Writers and Readers Publishing Co-operative, 1973b.

— *For Her Own Good: 150 Years of the Experts' Advice to Women*. London: Pluto Press, 1979.

Eichler, Margrit. *The Double Standard: A Feminist Critique of Feminist Sociology*. London: Croom Helm, 1980.

Eliot, George. 'Margaret Fuller and Mary Wollstonecraft', reprinted in

Pinney, ed., 1963, below.

Ellmann, Mary. *Thinking About Women.* London: Virago, 1979.

Engels, Friedrich. *The Origin of the Family, Private Property and the State.* Edited with an introduction by Eleanor Leacock. New York: International Publishers, 1972.

Enloe, Cynthia. *Does Khaki Become You? The Militarisation of Women's Lives.* London: Pluto Press, 1983.

Faderman, Lillian. *Surpassing the Love of Men: Romantic Friendship and Love Between Women from the Renaissance to the Present.* New York: William Morrow, 1981.

Farley, Lin. *Sexual Shakedown: The Sexual Harassment of Women on the Job.* New York: McGraw Hill, 1978.

Feminist Review. Many Voices One Chant: Black Feminist Perspectives. Vol. 17 (Autumn 1984).

Firestone, Shulamith. *The Dialectic of Sex.* London: The Women's Press, 1979.

Freeman, Jo. *The Politics of Women's Liberation.* New York: David McKay Co., 1975.

Friedan, Betty. *The Feminine Mystique.* Harmondsworth: Penguin, 1965.

Friedman, Scarlet, and Sarah, Elizabeth, eds. *On the Problem of Men.* London: The Women's Press, 1982.

Frye, Marilyn. *The Politics of Reality: Essays in Feminist Theory.* New York: The Crossing Press, 1983.

Gage, Matilda Joslyn. *Woman, Church and State: The Original Exposé of Male Collaboration Against the Female Sex.* Watertown, Massachusetts: Persephone Press, 1980.

Gavron, Hannah. *The Captive Wife.* London: Routledge & Kegan Paul, 1983.

Gilbert, Sandra M., and Gubar, Susan. *The Madwoman in the Attic: The Woman Writer and the 19th Century Literary Imagination.* Newhaven and London: Yale University Press, 1979.

Gilman, Charlotte Perkins. *Women and Economics.* New York: Harper & Row, 1966.

— *The Home: Its Work and Influence.* Urbana: University of Illinois Press, 1972.

— *The Man-made World or Our Androcentric Culture.* New York: Charlton, 1911.

Gordon, Linda. *Woman's Body, Woman's Right: Birth Control in*

America. Harmondsworth: Penguin, 1977.

Gough, Kathleen. 'The Origin of the Family', in Reiter, ed., 1975, op. cit.

Greer, Germaine. *The Female Eunuch.* London: MacGibbon & Kee, 1970.

— *The Obstacle Race.* London: Secker & Warburg, 1979.

— *Sex and Destiny: The Politics of Human Fertility.* London: Secker & Warburg, 1984.

— 'Better No Sex Than Bad Sex'. *The Sunday Times* (15 January 1984).

— 'Sex Without Gadgets'. *The Sunday Times* (22 January 1984).

Griffin, Susan. *Pornography and Silence.* London: The Women's Press, 1981.

— *Woman and Nature: The Roaring Inside Her.* London: The Women's Press, 1984.

Gyorgy, Anna, and Friends. *No Nukes.* Boston: South End Press, 1979.

Hallinan, Hazel Hunkins, ed. *In Her Own Right.* London: Harrap, 1968.

Hamilton, Cicely. *Marriage as a Trade.* London: The Women's Press, 1981.

Harford, Barbara, and Hopkins, Sarah, eds. *Greenham Common: Women at the Wire.* London: The Women's Press, 1984.

Henley, Nancy. *Body Politics: Power, Sex and Non-verbal Communication.* Englewood Cliffs, N. J.: Prentice Hall, Spectrum, 1977.

Herschberger, Ruth. *Adam's Rib.* New York: Harper & Row, 1970.

Hess, E.B., and Baker, E.C., eds. *Art and Sexual Politics.* London: Collier Macmillan, 1972.

Hooks, Bell. *Ain't I a Woman: Black Women and Feminism.* London: Pluto Press, 1981.

Howe, Florence. 'Feminist Scholarship: The Expense of Revolution'. *Change,* 14, no. 3 (April 1982).

Hubbard, Ruth. 'The Emperor Doesn't Wear Any Clothes: The Impact of Feminism on Biology', in Spender, ed., 1981, below.

Huber, Joan, ed. *Changing Women in a Changing Society.* Chicago: University of Chicago Press, 1974.

Hull, Gloria T., Scott, Patricia Bell, and Smith, Barbara, eds. *But Some of Us Are Brave: Black Women's Studies.* Old Westbury, New York: The Feminist Press, 1982.

Janeway, Elizabeth. *Powers of the Weak.* New York: Alfred Knopf, 1980.

Jones, Ann. *Women Who Kill.* New York: Holt, Rinehart & Winston, 1980.

Jones, Lynne, ed. *Keeping the Peace.* London: The Women's Press, 1983.

Kanter, Rosabeth Moss. *Men and Women of the Corporation*. New York: Basic Books, 1977.

Kaplan, Cora. 'Introduction', in Barrett Browning, 1978, op. cit.

Kishwar, Madhu, and Vanita, Ruth, eds. *In Search of Answers: Indian Women's Voices from 'Manushi'*. London: Zed Press, 1984.

Klein, Viola. *The Feminine Character: History of an Ideology*. London: Routledge & Kegan Paul, 1946.

Kolodny, Annette. 'Dancing Through the Minefield: Some Observations on the Theory, Practice and Politics of a Feminist Literary Criticism', in Spender, ed., 1981, below.

Kramarae, Cheris. *Women and Men Speaking: Frameworks for Analysis*. Massachusetts: Newbury House, 1981.

Lakoff, Robin. *Language and Woman's Place*. New York: Harper & Row, 1975.

Lane, Ann J. *Mary Ritter Beard: A Source Book*. New York: Schocken Books, 1977.

Leghorn, Lisa, and Parker, Katherine. *Woman's Worth: Sexual Economics and the World of Women*. London: Routledge & Kegan Paul, 1981.

Lerner, Gerda. *The Grimké Sisters from South Carolina: Pioneers for Woman's Rights and Abolition*. New York: Schocken Books, 1971.

— , ed. *Black Women in White America: A Documentary History*. New York: Vintage Books, 1973.

Lockwood, Maren Carden. *The New Feminist Movement*. New York: Russell Sage Foundation, 1974.

Lorde, Audré. *Zami: A New Spelling of My Name*. London: Sheba Feminist Publishers, 1984.

— *Sister Outsider: Essays and Speeches*. New York: The Crossing Press, 1984.

Lowe, Marian, and Hubbard, Ruth, eds. *Woman's Nature: Rationalizations of Inequality*. New York and Oxford: Athene Series, Pergamon Press, 1983.

Lutz, Alma. *Created Equal: A Biography of Elizabeth Cady Stanton*. New York: John Day Company, 1940.

MacKinnon, Catherine. *Sexual Harassment of Working Women*. New Haven and London: Yale University Press, 1979.

Matthews, Jacquie. 'Barbara Bodichon: Integrity in Diversity', in Spender, ed., 1983a, below.

McWilliams-Tullberg, Rita. *Women at Cambridge: A Men's University – Though of a Mixed Type*. London: Victor Gollancz, 1975.

Mead, Margaret. *Sex and Temperament in Three Primitive Societies*. London: Routledge & Kegan Paul, 1977.

— *Male and Female*. Harmondsworth: Penguin, 1971.

Merchant, Carolyn. *The Death of Nature: Women, Ecology and the Scientific Revolution*. London: Wildwood House, 1982.

Mill, John Stuart. *The Subjection of Women*, reprinted in Rossi, ed., 1970, below.

— *The Earlier Letters of John Stuart Mill 1812–1848*. Edited by Francis E. Mineka, Vol. 13 of *Collected Works of John Stuart Mill*. Toronto: University of Toronto Press, 1963.

Miller, Jean Baker. *Toward a New Psychology of Women*. Harmondsworth: Penguin, 1978.

Millett, Kate. *Sexual Politics*. London: Abacus/Sphere, 1972.

Mitchell, Juliet. 'Women: The Longest Revolution'. *New Left Review*, no. 40 (1966).

— *Woman's Estate*. Harmondsworth: Penguin, 1973.

— *Psychoanalysis and Feminism*. Harmondsworth: Penguin, 1975.

— *The Longest Revolution*. London: Virago, 1984.

Moers, Ellen. *Literary Women: The Great Writers*. London: The Women's Press, 1978.

Moraga, Cherrie, and Anzaldua, Gloria, eds. *This Bridge Called My Back: Writings by Radical Women of Color*. New York: Kitchen Table: Women of Color Press, 1984.

Morgan, Elaine. *The Descent of Woman*. New York: Stein & Day, 1972.

Morgan, Robin, ed. *Sisterhood Is Powerful: An Anthology of Writings from the Women's Liberation Movement*. New York: Vintage Books, 1970.

— *Going Too Far: The Personal Chronicle of a Feminist*. New York: Vintage Books, 1978.

— *The Anatomy of Freedom*. Oxford: Martin Robertson, 1983.

Newman, Louise. *Men's Ideas: Women's Realities*. New York and Oxford: Athene Series, Pergamon Press, forthcoming.

Nochlin, Linda. 'Why Have There Been No Great Women Artists?', in Hess and Baker, eds., 1972, op. cit.

Oakley, Ann. *Sex, Gender and Society*. London: Temple Smith, 1978.

— *The Sociology of Housework*. Oxford: Martin Robertson, 1974.

— *Housewife*. Harmondsworth: Penguin, 1976.

— *Becoming a Mother*. Oxford: Martin Robertson, 1979.

— *Women Confined: Towards a Sociology of Childbirth*. Oxford: Martin

Robertson, 1980.

— *Subject Women*. Oxford: Martin Robertson, 1981a.

— *From Here to Maternity: Becoming a Mother*. Harmondsworth: Penguin, 1981b.

— 'New Introduction', in Gavron, 1983, op. cit.

— *Taking It Like a Woman*. London: Jonathan Cape, 1984.

O'Brien, Mary. *The Politics of Reproduction*. Routledge & Kegan Paul, 1981.

Olsen, Tillie. *Silences*. London: Virago, 1980.

Orbach, Susie. *Fat Is a Feminist Issue*. London: Hamlyn, 1984.

Parker, Rozsika, and Pollock, Griselda. *Old Mistresses: Women, Art and Ideology*. London: Routledge & Kegan Paul, 1981.

Pinney, Thomas, ed. *Essays of George Eliot*. London: Routledge & Kegan Paul, 1963.

Quest Book Committee. *Building Feminist Theory: Essays from Quest, a Feminist Quarterly*. New York and London: Longman, 1981.

Reed, Evelyn. *Sexism and Science*. New York: Pathfinder Press, 1978.

Reiter, Rayna R., ed. *Toward an Anthropology of Women*. New York: Monthly Review Press, 1975.

Rich, Adrienne. *Of Woman Born: Motherhood as Experience and Institution*. London: Virago, 1977.

— *On Lies, Secrets and Silence*. London: Virago, 1980.

— *Compulsory Heterosexuality and the Lesbian Existence*. London: Onlywomen Press, 1981.

Roberts, Joan, ed. *Beyond Intellectual Sexism: A New Woman, A New Reality*. New York: David McKay Co., 1976.

Roberts, Joan I. 'Assimilation or Integration: The Woman Student, Women's Studies and the Transmission of Women's World View'. *National Women's Studies Association Newsletter*, Vol. 2, no. 3 (Summer 1984).

Robins, Elizabeth. *Ancilla's Share: An Indictment of Sex Antagonism*. London: Hutchinson, 1924.

Rogers, Katherine M., ed. *Before Their Time: Six Women Writers of the Eighteenth Century*. New York: Frederick Ungar, 1979.

Rossi, Alice S., ed. *Essays on Sex Equality by John Stuart Mill and Harriet Taylor Mill*. Chicago: University of Chicago Press 1970.

— , ed. *The Feminist Papers: From Adams to De Beauvoir*. New York: Bantam Books, 1974.

Rothschild, Joan, ed. *Machina Ex Dea: Feminist Perspectives on*

Technology. New York and Oxford: Athene Series, Pergamon Press, 1983.

Rover, Constance. 'Interview with Dale Spender', in Spender, 1983b, below.

Rowbotham, Sheila. *Women's Liberation and the New Politics*. Nottingham: Spokesman Pamphlet, 1971.

— *Woman's Consciousness, Man's World*. Harmondsworth: Penguin, 1973.

— *Women, Resistance and Revolution*. Harmondsworth: Pelican Books, 1974.

— *Hidden from History: Three Hundred Years of Women's Oppression and the Fight Against It*. Harmondsworth: Pelican Books, 1975.

— *Stella Browne: Socialist Feminist*. London: Pluto Press, 1977.

— *Dreams and Dilemmas: Collected Writings*. London: Virago, 1983.

Rowland, Robyn. *Women Who Do and Women Who Don't – Join the Women's Movement*. London: Routledge & Kegan Paul, 1984.

Rush, Florence. 'The Sins of the Fathers'. *The Women's Review of Books*, 1, 7 (April 1984).

Russ, Joanna. *How to Suppress Women's Writing*. London: The Women's Press, 1984.

Russell, Dora. *The Religion of the Machine Age*. London: Routledge & Kegan Paul, 1983.

Ruth, Sheila. *Issues in Feminism*. Boston: Houghton Mifflin, 1980.

Sarah, Elizabeth. 'Female Performers on a Male Stage: The First Women's Liberation Movement and the Authority of Men, 1890–1930', in Friedman and Sarah, eds., 1982, op. cit.

Scott, Hilda. *Working Your Way to the Bottom: The Feminisation of Poverty*. London: Pandora Press, 1984.

Showalter, Elaine. *A Literature of Their Own: British Women Novelists from Brontë to Lessing*. London: Virago, 1978.

Smith, Barbara, ed. *Home Girls: A Black Feminist Anthology*. New York: Kitchen Table: Women of Color Press, 1983.

Smith, Dorothy. 'A Peculiar Eclipsing: Women's Exclusion from Man's Culture'. *Women's Studies International Quarterly*. Vol. 1, no. 4 (1978).

Solanas, Valerie. *Scum Manifesto*. London: Matriarchy Study Group, 1983.

'Sophia, a Person of Quality'. *Woman Not Inferior to Man*. London: Bentham Press (facsimile reprint), 1975.

Spender, Dale. *Man Made Language*. London: Routledge & Kegan Paul, 1980.

—, ed. *Men's Studies Modified: The Impact of Feminism on the Academic Disciplines*. New York and London: Athene Series, Pergamon Press, 1981.

— *Women of Ideas – And What Men Have Done to Them*. London: Routledge & Kegan Paul, 1982a.

— *Invisible Women: The Schooling Scandal*. London: Writers and Readers Publishing Co-operative, 1982b.

—, ed. *Feminist Theorists: Three Centuries of Women's Intellectual Traditions*. London: The Women's Press, 1983a.

— *There's Always Been a Women's Movement This Century*. London: Pandora Press, 1983b.

— *Time and Tide Wait for No Man*. London: Pandora Press, 1984a.

— 'A Difference of View: Reviewing the Reviews of Women's Books'. Paper presented to Cambridge University, April 1984b.

— 'Sexism in Teacher Education', in Acker and Piper, eds., 1984 op. cit.

— and Spender, Lynne, eds. 'Gatekeeping: The Denial, Dismissal and Distortion of Women'. Special Issue, *Women's Studies International Forum*, Vol. 6, no. 5, 1983.

— — *Scribbling Sisters*. Sydney: Hale & Iremonger, 1984.

— — *Loving Husbands: Can We Afford Them?* Forthcoming.

Spender, Lynne. *Intruders on the Rights of Men: Women's Unpublished Heritage*. London: Pandora Press, 1983.

Stacey, Judith. 'The New Conservative Feminism'. *Feminist Studies*, 9, 3 (1983).

Stanley, Liz, and Wise, Sue. *Breaking Out: Feminist Consciousness and Feminist Research*. London: Routledge & Kegan Paul, 1983.

— *Kiss the Girls and Make Them Cry*. London: Pandora Press, forthcoming.

Stanton, Elizabeth Cady. *Eighty Years and More: Reminiscences 1815–1897*. New York: Schocken Books, 1975.

—, Anthony, Susan B., and Gage, Matilda Joslyn, eds. *History of Woman Suffrage*. Vol. 1. New York: Arno and The New York Times, 1969.

— (and The Revising Committee). *The Woman's Bible*. Seattle: Coalition Task Force on Women and Religion, 1978.

Steinem, Gloria. *Outrageous Acts and Everyday Rebellions*. London: Jonathan Cape, 1984.

Stone, Merlin. *The Paradise Papers: The Suppression of Women's Rites*. London: Virago, 1977.

Strauss, Sylvia. *'Traitors to the Masculine Cause' – The Men's Campaign for Women's Rights*. Westport, Connecticut: Greenwood Press, 1982.

Symons, Kay. 'Women and Publishing: Some Interesting Facts'. London: *Wiplash* (July 1984).

Thompson, Dorothy, ed. *Over Our Dead Bodies: Women Against the Bomb*. London: Virago, 1983.

Thompson, William. *Appeal from One Half of the Human Race, Women, Against the Pretensions of the Other Half, Men, to Retain Them in Political and Thence in Civil and Domestic Slavery, in Reply to a Paragraph of Mr Mill's Celebrated Article on Government*. London: Longman, Hurst, Rees, Orme, Brown and Green, 1825.

Trilling, Diana. 'Mill's Intellectual Beacon'. *Partisan Review*, 19 (1952).

Urbanski, Marie Mitchell Olesen. *Margaret Fuller's 'Woman in the Nineteenth Century': A Literary Study of Form and Content of Sources and Influence*. Westport, Connecticut: Greenwood Press, 1980.

Wagner, Sally Roesch. 'Introduction', in Gage, 1980, op. cit.

Walker, Alice. *In Search of Our Mothers' Gardens: Womanist Prose*. London: The Women's Press, 1984.

Walkowitz, Judith R. *Prostitution and Victorian Society: Women, Class and the State*. Cambridge: Cambridge University Press, 1980.

Weisstein, Naomi. '"Kinder, Küche, Kirche" as Scientific Law: Psychology Constructs the Female', in Morgan, ed., 1970, op. cit.

Winn, Denise. 'Fathers – Keep Out'. *The Sunday Times* (29 July 1984).

Wollstonecraft, Mary. *A Vindication of the Rights of Woman*. London: Joseph Johnson, 1792.

Woolf, Virginia. *A Room of One's Own*. Harmondsworth, Penguin, 1974.

— *Three Guineas*. Harmondsworth: Penguin, 1977.